To Joyce and the teen within!

Positive Discipline for Teenagers

Jane Nelsen

Jane Nelsen, Ed.D.
Lynn Lott, M.A., M.F.C.C.

Prima Publishing
P.O. Box 1260BK
Rocklin, CA 95677
(916) 632-4400

Library of Congress Cataloging-in-Publication Data

Nelsen, Jane.
[I'm on your side]
Positive discipline for teenagers : resolving conflict with your teenage son or daughter / Jane Nelsen and Lynn Lott.
p. cm.
Includes index.
ISBN 1-55958-441-6 (pbk.)
1. Parent and teenager. 2. Interpersonal conflict. 3. Adolescent psychology. I. Lott, Lynn. II. Title.
HQ799.15.N45 1994
649'.125—dc20 93-36383
CIP

97 AA 10 9 8

Printed in the United States of America

To my children, who continue to teach me there is always more to learn, and that learning from mistakes is a lifelong process.

Jane

To Casey, who broke me in; to Corey, who set me straight; and to David, who reminded me how much fun it is to be a mom.

Lynn

Other Books in the Developing Capable People Series:

Positive Discipline A-Z: 1001 Solutions to Everyday Parenting Problems
Jane Nelsen, Lynn Lott, and H. Stephen Glenn

Positive Discipline in the Classroom: How to Effectively Use Class Meetings and Other Positive Discipline Strategies
Jane Nelsen, Lynn Lott, and H. Stephen Glenn

Positive Discipline for Single Parents: A Practical Guide to Raising Children Who Are Responsible, Respectful, and Resourceful
Jane Nelsen, Cheryl Erwin, and Carol Delzer

Raising Self-Reliant Children in a Self-Indulgent World: Seven Building Blocks for Developing Capable Young People
H. Stephen Glenn and Jane Nelsen

Clean & Sober Parenting: A Guide to Help Recovering Parents Rebuild Trust, Create Structure, Improve Communications, Learn Parenting Skills, and Give Up Guilt and Shame
Jane Nelsen, Riki Intner, and Lynn Lott

Contents

Foreword

It has been said that "we are born twice: once our mother does the labor; the second time we do the labor during our adolescence—and the second time is frequently harder on us and our mothers." Throughout history, the developmental state that we call adolescence has been noted as a time of great stress and turmoil, both for those passing through it and for those who must raise and educate adolescents.

When we look at human development, we see that individuals are born with no established identity. The task of the first five years is to accumulate data about oneself. The next five years are spent refining this data and learning to behave in ways that reflect this sense of self. Between ten and twelve years of age, most human beings formulate beliefs about themselves and the world that govern their actions (morals and ethics). Just when we know who we are and what we believe, along comes puberty and "everything we know about life and ourselves is swept away in a rush of surging hormones and we have to start over."

Bodies change dramatically—or don't change—when everyone else's do. Either can be quite traumatic! Look at any group of twelve year olds and you will see up to six years difference between their minds and their bodies (in either direction). They are subjected to a wide range of feelings and impulses they don't understand and have never encountered before. They must separate from their parents who are teaching them to be "*their* child in *their* family" and rediscover themselves as people in their own right.

What they most need during this time is close supportive contact with more mature people who make them feel listened to, understood for their thoughts and feelings, and affirmed as unique and significant people. They need room to test and validate themselves as people. They need patience and stability from those around them and opportunities to develop these characteristics within themselves.

Unfortunately, in America, just as all these changes begin, we choose this moment within the educational system to take them out of a relationship with a primary teacher that they know and trust, a stable group in which they feel secure, and an educational model they understand; and we make them part of a constantly rotating group of educational migrants that move from teacher to teacher on an hourly basis with bells ringing and groups changing constantly. Because of our mobility and urban lifestyle, extended family and long-term family friends, which were once the most critical socialization resources for the adolescent, are unavailable to most young people.

Opportunities for practical experience in life and the workplace, which are also essential needs of the adolescent, are no longer provided by our lifestyle in general. In the 1930's a 16-year-old was more likely to be employed full time in an apprenticeship of some kind or working on the family farm than to be attending school full time in total isolation from the realities of the adult world.

The label "teenager" first appeared commonly in American culture about 1955. That's why we know so little about them—they were invented in 1955. Always before we had dealt with "children" and "young people" and knew what to do with each. Only when millions of "baby boomers" entered adolescence with no meaningful role to play and without the support of extended family . . . in a world where parents had planned to support them through four years of college . . . did we begin to experience the "universal craziness" that we see today in young people assigned to limbo during this critical developmental stage. So we labeled them "teenagers."

If we think about it, this is a stereotype which says the most significant thing about a young person between 13 and 19 years of age is the "1" in front of their age. It says that we do not discriminate between the worth, significance and needs of a pre-pubescent 13-year-old and a 19-year-old man or woman. This is particularly problematic when we realize that the major task of adolescence is to break out of a stereotype (child) and achieve the status of individual. It is essential that we begin to perceive and refer to adolescents as *young people* in order to encourage and allow for the individuation process.

In *Positive Discipline for Teenagers,* the authors have drawn upon their extensive experience as counselors and workshop leaders in creating a very sensitive and practical resource for understanding and working with young people. The developmental insights are solid and helpful and the anecdotal material drawn from workshops and case studies gives warmth to the discussion.

The emphasis on firmness with dignity and respect highlights essential principles in teaching young people the nature of authority and helping to develop their own capacities of self-discipline, judgment and responsibility so essential in life. When this is coupled with the concept that "mistakes are wonderful opportunities to learn," we find a very rich and powerful set of tools for encouraging self-actualization and building healthy self-esteem in young people.

As a former director of the National Drug Abuse Training Center, I am encouraged by the special treatment of drug and alcohol abuse in this book. It is often difficult for people to recognize different patterns of use and abuse and the stages young people go through as they are exposed to drug and alcohol use/abuse in society. The task of using and developing sound judgment without being judgmental has always been difficult and the processes outlined in this book help to focus and simplify this task.

The guidelines for intervention are very sound and reflect our best understanding of this process to date. The emphasis on maintaining the relationship above all may be troublesome to those of a very authoritarian orientation. It might be helpful to consider this idea: "what good is a strong parental position if the child is alienated from the parent or is not converted to it?"

Overall, *Positive Discipline for Teenagers* will join the previous works of the authors as an important and very useful resource for working with and understanding young people and ourselves.

H. Stephen Glenn

Introduction

Going through the teen years can be like going through a war zone for both parents and teens. Since adolescence is such an important part of the individuation process, during which kids find out who they are, separate from their parents; since it's an opportunity for parents to explore their own unresolved teen issues; and since parents tend to do so many things during this time that make things worse instead of better, we wrote a book to help parents educate, challenge, and support their young people in an atmosphere of mutual respect, which affirms the self-worth of youth and parents.

Notes from Jane

I wanted to write this book because of the challenges and difficulties I faced as the parent of teenagers. During that time—even though intellectually I knew otherwise—I felt that my teenagers should be perfect by now, after all their years of being raised on the principles I teach in my book, *Positive Discipline*. Actually, they *were* perfect—perfect in their individuation (rebellion) process.

Since I forgot all I ever knew about individuation when it came to my own kids, I panicked. Instead of respecting their individuation process, I took their rebellious behavior personally and felt like a failure. Everything seemed out of control; I began to question everything I had been teaching for years. Maybe the authoritarians were right—maybe I *should* become a controlling parent. Was it possible that control would keep my teenagers from being so obnoxious, would save them from making mistakes that could be drastic for the rest of their lives—if they lived? No, I knew better than that. I knew that control was not the answer even though it sometimes provides the illusion of success on a short-term basis.

I later learned that children who are raised respectfully and democratically feel free to rebel under their parents' noses instead of going underground; but at the time I was extremely discouraged. Philosophically I knew what to do, but instead of showing respect, I lectured. Instead of working out logical consequences and following through, I became controlling. Instead of allowing the natural consequences of my children's choices to occur, I rescued and then became resentful and angry.

I was ready to throw in the towel. However, one thing I've learned about myself is that when I'm discouraged, instead of giving up, I look for help, for answers, for principles that work—and then I love to share what I've learned with others.

I went to a workshop on teenagers presented by Lynn Lott and knew I could find the answers I needed with her. Thanks to my work with Lynn, I was able to go to an even deeper level of understanding of all the principles I had been teaching. Working with my teenagers became an opportunity to relearn the meaning of mutual respect. It was a real test to respect differences between what were my issues, and what were theirs. When I let go of that, I was able to see what fascinating individuals my children are.

Notes From Lynn

At a series of workshops for sixth to eighth graders, I was appalled to discover that their parents were more protective and controlling of them than the parents of the younger kids I had worked with. When I suggested to these parents that they could still allow their kids to do what they'd done when they were little —like letting their kids choose their clothes each day— they fought me tooth and nail! I tried "making" these parents see the light, just as they were trying to "make" their children do what they wanted. Of course, this didn't work for any of us.

Out of that experience, I started developing techniques to help parents of teens let go and empower instead of fighting and arguing with them. It was at one of my workshops on teen empowerment that I met Jane Nelsen. In her sparkling, positive way she approached me and said, "We're going to write a book together on teens." With my crazy schedule, that was the last thing I ever thought I'd do—but with Jane's encouragement, we started the project.

While working together, Jane encouraged me again and again to model what I was teaching—to empower, not to overpower. Jane and I helped each other apply in our own families what we were formulating for other parents, and we helped each other go back and do some healing from our own teen years.

It's upsetting to me to feel like a second-class citizen or to treat anyone that way. Much of the conventional wisdom on teenagers invites behavior from parents that is disrespectful and puts our kids or ourselves in a one-down position. After writing this book, I am more convinced than ever that information based on the Dreikurs/Adlerian model with its base in mutual respect can help us parent in a win-win way, even with teenagers.

From Both of Us

Our experience working together has been so wonderful that we hated to see it end almost as much as we were thrilled to finally be finished with the book. Together and separately we went through all the processes we teach while working through some of our own unresolved teen issues. Since we wanted to test everything we teach, we organized Empowering Teens and Yourself in the Process workshops to help others understand the individuation process and practice the skills of listening, letting go, spending quality time with teens, problem solving, following through, and knowing what to do concerning drug and sex issues. Many of our examples come from these workshops. (In order to protect the identity of individuals, the examples we give are fictitious composites of the many stories we've heard over the years.)

We have shared our growth and understanding because we know your journey with teenagers may be just as challenging. We hope that with our encouragement you'll be able to grow with us while resolving conflict with your teenage son or daughter.

SECTION

I

The Individuation Process

Chapter 1

Whose Side Are You On?

Understanding Your Teen's World

Mr. Conrad completed a parent study group where he had become convinced of the importance of "getting into the world" of his teenage son, James, of understanding his son's life tasks, and of supporting him through the "rebellious" stage of his growth in ways that would develop confidence and life skills. However, when he learned that James had been skipping school, Mr. Conrad forgot all his new resolutions—he cornered James in his room and lectured him about his irresponsible behavior. James responded by telling his dad to "get off my back."

That hooked Dad into escalating his lecture into a heated scolding about James's disrespect to his elders.

James retorted, "I don't see you being respectful to me."

Dad was now so angry he felt like hitting his son for speaking to him that way. Instead, suddenly flashing back to his parenting group, he realized what was happening and changed his approach. "Son. Do you know I'm on your side?"

James retorted, "You could have fooled me." Then, with tears stinging his eyes, he said, "How can I think you're on my side when you're always putting me down?"

Dad put his arm around his son and, fighting tears of his own, said, "I see your point." Dad had become sensitive enough to know this was not the time to say any more.

It is easy to forget whose side we are on when we allow our fears, judgments, and expectations to take over. How could James know his Dad was on his side when he was being bombarded with lectures and scolded about his deficiencies? Fortunately, Dad had learned enough to catch himself behaving ineffectively and was able to change his approach. When he left his son's room he said, "Why don't we talk about this later when we're both in a better mood?"

Of course, as parents, we *are* on our kids' side. However, too often our behavior could fool any astute observer. Although we want our children to do well, how do we help them? We criticize, scold, lecture, correct, put them down, and let them know how disappointed we are in practically every move they make. In the name of "for their own good," we do everything we can to make them live up to our expectations. In the name of being "on their side," we lose sight of who they are and what their side *is*.

Can you imagine yourself in the shoes of your teenager? How would you feel if you were treated the way you treat him or her? Would you feel inspired and encouraged to do better? Would you feel confident about your capabilities to explore the world and decide for yourself (sometimes through mistakes) what makes sense to you? Would you feel that your parent was "for you" or "against you?"

Dad was caught up in the trap of thinking he knew what was best for James. He then tried to accomplish this through humiliating lectures and angry reprimands. When Dad became aware that he was acting as though he were against his son, he decided to really *show* that he was on James's side by using the skills he had learned in his parenting group.

▼ *To get into your teen's world, listen and be curious.*

To get into his son's world, Dad's first step was to find out why James didn't want to go to school. He approached James in a spirit of support rather than aggression. He asked his son if he would like to drop out of school, since at seventeen years old he didn't legally have to attend. Suspicious of this new approach, James asked, "And do what?"

Dad was honest. "I don't know. Maybe just do what you're doing—sleep in, work in the afternoon, spend time with your friends in the evening."

For the first time in a long time, James dropped his defensiveness and seemed willing to share his thoughts with his dad. "I don't really want to drop out, but I would like to go to a continuation school."

Dad wondered, "Why?"

James explained that in continuation school he could take the classes he'd failed in his regular school (if he remained where he was, he'd have to take those courses during the summer). In addition, since continuation school allows students to progress at their own speed, James felt he could not only catch up but do much better.

Now committed to being on James's side and supporting his idea, Dad decided to suspend his fears about what other people might think. He also put aside his stereotype of kids who go to continuation schools as kids who can't make it in regular schools. Instead, he looked at the benefits. He told his son that he believed James was able to do extremely well when allowed to progress at his own speed in an atmosphere of mutual respect. Dad agreed to call both schools and see what could be done about a transfer. (In his next study group, he learned that it would have been even more effective to make the calls *with* James rather than *for* him.)

Later, Dad told his parent study group, "I have no idea how this will turn out. I know I felt closer to my son because I got into his world and supported him in living his life as he sees it. I got out of the power struggle that was making us both feel like losers so we could look for solutions that would make us both feel like winners. I took a look at my own issues about being a 'good' parent. Whenever I try to 'make him do what I think is best,' I become a lecturing, moralizing father—but when I try to support James in being who he is, he's willing to talk to me and look for solutions. Whenever I worry about what others think (usually people whose opinion I don't really respect anyway), I create distance from my son."

▼ *Humiliation invites distance and resistance—respect invites closeness and cooperation.*

This dad had learned the difference between supporting his son and thwarting him. He learned that humiliating James did not bring him closer or give the impression that he was on his side. Instead, Dad invited cooperation by respectfully using his awareness and new-found parenting skills—and making sure the message of love got through by being on his sons's side.

▼ *Make sure the message of love gets through.*

A mother from the same parent study group shared her success. Her son, Matt, did not come home one night. Although she was both angry and afraid that he might be involved in drugs, she remembered from her parenting group that mistakes can be opportunities to learn. She also remembered that we create distance by scolding and lecturing. Instead of focusing on her fear and anger, which would make her son feel she was against him rather than on his side, she decided to focus on love.

When he came home the next morning, Mom said, "I'm glad you're okay. I was worried about you. Before you say anything, I want you to know that I love you, and I'm on your side." Matt seemed genuinely apologetic and said, "I'm really sorry, Mom. I was watching television at Steve's and fell asleep." Mom said, "I can see how that could happen, but I would have appreciated a call as soon as you woke up—even if it was in the middle of the night, so I would have known you were okay." Matt gave her a hug and repeated, "I'm sorry, Mom."

Enjoying the closeness she felt with her son and feeling more comfortable with her new skills, she continued, "I can see that you might not want to call after you've made a mistake if you're afraid I'm going to scold you like I usually do. I want you to know I'm not going to do that any more. No matter how many times you make a mistake, you can still call me and I'll be on your side, not against you."

Matt said, "Really?"

▼ *Work on agreements rather than demands.*

Mom could see that she had now created enough closeness to work on an agreement, "Could we work on an agreement about you calling me if you're going to be late?"

Matt said, "What if it's really late and you're asleep?"

Mom said, "Even if I'm asleep, I'm not sleeping well when I don't know if you're okay. You can call me anytime."

Matt agreed, "I hadn't thought about you worrying about me. I always just thought about you being mad at me. You don't need to worry about me, Mom, but I *will* call you whenever I'm going to be late."

That night when he got home, Matt went to his parents' bedroom and hugged them goodnight—something he hadn't done in months.

Later, Mom told her parenting group, "What a difference! Before, I never thought how Matt would feel about my anger at him whenever he was inconsiderate. I'd just yell and accuse him—and he'd feel that I was against him. This time, I let him see how much I love him, and we were able to come to an agreement. I still don't know if he was telling the truth about falling asleep on his friend's couch—but the way I used to act didn't encourage the truth at all. It created a great chasm in our relationship instead. This feels so much better to me. Matt's need for independence still scares me, but at least we have a basis for communication and some consideration this way."

▼ *Remember the difference between your world and theirs.*

Think back to your teen years. What were your issues? What did you think about all day? Take time to make a list of things that were important to you, then compare your list to the following issues mentioned by teens today:

Am I going to get invited to the dance?

What will I wear?

How can I find time for studying?

How can I be popular, or at least included?

How can I get a car?

What am I going to do about drinking, drugs, sex?

What is happening to my body? Will my breasts/penis be as big as the other kids'?

Will the kids think I'm cool?

How can I get my parents off my back?

Should I go to college?

What is there to do? (I'm bored!)

What should I wear?

What are the kids saying about me behind my back?

How can I ever please my parents? (All they care about is grades and chores.)

Notice they do not include?

Clean rooms

A clean house

Doing chores

Spending time with family

Being considerate

Being nice to brothers and sisters

Parents often think that their teens are doing or not doing something because they want to hurt their parents. As we can see from the two lists above, teenagers usually aren't even thinking about their parents. Parents need to accept and respect the fact that, for instance, chores are not a priority for kids. That doesn't mean they shouldn't do them. It does mean we'll have better results if we acknowledge to our kids, "I can understand that chores aren't a priority for you, but they need to be done anyway. Let's work on a plan to make it as easy as possible."

Teens want their parents to love them and leave them alone to pursue their life tasks. It's easier to leave them alone when we get into their world and understand them.

The Teen's World

To be on our teenager's side, we have to know who our teenager is. We can't be supportive unless we get into our kids' world and understand what is important to him or her. Each teenager is different, with some characteristics that are unique. To avoid stereotyping our teenager takes special listening, understanding, and respect for separate realities. However, other characteristics are almost universal for teenagers.

Privacy

Teens have a tremendous need for privacy, which parents often don't recognize. An important part of teenagers' maturation is finding out where they stand in relation to the various issues and values that life presents. They need privacy in which to experiment so that they won't make us or themselves feel as if they're bad for experimenting. If teenagers want to do something that runs counter to our attitudes and values, they try to do it so we don't find out. This protects them from experiencing our disapproval and protects us from feeling disappointment. Usually, teens return to the values they were taught at home—but they must be able to do this on their own, not because we want them to but because they themselves want to.

Parents often have a hard time with this process.

Although we don't want to tell our teenagers everything we ourselves think and do, we frequently demand this from our children. When our kids refuse, we say, "You're lying to me. How can you sneak around like that—after all I have done for you."

Talking on the Telephone

It's very scary for most adolescents to interact with their peers face to face. The telephone provides one of the safest ways for them to get to know each other. During their phone conversations, they can check out various ideas, attitudes, and feelings—and since they're in the process of maturing, they have a lot to check out! Teenagers need a lot of telephone time—which many parents find difficult to accept.

Dating

Junior high courtship is a very intricate process. What dating or "going with" someone means to adults and what it means to adolescents are two very different things. There are some adults who picture this as the first step to pregnancy. However, most teenagers see it as validation of their worth—a status symbol with their friends.

Let's say a boy wants to "go with" a girl. He first tells several of his friends, who then pass it through the grapevine so that the message quickly gets to the girl. She either says, "Totally cool" or "Gross." Either way, the message soon gets back to the boy. If the message is "totally cool," he tells his friends exactly when he is going to call her up and ask her. (To ask her face to face is not even considered.) She then sits by the phone, usually with several friends, waiting for the call. He calls, asks, she says yes, hangs up, and then screams in delight.

During their "courtship," they will probably break up and make up as many times the same way, through the grapevine, over the phone, with an audience.

Lying

Kids often lie because they love you. They want to be able to do what they do without hurting your feelings. While they sometimes lie to protect you, other times they lie to protect themselves—from your harsh opinions and possibly harsh actions.

If we are aware of the private logic behind our teens' behavior—such as that behind lying—we can deal with most problems and issues much more creatively. Such awareness—and understanding—takes creative listening rather than authoritative lecturing.

Understanding Your Teen's Point of View

▼ *It's important that you listen to, rather than lecture, your teen.*

Mr. Jenkins was giving his son Kirk a routine lecture on being more responsible about doing his homework. Kirk said, "Oh, Dad, you're never satisfied."

Dad was tempted to say, "What do you mean I'm never satisfied? If you would do it right I *would* be satisfied." However, since he had just learned about getting into the world of his teen and understanding his private logic by listening instead of lecturing, little bells rang in his head. He asked his son, "Do you think the only reason for doing or not doing your homework is for me?"

Kirk said, "Why else would I do it?"

Dad said, "I think we've found the problem. If you

don't see anything in it for yourself, no wonder you don't want to do your homework! Would you like to talk to me about what might be in it for you?"

Kirk reluctantly said, "I guess."

Dad hesitated, "Well, I'd rather not discuss it unless you really want to—I don't want this to sound like just another lecture from me. But I'm really interested in your ideas and what you see as valuable or not—but only if you want to."

Kirk agreed with a little more enthusiasm, "Okay."

Father and son spent about half an hour going over the pros and cons of an education. They agreed that it was possible to be an eighth-grade drop-out and still be a millionaire—but chances were slim. Kirk took a look at all the people he knew who had no education and were really struggling. He also acknowledged that he could never be the engineer he wanted to be without an education.

At the end of the conversation, Kirk said, "Well, okay, I'll do it, but I'm not going to like it."

Dad said, "I know how you feel. There are a lot of things I do even though I don't like to—but sometimes it is necessary to get what I want."

What About the Really Serious Problems?

Mr. Sylvan got a call from juvenile hall telling him that his son had been picked up for vandalizing. In his parenting group, Mr. Sylvan later shared how he got hooked, went crazy, and catastrophized: "'I'm a failure as a father. My son is amoral, will end up a criminal, and spend the rest of his life in prison.' I was so angry I told him he could stay in juvenile hall and rot for all I cared. Then I went to the other extreme and bailed him out—but not without a price. The price was a class 'A' guilt trip, 'How could you do this to me? I'm a failure. You're a failure. I have a thief for a son.'"

Imagine yourself in Mr. Sylvan's position. What else could you have done?

▼ *Remember to empathize.*

"What a bummer! I'd be pretty upset if that happened to me. Were you scared? How did they treat you? How did you feel?"

▼ *Decide what you will do—and do it with dignity and respect.*

If it's the first time your son has been in juvenile hall, you might bail him out. Then allow a cooling-off period before discussing the situation with empathy, dignity, and respect.

▼ *Talk with your teenager—not to, at, or for him or her.*

This is a tricky skill for most parents. It means forgoing lectures, judgments, guilt trips, and assumptions. It means really wanting to know and understand your teen's perspective, even though it may be very different from your own. Most important, it means asking your teenager if he would like to discuss the experience with you and stifling yourself if he says no. And he *will* say no if you lecture, judge, guilt trip, or assume you know what he thinks or should think.

If he agrees to talk with you, ask "what and how" questions that are totally void of judgment, but that express a sincere desire to understand his point of view. "What happened? What were you thinking of? What were you trying to accomplish? How was it for you? What was the most important thing you learned from this experience? How do you think you might handle this kind of thing in the future?"

You may want to share a similar experience of your own before asking these questions.

▾ *Share a time when you might have had a similar experience.*

Mr. Sylvan agreed that he could tell his son the following story: "I can remember a time when I was twelve years old. The police came to our house (we didn't have a juvenile hall in the small town where I was raised) because some friends of mine and I had thrown rocks through the windows of a neighbor's warehouse. I was just having fun with my friends. It didn't even occur to me that it would cost a lot of money to replace those windows. I felt so ashamed of myself and embarrassed for my parents. I knew I wasn't a bad kid. I had just done a stupid thing."

▾ *Use your experience to explore his or hers.*

Mr. Sylvan then might ask his son some of the following questions to draw him out: "I wonder if you had any feelings similar to mine. I wonder if you were just going along with the crowd, or had other motives. I wonder if you didn't think about the other person like I didn't. I wonder if you felt embarrassed like I did, or just angry about getting caught. I would really like to know if you feel like sharing with me."

If your teenager trusts you enough to share his or her perceptions with you, it's imperative that you don't judge or condemn.

▾ *Share what you learned and what you will do—not what you are going to try and make your teenager do.*

Mr. Sylvan wanted to practice how he would like to handle a similar situation if it happened again. Deciding he would like to talk with his son in advance about what he would do, he practiced in a role-play with another member of his study group: "This was scary for me, son. I felt like bailing you out this time, but I know I'll feel resentful if I bail you out again. I'd like you to know that if you make choices that lead you to juvenile hall again, I'll respect your right to experience the consequences. I'll support you in other ways. I'll visit you, and I'll always love you. However, it will be up to you to work things out with the juvenile justice system."

Mr. Sylvan was cautioned not to make this kind of statement unless he was willing to follow through. (See Chapter Ten for more information on the importance of following through and how to do it.)

▼ *Remember the difference between support and punishment.*

The above scenario illustrates the difference between support, which helps to teach life skills, and punishment. Usually, when kids make mistakes parents punish them. By doing this, we miss many opportunities to teach kids to deal with something that they'll encounter all their lives—they will make *mistakes*.

We have to remember that once a mistake has been made, it can't be undone. We might be able to learn from it, and we might be able to fix it, but we can't undo it. However, the process of "learning" and "fixing" can be so valuable that situations and relationships can even be *better* because of the mistake. But when we focus on the mistake rather than what can be learned from it, we miss great opportunities to learn and grow.

When we punish instead of support we are totally in our own world and our own perceptions. We forget about the world and the perceptions of our teens. Usually, we forget what life was like for us when we were teens—and when we do remember, we often don't understand how life is different for teens today.

Issues Related to Teen Stress Today

Parents spend too much time focusing on their own perceptions and remembering a world that is long past. Times change. Norms and values are different today from when we were teenagers. Unless we take the time to find out what is going on in their world today, we can't be on our kids' side.

Things that were unacceptable when we were kids may be perfectly acceptable for kids today. A good example is pierced ears. When some of us were growing up, if someone had their ears pierced it meant they were a punk or cheap. Unless you wanted to be perceived that way, you didn't get your ears pierced—it was only acceptable for mature women (in their thirties or forties). Now it's different. Pierced ears are a respectable fashion statement. But when our eight-year-old wants her ears pierced, we think, "No child of mine is getting her ears pierced. Not at eight. Do you want people to think you are cheap?" (We found an extreme example of changing times when we read a book written on adolescence in 1890. One of the greatest concerns of that day was to avoid being seen eating in public!)

The difference between what parents feel is acceptable and what their teens feel is acceptable can create stressful issues for both parents and teens. These are only some among many issues contributing to teenage stress.

We had the opportunity to ask several teens to brainstorm the following question: What kinds of things cause you stress? Their list appears below:

Friendship Issues

Peer pressure

Cliques

Belonging
Popularity

School Issues

Grades
Teacher expectations
Peer competition and class ranking
Athletics
Being stereotyped
Being "good"
Teachers favoring kids who are good
Being trusted

Family Issues

Relationship with parents
Parent expectations (for their teen "to have it all together" or to fulfill parents' unfulfilled dreams)
Fear of disappointing parents
Lack of respect from parents (for their teens' opinions, decisions, choice of friends)
Parents saying, "when I was a kid" and "because I said so"
Stepparents
Getting the runaround from parents
Being compared with siblings
Being stereotyped
Being "good"
Being trusted

General Issues

Freedom and responsibility

Money

Lifestyle

Equating mistakes with failure

Being given solutions rather than being allowed to find solutions themselves

Career decisions

Personal decisions regarding drugs, sex, trust

▼ *Remember that the grass is greener—even for teens.*

Like most members of the human species, teenagers often want what they don't have and take for granted what they do have. Kids who have a mother who stays home often wish she would go to work like the other kids' mothers. Those who have mothers who work often fantasize about having a mom who stays home and bakes cookies. Teens who have lost one parent might spend a lot of time thinking life would be better if only they had both parents. Kids who have both parents often don't appreciate them and just wish they would get off their backs. We can save ourselves much grief if we are willing to accept this normal human predicament in our teenagers. Teens create their own private logic based on how they interpret their particular situation in life.

Too often we focus on our agenda for our kids without even considering their concerns, their perceptions, and their separate realities. To be on the side of our teenagers, we need to consider these things.

We make many assumptions about teenagers—about our own kids—without ever really knowing what is going on inside their heads. And when they do tell us, we either take it personally or judge it negatively. To avoid these reactions, we need to remember how we ourselves felt as teens; if we look at the above list of teen concerns we'll find many similarities. In addition, we can focus on what the true goals of parenting are. "*Whose side am I on?*" is a good question to help us stay on track, or get back on track, so we can be truly supportive and helpful to our teenagers.

CHAPTER

2

A Growing Process

Parenting teens is a growing process for parents as well as for their teenagers. When parents learn to let go they allow their teens to develop according to their uniqueness—rather than trying to mold them into who the parents want them to be. For many parents, this is difficult and takes growth on their part. Often, we may feel that we and our teens are failures if our kids don't conform to society's norms. Conflict with teenage sons and daughters begins when fear of failure is the basis of parenting. Conflict escalates when parents increase control and pressure tactics, giving teenagers no choices except to rebel or to become "approval junkies" (when they feel they must win their parents'—and society's—approval at almost any cost).

The growing process we advocate in this book is illustrated most beautifully by Kahlil Gibran in *The Prophet*:

> Your children are not your children.
> They are the sons and daughters of Life's longing for itself.

They come through you but not from you,
And though they are with you yet they belong not
to you.

You may give them your love but not your
thoughts,
For they have their own thoughts.
You may house their bodies but not their souls,
For their souls dwell in the house of tomorrow,
which you cannot visit, not even in your dreams.
You may strive to be like them, but seek not to
make them like you.
For life goes not backward nor tarries with
yesterday.

Most parents are moved by this passage's beauty and simplicity but do not know how to apply it to their lives. To many it seems permissive and passive. This book shows how to apply Gibran's wisdom with a very active, supportive style of parenting that is neither permissive nor controlling. We teach parenting skills and attitudes based on understanding the growing process of teenagers. We include many suggestions on "what to do" in the areas that concern most parents of teens. Everything we teach is based on respect—respect for our teenagers, for ourselves, and for the growing process itself.

Adults in Training

Part of the growing process means teaching kids the skills they need to be successful grown-ups—people who know how to handle money, to solve problems, to learn from mistakes; people who possess negotiation skills and the skills of listening to, respecting, and cooperating with others. What we want most of all is to be able to help them to become people who know who they are, what they feel, what they want, and how to get what they want in a way respectful to themselves and others.

Although teenagers need to learn successful grownup skills, support in learning these skills is not what they usually get from us. Teenagers need more freedom and a different kind of guidance than younger children. Instead, we often attempt to control our teens, to limit their freedom, thereby prohibiting them from learning the skills necessary to successful adulthood. We do this primarily because we don't understand the importance of individuation, the process through which every adolescent must go to become a self-actualized human being able to reach his or her full potential.

Many of us were not supported during our teenage years to be fully functioning human beings and to develop our unique potential. Instead, we became approval junkies or rebels—and we therefore have many unresolved issues from that time. It's almost impossible for us to deal effectively with our teenagers until we resolve our own teenage issues. In this book, especially in Chapter Seven, we'll help you discover and resolve your own issues so that you may support your teenagers more effectively.

▾ *Parents have to grow themselves before they can help their kids grow.*

The following are attitudes which allow parents to better support their teens' growth:

1. Desire to grow and change.
2. Willingness to look at what you're doing that is effective and what is not effective.
3. Accepting mistakes as opportunities to learn.

4. Willingness to look at and try alternatives.
5. Learning about unresolved issues that get in the way of your effectiveness.
6. Willingness to make new decisions and interpretations from childhood experiences. (We will teach processes to help you with this in Chapter Seven.)
7. Seeing beyond your own past issues so you can listen and understand your teen today.
8. Letting go—having faith in yourself and your kids.

An important part of this book is providing information, methods, and encouragement for parental growth so that parents can better support their kids' growth.

Short-Sighted Parenting

Common methods for parenting teenagers are to tighten the reins of control with punishment, grounding, lectures, removal of privileges—or to give up in total frustration and feelings of helplessness; in short, to be authoritarian or permissive. We call this short-sighted parenting.

Short-sighted parenting limits the growth process. Short-sighted parents look for immediate solutions that seem to control the behavior of children; they do not consider long-range results or long-range goals. We say "seem to control" because short-sighted parenting *does* seem to get results, even though these are short term. Grounding or removing privileges does give temporary relief from a problem behavior. A grounded teenager may do his or her homework for a while—but at what price? If the long-range results are rebellion or low self-esteem, then we must beware of what works.

In the other extreme of short-sighted parenting—permissiveness—we "stick our heads in the sand and hope it goes away." We do not even consider teaching life skills for long-range results.

Control

Trying to gain control through punishment or lectures makes parents feel that they have done their job. This is the most popular form of short-sighted parenting. If all power is taken away from teenagers, they never have the opportunity to make their own mistakes and learn from them; they never have the opportunity of finding and setting their own limits. And many teens are provoked to rebel continuously against such control, making for little familial understanding or happiness.

Example: A parent attending one of our workshops challenged us on the issue of giving up control. He explained that his fifteen-year-old daughter habitually came home later than the curfew he had set for her. The last time she came home an hour late he grounded her for a week. When he was asked what he thought she learned from this, he said, "She learned that she can't get away with this behavior." When asked how he felt about this, he said, "I feel good. It's not my job to be her buddy. It's my job to be her parent."

Further exploration revealed that even though this father hated it when his parents grounded him, he believed it was the parent's job to set rules and restrictions and to punish kids when they disobey. He felt a sense of accomplishment that he had done his job, although he admitted that grounding did not solve the problem. His daughter continued to come home late and he continued to ground her. Later, he realized that he still hates his father, and that grounding didn't do him any good. He said, "Come to think of it, I acted like my daughter and continued to defy my father as long as I lived at home. I didn't keep curfew until I left home and felt like getting home early so I could get a good night's sleep. And I still don't want to have anything to do with my father. Good grief, I don't want that kind of relationship with my daughter. Okay. I'm ready to learn alternatives."

Giving Up

Giving up is the other common form of short-sighted parenting. Instead of controlling, parents simply try to ignore their child's behavior, hoping fervently that it will go away by itself. It usually doesn't. However much teenagers say they want to be left alone, in reality they need and want *some* guidance. They still need a co-pilot. Even though they act as if they would like to throw you out of the plane, they feel abandoned when you go.

Example: One mother could see that control was increasing rebelliousness in her son without teaching him life skills. She made the mistake of giving up control and not replacing it with other methods; instead of moving to the co-pilot seat, she got off the plane—and it floundered badly. Her son had been staying out late. Now he began staying out all night. Instead of punishing him the way she used to, she wavered between doing nothing and buying him things to show she loved him. Although she tried to get him to talk to her about his feelings, he refused. She blamed herself and her ignorance: things would get better if she could only figure out what to do. So she "did nothing" out of feelings of frustration and inadequacy.

Eventually, this mother quit blaming herself and quit trying to buy her son's love. Instead, she purposely decided to "do nothing." There is a difference between doing nothing out of frustration and doing nothing on purpose. The former conveys the message: "We're both failures, and it's mostly your fault. How could you do this to me?" The latter conveys the message: "I respect you and have faith in you. I also have respect for and faith in myself. I'm here if you need me, but I won't force my judgments and criticisms on you. I'll tell you how I feel without demanding that you tell me how you feel." This mother decided to love her son no matter what he did, and she told him, "I hope someday you'll talk to me about whatever is going on for you instead of being such a jerk to me." She told him she had faith in him to learn from his own experiences. We don't know the "end" of this story. That's what faith is all about. Sometimes all a co-pilot can do is offer love and faith.

Did we say *all*? That *all* may not get the immediate results of short-range parenting, but the payoff for both parent and teen is tremendous for long-range results.

Neglect

Neglect is another form of short-sighted parenting. Although it can take many forms—some quite severe (for instance, complete indifference to a child's physical, emotional, or mental welfare)—many forms of neglect, such as aloofness, emotional unavailability, and lack of communication, occur out of ignorance or misguided beliefs.

Example: One mother complained that her husband refused to parent her son and daughter from a previous marriage. He expected her to handle all their discipline, but criticized her parenting methods. Although he complained vehemently about their behavior, he refused to deal directly with the kids. As a result, the kids felt unloved and unimportant—and lacked respect for this grownup who had lived with them since they were preschool age. The father was unable to see his behavior as neglectful: he provided for the family's economic welfare, advised the mother on raising her children, and co-parented his younger biological child. But when he realized that, in fact, he *had* been neglecting his stepchildren, he told them so, saying he'd made a mistake. He told them that he loved them, that they were important to him, and he found ways to spend quality time with each of them. Instead of turning his back on what happened with these children (and later complaining to the mother), he involved himself in their lives by sharing his feelings and ideas directly with them.

Sometimes neglect looks like the above example. Sometimes it takes the form of parental chemical dependency or workaholism. Sometimes it's the result of despair—the belief that no matter what you do it will not work so it's better to do nothing at all.

Overprotection and Rescuing

Another form of short-sighted parenting, overprotection and rescuing, makes parents feel that they've done their job because they protect or rescue their children from pain or suffering. However, this short-sighted parenting robs their teenagers of learning the life skills for self-reliance.

Example: Gina called her ex-husband, Tony, early one morning and asked him to rush to her house, 100 miles away, with a picture that their son Chris needed for a project due the next day. Tony refused, saying in a firm and friendly manner, "I'm not willing to rescue Chris. I'm sure he knew earlier in the semester what he needed for this project. He's chosen not to do what needed to be done. I don't know why you're on the phone with me doing Chris's work. If he has a problem and needs some help, he can give me a call. I'll be glad to bring the picture next weekend when I come down. In the meantime, I'm sure Chris can figure out another solution."

Although Chris is a freshman in college, his mother still runs around doing his homework. He will never learn to be on his own as long as she is willing to take care of him.

Tony later shared with his parent study group that it was hard for him to stay out of the plan to rescue his son. However, he recently learned that his own habitual procrastination and frequent inability to finish projects resulted because his mom used to rescue him, and he let her. He told his group, "My mom typed my papers. I never learned to write because I would wait until the last minute and plagiarize. I never learned to spell because my mother corrected all my spelling."

Overprotection and rescuing may make you appear a saint. Your kids may even love it—but it doesn't help them learn to fly on their own. When you avoid overprotection and rescuing, your kids may momentarily think you don't care; they may even accuse you of not loving them. But this doesn't last—they know better in the long run. Many grown-ups are angry at their parents for not allowing them to learn the skills that serve them in their marriages, jobs, and life in general.

Another Way

Most parents focus on short-term rather than long-term goals. I may rescue my daughter by giving her money for skiing because my short-term goal is to save her from experiencing pain and disappointment—but I've totally wiped out my long-range goal of teaching her to be financially responsible. I may ground my child for coming home late because my short-term goal is to let him know he can't get away with being irresponsible and inconsiderate—but I've wiped out my long-term goal of teaching him communication, negotiation, and creative planning skills.

All short-sighted parenting methods offer short-term results and do not teach our children the skills they need to become successful adults. Some short-sighted parenting methods, such as control, are not really effective even short term. A parent who has used punishment or other forms of control may think he or she has been effective in eliminating certain behaviors, when the fact is that the child has only been forced "underground." By conscientiously giving up control, you will discover that you have not given up anything but the illusion of control.

If you are feeling defensive, ask yourself, "What are my long-term goals—to control behavior or to teach life skills?" The next question is, "Does what I'm doing work to achieve my goals?"

Long-Term Goals

Many parents have shared with us some version of the following list of characteristics that embody their long-term goals for their children: courage, responsibility, cooperation, self-esteem, respect of self and others, success, and a sense of humor.

We have found, however, that most parents haven't given a lot of thought to what exactly constitutes these characteristics. We offer the following definitions:

1. *Courage:* The ability to hang in there when the

going gets tough and to have enough faith in themselves to know they can make it. Too many kids fall apart when the going gets tough. Some even commit suicide as a permanent solution to a temporary problem.

2. *Responsibility:* Knowing they can learn from their mistakes and that they can try again. Often, parents assume responsibility for their teens' mistakes by punishing their kids without giving them the chance to learn and make adjustments. When our kids stay our late, instead of saying, "You made a mistake. Let's figure out what we can learn from this and what we can do differently next time," we say, "You made a mistake. Now you're grounded for the next six months!"

3. *Cooperation:* The ability to get along with others. Without realizing it, we cut off many of the opportunities our kids have for learning how to get along with others. We do this by insisting they adhere to our rules governing which children and which activities are acceptable and which are not, rather than engaging our teens in working out solutions to conflicts. We give such orders as "No, you can't go out with that person" or "I don't want you wasting so much time on the phone talking to your friends." (We say this at the time when talking on the phone provides one of the best opportunities for teens to learn how to get along with others.)

4. *Self-esteem:* To know, accept, and value their own thoughts and feelings. To respect and value differences in themselves and others instead of seeing these competitively or judgmentally. To take care of themselves, including how they treat their bodies.

5. *Respect for self and others:* Having a high level of social interest, which means wanting to contribute to society and knowing they can be significant in a positive way.
6. *Success:* Being happy, contributing members of society by doing what they enjoy in life while benefiting, or at least not hurting, others.
7. *Sense of humor:* Not taking themselves, or others, too seriously.

It's important to note that many of these qualities can occur in negative ways as well. Delinquents can have courage, be responsible, get along with others, like themselves, and contribute to a group. Our emphasis is to help our kids develop these qualities positively instead.

If what you're doing is not working to meet these long-term goals, then it's time to try something different.

Long-Range Parenting

Long-range parenting means being more interested in long-range results and long-range goals rather than in immediate short-term solutions. One of the first issues to overcome if we wish to move in the direction of long-range parenting is our aversion to mistakes. Although it's human to make many mistakes during the growing process (and indeed we continue to make mistakes throughout life), we often equate these with failure rather than with an opportunity to learn. Because of this, we try to protect our children from making mistakes and thus deprive them of valuable experience. It is not our job to control or overprotect our children; instead, we can support them in their growth. By allowing them to make mistakes and supporting the learning that ensues, we can nurture our teens' growth. If we attempt to protect them by using one of the short-sighted parenting methods, we may fan the flames of rebellion or create approval junkies and the disease of perfectionism.

Sitting back and watching our children make mistakes can feel very uncomfortable, unless we have our sights on future benefits. Long-range parenting means being more interested in the skills our teens learn than in the mistakes they make. Long-range parenting means being available as a teacher and consultant rather than being a controlling director and punitive dictator.

Parents with short-term goals are concerned with controlling their teens' behavior right now (or else hoping that the behavior will change by itself). They do not examine the future results of their present concerns. However, parents with long-term goals are interested in helping their children grow into independent adults, and they examine their parenting methods with this in mind.

Change Can Be Uncomfortable

The more uncomfortable you feel, the better you are doing. You may feel comfortable punishing, rescuing, or overprotecting because you are used to it and believe that it is right. And you will probably feel very uncomfortable saying, "No, you can't have money for skiing" or "I'm uncomfortable about you coming home so late last night and I want to talk with you about it." It takes understanding and a leap of faith to feel confident that you're doing a better job of parenting when your actions relate to your long-term goals.

You may have heard the story about the little boy

who was watching a butterfly struggle to break out of a cocoon. Feeling sorry for the butterfly, the boy opened the cocoon and set the butterfly free. But after flying only a few yards, the butterfly fell to the ground and died. The little boy hadn't realized that the butterfly needed the struggle to gain the strength that would allow it to fly and live.

Long-range parenting gives kids the strength and skills to leave home and make it on their own.

Parental Courage

If you ask teens whether they want their parents to stop grounding them, they may say, "No. I don't want that kind of responsibility for my life. It's way too scary." Kids often want their parents to take responsibility for them through overprotection or overcontrol. This frees teens to do what they want and blame the consequences on their parents—or it protects teens from the risks of trying, failing, and learning.

Our goal is to help parents develop the courage and the skills for long-range parenting so that their children can develop courage, responsibility, cooperation, self-esteem, respect for self and others, and a sense of humor. The growing process can be an enriching experience for both parents and teens.

Chapter

3

Adolescence and Individuation

You know you have adolescents when you hear yourself complaining, "They have no purpose. They won't help. They only care about their friends. Their room is a mess. I can't trust them. There is no control. I can't stand their hair, their clothes, their makeup, or their music. They waste their money. They resent me and idolize rock stars. They are on drugs and treat me like dirt. They are moody and self-centered."

You know you have adolescents when you hear them complaining, "My parents treat me like a kid. They think I'm having sex all the time. They butt in. They hate my friends. They give advice. They try to live my life for me. They are never satisfied. All they do is ask questions and control my life."

In our workshops on teenagers, we asked one group to draw a "normal" teen—how most parents see their teens. Their composite teen was messy, self-centered, listened to loud music, defied authority, preferred friends to family, decorated room with posters, valued cars and an independent lifestyle, needed to conform to clothing styles of peers (no matter how gross), smoked and drank.

Comments from the group included, "Well, this is an exaggeration. All teens aren't like this." "But, it sure does depict the rebelliousness because most of them are a lot like this." "It helps to be reminded that my teen would not be normal if he cleaned his room." "Come to think about it, I was like that once." (This last comment was a nice reminder to the group that we continue to grow and change beyond adolescence.)

Another group was asked to draw a "dream" teen —how most parents want their teens to be. Their composite teen was a prom queen or king, someone who kept agreements ("I promise to be there on time, as always"), volunteered to help, loved to talk to parents ("Let me tell you everything about my life"), ate only healthy food, didn't watch TV, was very athletic, earned two scholarships (one athletic and one academic), scored high on the SAT, got a job for the summer all lined up in January, supplied own money for hair or makeup and saved the rest for college and a car, respected everyone, loved brothers and sisters, was respectfully assertive, and was an A student.

One participant commented, "A teen like this wouldn't have any friends. No one could stand her." Another commented, "I have friends who have a teenager like this and I can't stand her."

This exercise revealed that while we may fantasize about a dream teen, we instinctively know that such a creature would be abnormal and undesirable. However, the reality of living with a "normal" teen can be quite painful for parents, unless they are able to come to a deeper understanding of what is going on during adolescence.

Another source of anxiety for parents during this time is that they tend to think that the way kids behave as teenagers is how they have *become* and will *be* for the rest of their lives. Parents panic when they think their teens have grown up to become terrible people. But teens are *not* grown up. Their behavior is temporary as they struggle to find out who they are and how they *will* grow up.

Individuation: The Teen Life Task

Many life tasks are inherent in child growth and development. These tasks may be physical, intellectual, emotional, social, psychological, or spiritual. During adolescence, individuation is the primary task, as outlined below.

1. Adolescents have a need to find out who they are, how they are different from their family, how they feel about things, what their own values are, and what they think about things. This process of separation from the family in preparation for an independent adulthood is called individuation.
2. Individuation usually looks like rebellion to parents. Although most parents worry when their teenagers rebel, it would be more appropriate to worry if they didn't. Teenagers must begin their separation from their family, and rebellion gives them the energy to do this. At first, teens may rebel by looking at what is important to us or what we want, then doing exactly the opposite. Later, they may rebel in other ways—but at first,

individuation is primarily a reaction against their parents.

3. Whether they like it or not, adolescents are maturing physically and sexually, undergoing biological processes that are essentially out of their control. In addition to the tumultuous, contradictory feelings these major changes cause, adolescents may feel anxiety regarding their rate of change—they may feel their physical maturation is too quick or too slow in relation to that of their peers. (Most parents would prefer their kids to mature slowly, but nature has her own patterns!)
4. The physical maturation process, with its sudden and powerful hormonal changes, causes mood swings. Without premeditation, teens are delightful one minute and biting our heads off the next. In addition, some teens are in such a rapid rate of physical growth that they experience real "growing pains" where their bodies actually hurt.
5. Teens need to work out their relationships with peers to find out if and how they fit in. Friendships take the place of time spent with the family. While this helps teens in their task of separation, it is often interpreted by parents as rejection or rebellion.
6. Teens have a strong desire to find out what they're capable of—they need to test their power and importance in the world. This means that they want to decide what they can do for themselves without being directed and ordered. However, some teens find this so intimidating that they *want* others, usually their peers, to tell them what to do.

7. Teens have a great need for privacy so they can work out a lot of the already-mentioned tasks without an audience. Since their rate of development moves so fast and is out of their control, it can be embarrassing to have their parents watching and knowing. In addition, to figure out what's important to them, teens may do things their parents wouldn't approve of before deciding for themselves that they might not want to do them either. They need the room to test these things without getting in trouble or disappointing their parents.
8. During this period, teens tend to put their parents down and try to show them how "stupid" they are. Sometimes teens act embarrassed around their parents and families in public or may even refuse to be seen with them. The affection that may have been a normal part of family life may suddenly become taboo.
9. Teens think of themselves as omnipotent and all-knowing. Parents who try to tell them how to dress or eat or what they can or can't do just don't seem to understand that the teen *never* gets sick, *doesn't* get cold, *doesn't* need sleep, and can live *forever* on junk food or not eat *at all*.

Understanding Individuation

All individuation (or rebellion) does not look alike. It may take as many different forms of behavior as their are different teens. But there *are* some general behaviors that most teenagers exhibit, such as not wanting to be with their families, not wanting to have clean rooms, and listening to music parents hate. Some rebel mildly or passively, some severely and aggressively.

The most difficult type of rebellion for parents—also the most typical—is that directed against the things that are most important to them. If you're a math teacher, it's possible that your teenager will fail in math. If piano lessons are important to you, prepare for a fight. If religion is important to you, guess what? For us as therapists, it's difficult to watch other teenagers flock to our doors, while our own kids think "shrinks are stupid" and refuse to share anything important with us. It can be especially hard when you've felt close to a child who once told you "everything" and now sneaks off to concerts or other forbidden places rather than face your disapproval or disappointment.

Individuation often becomes all-out rebellion when parents invalidate the normal growth process in the following ways:

1. When we don't understand this individuation process.
2. When we take the individuation process personally: "How could she do this to me?"
3. When we feel guilty: "This wouldn't be happening if I had been a better parent."
4. When we get scared about the mistakes our teens make as they try different behaviors and different values.
5. When we try to stunt their individuation through control, punishment, overprotection, or neglect.
6. When we think that what they're doing is what they've *become* and who they will be *forever*.
7. When teens *do* stick with some of these behav-

iors "forever" and we don't respect their right to be different from us.

8. When we don't respect and support the individuation process.

In other words, individuation might not escalate into open rebellion if parents could eliminate all the above behaviors—but we don't know many parents who can do this. It's also true that teenagers sometimes think they *have* to rebel to individuate, even when parents are supportive of their individuation. With all this in mind, we'll continue to use *individuation* and *rebellion* interchangeably, since all the above behaviors are as normal for parents as resulting rebellion is for teenagers.

Support Through Understanding

Understanding what constitutes a normal teen life task and what does not can be a great relief for both parents and teenagers. With such an understanding, teens won't feel as guilty and conflicted by wanting to please their parents and yet wanting to behave in ways that won't please their parents. Parents don't have to take all their teens' behavior personally. We can stop wondering if our teens are doing this just to hurt us and we can stop feeling guilty about not being good-enough parents. We don't have to worry that we've failed. We can look at their behavior as something they are doing *now*, as part of a normal developmental task, and not necessarily indicative of who they will be when they grow up.

Tammi is fourteen. She doesn't understand why she does some of the things she does. She loves her parents and doesn't want to hurt their feelings, so she can't understand why she goes to the beach with her friends when she knows her folks don't want her to. She feels guilty because, in addition to disobeying, she also lies, telling them she's going to a friend's house because she knows her parents won't mind that.

Tammi's counselor asked her, "Would you be puzzled if you were eleven months old and you started pulling yourself up on the furniture and tried to walk? Would you wonder why you were doing that?"

Tammi said, "No."

"Well, then you can stop wondering and feeling guilty about what you are doing now. You are doing your job. What you are doing is normal adolescent behavior."

Tammi heard this with a sigh of relief—but it's not that easy for her parents. Nor is it easy for most parents. Why? Because we treat the life tasks of a teenager much differently than we treat the life tasks of a toddler. Why? One reason is our ignorance of the individuation process. Another reason is our fears (some of them well-founded—such as life-threatening mistakes—and others based on our own hopes for our children). We also carry many unresolved issues from our own teen years that can get in our way. And, finally, teens can be terribly irritating to live around. Nevertheless, irritating teen behaviors are a normal part of the teen developmental process. Ignoring there behaviors in the hope that they'll go away doesn't work, but understanding them can help us and our teens live through this stage with more ease—and even some enjoyment.

Not Permissiveness

The reaction of many parents who hear us talking about the ineffectiveness of control, punishment, and overprotection believe we are suggesting permissiveness. We do not advocate permissiveness. We will be offering many alternatives to control and overprotection in our section on nonpunitive parenting. For now, it's important to establish that permissiveness does not provide the support and life-skills training that adolescents need to develop their full potential. Doing everything for our children and protecting them from the consequences of their behavior robs them of opportunities to do for themselves and learn from their mistakes. Understanding the developmental life tasks of our children is the first step we must take before knowing how to give them the support they need. We often react inappropriately when we don't understand those developmental life tasks.

Different Reactions to Developmental Life Tasks

Let's look at how differently we handle the life task of a toddler and the life task of a teenager. Ten-month-old Michael is learning to walk. He falls down and bumps his head. He cries. Mom doesn't spank him and say, "Bad boy! You shouldn't try to walk. See how much it hurts you," because she knows that learning to walk is a developmental life task for children during this period. Since children don't master this task for awhile they are called toddlers. Parents understand this and, knowing that many mistakes will be made during the process, they comfort, support, and encourage. "Come on, you can do it. Hooray! Isn't that wonderful? Let's call Grandma and tell her Michael took his first step today." Michael feels proud and elated.

Now let's look at a similar developmental task for a teenager. Michael, now age sixteen, comes home after his first time using the family car with a dent in the right fender. Furious, Mother says that he won't be able to use the car again until he can prove he's responsible. She also tells him that she will keep his allowance until the deductible for the insurance is paid and that if the insurance rates are raised he'll have to pay for it himself. Dad comes home and questions Michael to find out if he was drinking, talking to his friends instead of paying attention to his driving, or putting a tape in the car stereo instead of watching the road. Of course, Grandma is not called. Michael feels angry and stupid.

Dangers of stunting adolescent development. As parents, do we help our teenagers learn from their mistakes with encouragement and support or do we slap their hands and try to "keep them in their playpen?" Do we stunt their growth by insisting that they "crawl" instead of walk?

Let's go back to ten-month-old Michael. Imagine that suddenly you decided learning to walk was bad. Every time Michael pulled himself up on the table, you knocked him down or put him in his playpen or lectured him about being a bad boy. Suppose you even went so far as to forbid him to stand and insisted that he only crawl. Now picture this child at four years of age. He would be severely developmentally stunted, not only physically but emotionally. By being thwarted in something as natural and necessary as walking, baby Michael could suffer the consequences the rest of his life.

Although the above example is extreme, our sixteen-year-old Michael could experience damage as well. Teen developmental tasks can be so scary and upsetting to parents that they often do everything they can to reverse the process. When they succeed, their teenager may become extremely rebellious or extremely compliant. Extremely rebellious teens put most of their energy into cover-ups, power struggles, and manipulation rather than into individuation and development of their full potential. Extremely compliant teens become approval junkies, whose main life task is trying to live up to the expectations of others—and never quite making it.

Parents with long-range goals do not want to retard natural individuation (even when it looks like rebellion) for some other very important reasons. When teenage development is thwarted, teens may take extreme measures—such as suicide, drug abuse, dropping out, or running away—to ease the frustration or pain of not being able to do something that is natural and necessary to their development.

Was your growth stunted? Many adults have never individuated. We grew up in our families as "good" little boys and girls who went on to marry someone who would tell us what to do and how to feel. Or we went to a job where we could follow orders and do what we were told. Many of us never feel comfortable being "who we are" because we feel that we might not live up to the expectations of "someone else." Others had to work so hard to break through oppressive control that they continue acting out and rebelling throughout their adult lives. Some of us have had years of therapy and workshops to help us grow up and individuate because we didn't do it when it was developmentally appropriate. These feelings were poignantly expressed in the following poem written by a woman in one of our workshops.

When I was a kid
My Dad would come in my room at night
And tell me I couldn't read
That I had to shut off the light
And go to sleep.

My folks would tell me
Where I could drive my car

Who I could pick up in it
When I had to be home
And make sure I never took any trips alone.

When I was in college
My Dad was hysterical
When I smoked or drank coffee
And when I stayed up late to study for finals
He came in and yelled at me to go to sleep
And turn out the light.

Now I'm a grown-up married woman
And I can't read in bed
Or drive where I like
Or do what I want
Or be who I am.

If we didn't rebel, or individuate, as teens, we have to work it out somewhere along the line; sometimes the costs are much higher than the consequences of the mistakes we might have made as teens. Unhappy marriages, divorces, job dissatisfaction, lack of creativity, failure to deal with money, inability to have close relationships, inability to respectfully stand up for our needs and wants, and poor mental and physical health are just a few of the problems that may be left over from our teen years if we were not encouraged in our developmental tasks.

Parents often see "the good kid" as the standard. These kids need help too. They've often sold out and become pleasers and approval junkies. Their parents used them as the standard and said to the others, "Why can't you be more like your brother or sister? At least I have one that doesn't give me any trouble." The good kid felt significant only if he or she was getting this kind of praise. Many of these kids fall apart when they make their first big mistake. Some cannot handle the competition of finding they are not the only special kid in college. Unable to handle this pressure some even commit suicide because they don't think they can stay on top.

We don't want to give our teenagers such a legacy. If we attempt to discourage their individuation, we may stunt their development and prevent them from finding out who they are independent of others. They won't learn self-evaluation: "What do I like? What do I want to do? What works and doesn't work for my personal joy and satisfaction? What do I have to offer?" If we don't allow our kids to make their own mistakes—or if we treat their mistakes as failures—they may adopt an extremely distorted view of what it means to make a mistake. Instead of valuing mistakes as opportunities to learn, they see them as failures in their ability to live up to the expectations of others.

If I've raised my kids on the principles of positive discipline, will they still rebel? Let's assume you've been using the democratic model of parenting. You've been kind and firm. You've used problem-solving skills in family meetings, and your kids have become very responsible and cooperative. You have a great relationship with them and are convinced they can go through adolescence smoothly. Not true. A teenager *has* to be a teenager. There is no technique in the world that can tame hormones—and when they start jumping around, your kids will begin their developmental tasks.

▼ *Don't Panic.*

This is not the time to question everything you've been doing as a parent or to think "maybe this democratic stuff doesn't work." Maybe, you tell yourself, you should have given more lectures on morality and taken more control so your kids wouldn't be so inconsiderate and disrespectful now. Maybe, you wonder if you should tighten the reins before it's too late. This is not an easy time for any parent.

It can help to know that kids raised under the democratic model often feel freer to rebel under their parents' noses. They may even use many of the messages we gave them to fuel their rebellion, such as, "But I thought you told me you wanted me to think for myself and listen to my own inner voices," and "Why are you so upset? You always taught me that mistakes are opportunities to learn. We can fix the dented fender."

During the individuation process, kids want to, and *need* to figure things out for themselves—they can't have parents do it for them. Our teens are saying the kind of help I want is to know you are there, you won't abandon me, and you love me. Other than that, I'd like to work this out myself. If I want to tell you something, I will; but I don't want you asking me what I'm feeling and what's going on.

Raising Teenagers To Be Who They Are

A master gardener knows there is no way she can make petunias grow into roses. To help flowers be what they are meant to be, she simply plants them in a good environment with the right amount of sun and shade. She then waters, weeds, fertilizes, and maybe even talks to them. In other words, she adds nurture to nature.

We begin our workshops on parenting teens by giving every participant a plant. Some are gorgeous, some not so gorgeous. Some have wilting flowers, some broken stems. We then ask the following questions, which we would like you to consider: How many of you got your favorite plant? If you got a petunia but wanted a rose, is there anything you can do to make that petunia grow into a rose? What if you got a plant that you don't think the neighbors or your relatives will like? What if you got a cactus and you live in Alaska? What if you got an unhealthy or damaged plant? Since you got what you got, what do you need to do to help your plant grow into the best it can be?

Growing human beings is a lot more complicated than growing plants, but some of the principles are the same: we need to figure out how to provide the kind of nurturing atmosphere that helps them grow to their full potential, and we need to understand what their potential is as well as what their limitations are. Without such understanding, we sometimes stunt their growth by improper nurture or by trying to change a petunia into a rose.

We get in the way of nurturing our teenagers to become the best they can be when we try to control who they are; when we try to force them to be who we think they should be "for their own good"; when we catastrophize mistakes; and when we take everything they do personally. We help them achieve their potential when we provide unconditional love, support through mistakes, and a safe environment in which to make their inevitable mistakes and to explore who they are—and when we take care of ourselves so that we continue to grow into the best we can be.

Many parents have a picture of how they want their kids to grow up. Their picture may not fit their children's picture at all. Some don't want to go to college, join the family business, be a doctor, or whatever else their parents may have in mind for them. Some go along and many grow up as adults who are distorted and stunted in their growth, like bonsai trees, which are seen as wonderful specimens of successful parenting—and they are not. They don't know how to think for themselves. They don't know how to deal with money.

They don't know how to deal with values. They don't know how to recover from mistakes by learning and growing. They have been given too much of the wrong kind of attention: too much control, too much pruning, too much protection, too much neglect, too many material possessions, too much of everything except unconditional love and the kind of nurturing that teaches them life skills.

Chapter

4

Mistakes Are Wonderful Opportunities to Learn

Have you ever wished you had a perfect teenager—a teenager who always obeyed your rules, was pleasant to be around, and didn't make any mistakes? As we saw in Chapter Three, if you had a perfect teenager, you wouldn't have a *normal* teenager—you might have a pleaser, an approval junkie, or a zombie, but not a normal teenager who is growing and learning from all experiences—including mistakes.

The Value of Mistakes

Where did we ever get the crazy idea that in order to make kids do better, first we have to make them feel worse? People cannot feel bad and learn at the same time. We only learn when we feel good. If we berate our children for their mistakes, they will simply feel bad —and be unable to learn from them. But if we can change our attitude and see mistakes as wonderful opportunities to learn, our kids might approach things differently the next time and have more faith in themselves.

"Misteaks r wunderfull opertuniteez to lern" is a motto we have emblazoned on T-shirts as part of a campaign against the destructive disease of perfectionism. Think of all the misery created in the world because of perfectionism!

Mistakes are a natural part of growing and learning. Consider a toddler learning to walk. She doesn't begin with perfect balance and skill, and she'll fall a lot. If she hurts herself, she may cry—but she won't think, "Oh, dear, I failed again. What will people think? I'm so inadequate. I'd better not risk humiliating myself again. I can't get it right, so I must be a bad person. I give up."

When does this same toddler start feeling self-conscious about mistakes? When does she start hearing that mistakes mean she is failing and inadequate rather than that mistakes are part of the learning process? Her perceptions about mistakes are shaped by the messages she receives from adults.

Sometimes negative messages about mistakes are overt: "Bad girl. You shouldn't touch the vase." The truth is that she's not "bad" for touching the vase; she wouldn't be normal if she didn't want to touch it.

Sometimes the messages are more subtle. How much damage is done to budding self-confidence and the joy of learning when we send our kids off to school or to play saying "Be careful" or "Be good"? By saying these things, the negative connotation about mistakes is implied. Imagine the different message that would be conveyed by saying, "Enjoy your adventures today and see how much you can learn from your mistakes." This creates a climate of freedom in which to learn and grow without any loss of self-esteem from the numerous mistakes that will always be part of living. Children raised with that kind of encouragement can still feel good about themselves as they learn from their mistakes.

Thomas Edison conveyed his understanding of the value of mistakes during an interview with a newspaper reporter, who asked him, "How did you feel about your 10,000 failures before you finally invented the light bulb?" Edison replied, "I didn't have any failures. I learned 10,000 things that didn't work. Each one of those discoveries gave me valuable information that eventually led to success."

Why Parents Fear Mistakes

Many parents who try to save their children from making mistakes have good intentions. They want to protect their children from pain, disappointment, and embarrassment. In addition, some parents are afraid their teenagers will make the kinds of mistakes that could "ruin" their lives. These parents argue, "But I can't let my child make a mistake that could really hurt him." Of course we have to use common sense. We don't want our children to learn from the mistake of running into a busy street. Nevertheless, too many parents use the "need to protect" excuse, which creates more damage than good.

Good intentions backfire when parents inflict pain on their children through their disapproval. While protecting their children from the pain of mistakes, they rob them of self-confidence, of a positive attitude about mistakes, and of skills that could be learned from making mistakes.

Other parents are more concerned with their own reputations than with the growth of their children. They're afraid that their children's mistakes reflect on them: "I'm so embarrassed about what you've done. What will people think?" We may never know what other people think, but we do know that children feel conditionally loved in such a situation. Their self-esteem diminishes, and they're more likely than ever to compound their mistakes rather than to learn from them. However, when our children are more important than "what other people think," we might ask, "What was that experience like for you?"

Sometimes it's not a concern for reputation but for the whole philosophical question of right and wrong.

One father commented, "I guess I'll just have to trust my son to make the right decisions." Although this father felt he had made progress by realizing he could not "make" his son do the "right" thing, he had just set another trap. What a burden for both parent and teenager to feel the "right" decision must be made. How much more liberating to know that if he made the "wrong" decision he could do his best to correct it and learn from it.

What Do Mistakes Mean to You?

Before we can teach our children the value of mistakes, we need to see their value ourselves. Usually to do this means examining the way we've handled mistakes in the past.

Leslie, a participant in one of our workshops on empowering teenagers, volunteered to look at this in the following exercise.

Facilitator: How would you like to have a perfect teenager?

Leslie: I wouldn't.

Facilitator: Well, most people would say yes, but let's go with that—since you wouldn't want a perfect teenager, why not?

Leslie: Because I want my kids to be who they are.

Facilitator: You are an unusually supportive parent. Let's write that one down. We can learn something from this. Can our kids be who they are if they can never make a mistake? If they can never make a mistake, who are they living for?

Leslie: Well, I don't want my kids to be perfect, but I don't like it when they make mistakes.

Facilitator: So you have a conflict here. You want your kids to be who they are, which means you know they won't be perfect, but you don't want them to make mistakes.

Leslie: No, they can make mistakes. There are just certain ones I don't want them to make.

Facilitator: So the key here is that they can make the mistakes that are okay with you, but you feel uncomfortable with the mistakes they make that are not okay with you. So we still have some issues with right and wrong and control. What happens when you feel good about your child making mistakes? Can you give us an example of a mistake your child made that you felt good about?

Leslie: My daughter went to two dances with people she couldn't stand. She spent a lot of money on the dances for dresses and other stuff. The two guys were totally obnoxious. One of them threw up in her car from being so drunk. But she felt it was important to go to the dances. I thought it was a mistake to go with someone you didn't like at all. But she decided that's what she had to do. But before the last dance of her senior year, she told me, "I don't really want to waste any more money going to dances with people I don't like. Right now there's nobody I really like so I'm not going to go to the dance."

Facilitator: What did you do to support her in making those choices?

Leslie: I listened. I didn't interfere. I didn't tell her what I thought. I didn't lecture. I didn't judge and tell her it was stupid. I just stood back and watched to see what would happen.

Facilitator: What would you guess she felt from you?

Leslie: Support. Freedom to explore. Safe. That her privacy was respected. She had room to blow it without anyone looking over her shoulder. She experienced unconditional love.

Facilitator: What do you think she learned from that?

Leslie: She learned that it's better to do something because you enjoy it rather than to impress others. She learned it's better to respect yourself.

Facilitator: So, she learned all those things from her experience.

Leslie: Yes, I think she did.

Facilitator: Do you think she would have learned all those things if you had tried to prevent her from making her mistakes? Would she have learned it from your lectures, overprotection, and so on?

Leslie: No. I think she'd learn to *not* trust her own judgment. She'd probably learn that to get my approval she'd have to memorize all the things I have judgments about and make sure she doesn't share anything with me that goes against these judgments. She'd learn to hold back on those things. And, she'd falsely conclude that my approval of her is conditional, which it is not. But she wouldn't know that.

Facilitator: Now give me an example of a time you did not want your child to make a mistake.

Leslie: Hmmm. That's interesting. It's more the mistakes I'm *afraid* she might make.

Facilitator: How often is that true—that we're more afraid of the mistakes they might make?

Leslie: It's really hard, because I have so much faith in her that even the things she's doing that I don't like, I think it's going to be okay.

Facilitator: Let's look at one you are afraid she might make.

Leslie: I think she might make a mistake about college. I'm not even sure what the mistake will be, but she didn't get accepted to Harvard and that was really important to her. Kind of in the back of her mind is that if she really wants to be a professional singer she shouldn't be going to college anyway at her age. She should be getting an agent and going for all that. I guess my fear is that this might be an excuse for her—that rather than go to another college, she might not go to college at all.

Facilitator: When you're afraid she might make a mistake, what kinds of things do you do?

Leslie: I might tell her how I feel. It's interesting that in the other one I didn't tell her how I felt. I listened to how she felt. I wouldn't tell her what to do. I'd be much more respectful than that. But about this college thing, I'd tell her how I feel to help her make the "right" decision. I'd have good intentions—that I am just doing this to help her.

Facilitator: You would want to help her?

Leslie: Yuk! I'm done. Gross!!! I can see now how that would be a manipulation to get her to do what I think is best.

Facilitator: You can't be done! We've got to finish the process so everyone else can learn. If you want to help her by telling her how you feel, what does she learn from that?

Leslie: Nothing! She'd feel a righteous indignation. She'd be justified to be angry with me, and it would give her rebellion steam. It'd be like throwing coals on her rebellion.

Facilitator: What would she learn from this?

Leslie: Whatever she learned, it wouldn't have anything to do with college. That's for darn sure. She would learn that her mother is an obstacle. It would nip away at her confidence and her faith in herself to make decisions. And . . . I wouldn't want to do that. I would rather have her make mistakes and feel confident from what she learns.

Facilitator: What did you learn from going through this process?

Leslie: I re-learned that whatever happens is going to be just fine. And that I'm happier when I'm listening than when I'm telling.

Facilitator: And how do you think she feels when you are listening instead of telling?

Leslie: Sometimes I read all this stuff about talking about feelings and I feel guilty if I'm not being "real" with my kids, telling them how I feel or what I think. I use this stuff the wrong way—like I "should" be more open with my kids. But I've learned that that is mischief. There are times when my "openness" is appropriate, and there are times when it's manipulative. When I share my feelings inappropriately, when my kids aren't ready to hear them, I can see how they feel criticized and judged. It will be very helpful for me to be aware of the difference. In this case, it would be appropriate just to listen to her. Then I think she would feel validated and loved unconditionally.

How to Model Learning from Mistakes

One of the best ways to teach children that mistakes are

wonderful opportunities to learn is to practice this principle ourselves. When we make mistakes, we can either feel inadequate, humiliated, and like a failure or we can look for the opportunities to learn. The Four Rs of Recovery can help us when our mistakes involve other people.

The Four Rs of Recovery

1. Recognition
2. Responsibility
3. Reconciliation
4. Resolution

Recognition

Recognition means not seeing ourselves as failures because we made a mistake but simply seeing that what we did was ineffective.

Responsibility

Responsibility means seeing what part we played in causing the mistake (without attaching blame to ourselves or others) and being willing to do something about it.

Reconciliation

Reconciliation means telling the other people involved that we're sorry if we treated them disrespectfully and hurt them in any way.

Once we've recognized our mistake, taken responsibility for it, and apologized, we've usually created an atmosphere conducive to resolving the problem.

Resolution

Resolution means problem solving with the others involved to come up with a solution that is satisfactory to all.

One day my teenager was bugging me while I was at a salon having my hair done. She kept asking me for money, wondering how much longer I was going to be, and generally interrupting my conversation with the beautician every five minutes.

When we finally got home, I was so angry that I called her a spoiled brat. She retorted, "Well, don't tell me later that you're sorry!"

I said, "You don't have to worry, because I won't!"

She stormed off to her room and slammed the door. And then I realized that I'd made a mistake calling her a spoiled brat. (I had made many mistakes during this episode, but that was enough to start with.) I went to her room to apologize, but she wasn't ready to hear me—she was too busy writing in her diary about how much she hated me.

When I tried to talk to her, she said, "You're such a phony! You teach other parents to be respectful to their kids and then you call *me* a name."

I quietly left the room. Within five minutes she came to me, gave me a hug, and said, "I'm sorry."

I said, "Honey, I'm sorry, too. When I called you a spoiled brat, *I* was being a spoiled brat. I was so angry at you for the way you behaved at the beauty salon that I lost control of my behavior."

She said, "That's okay. I really *was* being a spoiled brat."

"Yeah," I said, "but I can see how I provoked your behavior by not being respectful to you."

She said, "Yes, but I did interrupt you and bug you."

And that is the way it so often goes when we're willing to take responsibility for our part in creating a problem: our children learn from our example and take responsibility for their part.

My daughter and I resolved the problem by deciding that next time we would make a plan before I went into the salon. I would tell her how long I'd be, she would decide what she wanted to do during that time, and we'd meet when we were both done.

Using Mistakes to Improve Communication

Instead of perpetuating feelings of judgment and guilt by focusing on the mistake itself, our children would learn infinitely more if we taught them to evaluate how *they* feel about the result of their decision, to understand what the result was and how it came about, and to determine what they might do differently to achieve a different result next time. We can use this same process to evaluate our own mistakes.

Recently, Becky, a parent at one of the teen workshops, asked, "What could I have done? I know I made a mistake. My fourteen-year-old daughter wanted to eat her dinner in front of the TV. I told her she couldn't—that she had to eat at the table with us. She became very angry and said, "That's so stupid! I *hate* always eating at the table."

"I told her, 'Don't get smart with me, young lady. You'll sit at the table and be respectful or you won't go to your dance practice.' She sat at the table but refused to eat and was sullen and miserable. We were all miserable. Later, she left me a note saying, 'I feel no love at all for you.' I know I did it all wrong. I can see that I certainly didn't use a logical consequence by threatening her with a dance practice—but I don't know what else I could have done."

The facilitator responded, "Remember, mistakes are wonderful opportunities to learn, so let's not think of this situation as 'wrong.' Instead, see it as an opportunity to discover what you really wanted to happen, what did happen, what caused it to happen, and what you could do differently next time. Let's begin with a few questions:

Facilitator: Why did you want her to sit at the table with the family?

Becky: It's important to me. I like having my whole family together at dinnertime.

Facilitator: Do you think she got that message—especially that you would miss her if she wasn't there?

Becky: Well, no.

Facilitator: Let's store that information for now. We'll come back to it when we get to suggestions. Why do you think she wanted to eat in front of the TV?

Becky: I think she just wanted to see a program she was excited about.

Facilitator: Have you ever felt that way about something you wanted to watch?

Becky: Yes. I can understand that.

Facilitator: Can you see how you skipped the issues that were important to you and your daughter and got into a power struggle that escalated into a revenge cycle?

Becky: Yes. I felt bad after threatening to make her miss a dance practice—but I couldn't let her get away with talking to me like that. So I won the round, but she sure got back at me. I was very hurt and frustrated when I got her note.

Facilitator: Based on the issues we've brought to

the surface, can you think of any principles and strategies we've discussed in the workshop that might apply to this situation?

Becky: No. I feel really stuck. I can't imagine what logical consequence I could have used.

Facilitator: Great! If you can't think of one, it probably means a logical consequence is not appropriate in this case. As I've mentioned before, most of us are so enamored with the idea of consequences that we often try to apply them when they aren't appropriate. How about making sure the message of love gets through, sharing what you want, getting into her world and finding out what she wants, and then working out a plan where you both win? Would you like to role-play all that and see what it feels like?

Becky: Sure.

Facilitator: Okay. Would you like to play the daughter and I'll play the mom?

Becky: Yes. That feels easier to me right now.

Facilitator: Start with what your daughter said in the beginning.

Daughter: Mom, can I eat in the other room in front of the TV?

Mom: Honey, it's real important to me that we sit together as a family at dinnertime . . . I really miss you when you're not there. Is there something special about the TV program you want to watch?

Daughter: Yeah. It's something I've been looking forward to seeing.

Mom: Well, I can understand that. There are times when I look forward to a certain program, too. Would it be okay with you if we tape your show on the VCR tonight and discuss this at our next family meeting so we can work out a plan to accomplish both our goals?

Daughter: Sure. Thanks, Mom.

Facilitator: How are you feeling now as the daughter?

Becky: I feel loved and respected and willing to work on a plan with you at the family meeting.

Facilitator: What would you now like to work on at the family meeting?

Becky: I'd like to set a time for dinner that's agreeable to everyone so they'll make a commitment to be there. I'd also like to discuss exceptions to the rule and how often exceptions would be reasonable to everyone concerned.

Facilitator: It sounds to me like you're now on a track that sidesteps the power struggles and revenge cycles. This track is more likely to get everyone what they want while teaching perceptions and skills that will be useful to your daughter.

Correcting Mistakes in Communication

Following is a list of the perceptions and skills that help parents to improve understanding and communication after making the kinds of mistakes that lead to power struggles, rebellion, and revenge:

1. Get back to the spirit of the rule rather than the letter of the rule. (The spirit of eating together was to enjoy love and sharing. The letter of the rule was "be here or else.")
2. Treat children the way you would like to be treated—with understanding, dignity, and respect. (How would you like it if someone threatened to deprive you of something if you watched a TV program?)
3. Share what is important to you and why. (Make sure the message of love and respect comes through.)

4. Find out what is important to your child and why.
5. Be willing to make exceptions to rules. (This is not the same as being permissive.)
6. Make an appointment (family meeting or some other time) to work on a plan to meet the needs and desires of all involved, without forming a pattern of exceptions.

To correct our mistakes of communication, we need to change our attitudes from fear, anger, disrespect, and control to those of love and understanding. Then we can remember our long-range parenting goals and demonstrate interest in our teens' point of view and faith in their basic goodness and abilities. If we find ourselves involved in a conflict that creates distance between ourselves and our teenagers, we might ask, "Am I acting from my fear and anger or from my love and faith?"

Our illusionary fears about mistakes disable us and our teenagers, but the ability to learn from mistakes is encouraging—and enhances our relationships. Mistakes are a small price to pay for the valuable lessons that can be learned. Give yourself and your child a break and remember that "misteaks r wunderfull oppertuniteez 2 lern."

Chapter

5

Being on Your Own Side

In Chapter One, we discussed the value of being on your teen's side, not only in words but in action. It's just as important to understand the value of being on your own side to achieve the appropriate balance.

If you were to ask any parent of a teenager, "Are you on your teenager's side?" the odds are good that he or she would say, "Of course I am," even though the parent's actions might indicate otherwise. These same parents might also say, "Of course I'm on my side. You know what they say, 'if you don't take care of yourself, no one else will.'" At first glance, being on your own side may seem as obvious as being on the side of your teenager. However, we've already seen that there's often a wide discrepancy between what we say and what we do, especially when our fears become the basis of our thoughts and actions. Our actions then become the dance of the "mischief shuffle."

The Mischief Shuffle

The mischief shuffle consists of the things we think and do that get in the way of our long-term parenting goals. This shuffle not only keeps us from being on our teen's side, but keeps us from taking care of ourselves with dignity and respect. Some of the most common characteristics of this dance help us justify short-term parenting techniques (such as control or permissiveness):

1. A need to "fix" everything that goes wrong, rather than allowing teens to grow from "fixing" their own mistakes. This attitude helps distract us from fixing our *own* mistakes; but to be on our own side, we need to be able to learn from them.
2. A fear of what others might think, which makes "looking good" more important than "finding out what is best" for our teens—and for ourselves. We cannot be on our own side when we are busy trying to please mythical "others."
3. A need to protect teens from all pain, which also protects them from learning and growing into capable adults. Being on our own side means facing some of our own pain, forgiving ourselves and continuing to grow.
4. A fear of anger, which means giving up, giving in, or doing whatever it takes to avoid the wrath of our teens. This teaches teenagers that anger is bad and should be avoided or that it can be used to manipulate others—instead of showing that anger is a valid feeling and can be handled appropriately. Being on our own side will make our teens angry at times, especially when we say no when we believe it's right for us.

5. A belief that we are selfish if we aren't self-sacrificing, which means that we're never allowed to enjoy ourselves. Being on our own side means finding our own balance between doing things for ourselves and doing things for or with our teenagers.

Being on Our Own Side Usually Helps Our Teens

When parents stop dancing the mischief shuffle and instead focus on their long-term parenting goals, they find that they actually have a lot of power to influence their teens. We often find that taking care of ourselves and being on our own side is one of the best ways to influence our teens and thus be on their side at the same time. With this realization, we can decide what we want to say no to, how to express and honor our own limits, how to listen without having to fix or judge, how to ask for help, how to be our "own person," and how to give up guilt and manipulation.

Being on our own side means understanding our own individuality just as we understand the individuality of our teenagers—and supporting our own growth with dignity and respect just as we support our teen's growth with dignity and respect.

Skills that Support Being on Our Own Side

1. Deciding what you will do, not what you will make your teenager do.
2. Setting limits and following through.
3. Having confidence in doing what makes sense to you regardless of what others might think or do.

4. Sharing from your heart and gut what you feel and what you want, without expecting anyone else to feel the same or to give you what you want.
5. Supporting your own growth. Learning about your own unresolved issues and how to get past them.

Since it is normal for parents to want to control their teens instead of changing their own behavior, we are including several specific ways to be on your own side.

Just Say No—And Say Just No

Parents have many opportunities to encourage their teenagers to learn important life skills. Sometimes it's helpful for parents to "just say no." Often, however, they miss this opportunity because they're afraid to say no—or because they say more than just no, adding words and a manner that creates defensiveness and resistance instead of opportunities to learn.

The key is appropriateness. There are many times when it is appropriate to say no in order to be on our own side and teach life skills. The the question is *how* to say no.

My teenage son wanted to borrow five dollars because he spent all his paycheck in one week and had to wait another week for his next paycheck. It took self-discipline on my part not to rescue my son so he'd think I'm a "nice mother" and give him the money. By saying no, I allowed him to experience the consequences of his choice not to save for future needs. (One week can seem like forever to a teenager.) This experience may encourage him to develop the self-discipline of budgeting his money to make it last longer. Or he may choose to live a "feast and famine" lifestyle. Either way, he learns that *he* is responsible for the outcome of his choices and will have to deal with the consequences.

If I'd given him the money I would have robbed him of the opportunity to become a more capable person. Instead, I would have allowed him to feel successful at manipulating me and avoiding the consequences of his choices. In addition, if I'd rescued him, I would also avoid taking care of myself. I might loan him the money even when I didn't want to in order to prove what a wonderful person I am. In other words, I would be trying to buy his approval.

Teens give parents many opportunities to look at their own issues and life skills. The following example illustrates how I overcame the tendency to rescue and "buy" approval while avoiding the other extreme of self-righteous "teaching lectures." I was able to take care of myself *and* my long-range parenting goals.

For Christmas, I either take my kids on a shopping spree and let them buy what they want, or they give me a list and I buy them what I can afford from it. Last Christmas, my daughter chose the shopping spree. She had purchased several low-cost items but then decided she wanted a sixty-dollar bottle of perfume. Normally, I'd explain to my daughter why such expensive perfume is inappropriate for a teenager, and I'd justify this by saying I wouldn't buy it for myself, although I earn my own living. I'd probably get into a moral and ethical discussion about the price of perfume—none of which my daughter would understand—and we'd end up having a big fight. Although I wouldn't buy the perfume then, I'd feel so bad that I'd go back and buy it later. Then I would feel worse, not only because I had given in but also because I wasn't standing up for what I believed.

But this time I simply said, "No, I'm not going to

buy the perfume." I didn't explain or lecture. My daughter got incredibly angry, said something insulting under her breath, and announced, "I'm going upstairs," adding that she would meet me later.

Although I acted cool, I was so flustered that I left my credit card at the perfume counter and went upstairs to do some more shopping. By the time I found my daughter, she was over her anger and on to the next thing that she wanted me to buy. (It's hard for me to remember how quickly kids get over their upsets while I stew for a long time.)

Realizing I had forgotten my credit card, I went downstairs to get it. The saleslady said, "Was your daughter real angry?"

I said, "Yes."

The saleslady seemed very concerned and asked, "Well, was that okay?"

I said, "Sure. My daughter was angry because I was unwilling to spend sixty dollars on perfume. I could explain to her until the cows come home and, at this age, she wouldn't get it. But you and I understand, don't we?"

The saleslady nodded. She added that she'd noticed I also hadn't purchased the forty-dollar perfume I was interested in for myself and that, like her, I would probably wait for the holiday, hoping someone would buy it for me. Neither of us had grown up buying expensive things like that. I told her it was good to talk with someone who understood, especially since I couldn't have this discussion with my daughter.

I learned a lot from that experience. I saw how much less traumatic it was for my daughter to hear no than it was for me to say it. Although she got over her anger quickly, I remained upset much longer (out of fear of her anger, fear that she might dislike me, guilt that I might not be being a good mother, and fear about standing up for my beliefs). In addition, I realized how satisfying it was to discuss this with someone who understood my position.

I learned that it's much easier and more effective to decide what I'm willing to do and be firm about it. I learned that lectures and moralizing can create defensiveness and resistance rather than understanding and agreement. While my daughter might enjoy hearing about my "deprivation mentality" some other time, she won't be open to it when I'm trying to be "right" or trying to teach her a lesson.

I also realized that her mumbled insult was not meant to manipulate me but simply expressed how angry she was. (Feelings are frequently intense for teenagers.) Too often I take everything she does personally.

Teens handle their anger differently than adults do—and differently today than was acceptable a generation ago. (If I had mumbled an insult to my Dad, he would have washed my mouth out with soap.) This doesn't mean that I should ignore the insult. Later on I might say to my daughter, "Look, I know you were angry and I understand it, but I wish you'd find another way of expressing it rather than insulting me. It's really disrespectful and hurts my feelings." However, it's important to discuss this *after* the conflict is over—otherwise it's like talking to a volcano!

Finally, I learned that it's not my job to take away her feelings, or to fix them, or to fix her, or to fix the situation.

Things often get worse before they get better if your teen isn't used to hearing no. So hang in there. And find a sympathetic ear to help you through this trauma, so you can leave your kids alone to learn from their own experience while you learn from yours.

In Chapter 8, we give specific advice about the

importance and limitations of saying no once in a while to teenagers. For the purposes of being on your own side, find a time when saying no is an important way to take care of yourself, because of something *you* don't want to do, rather than because you are trying to teach your teenager something.

Another way to take care of yourself is through the concept of give and take.

Be on Both Sides Through Give and Take

During a family vacation at Lake Tahoe, we had done everything the kids like to do. We had taken them on a jet-ski trip, taken them to play golf, and had rented movies of their choice. But when we adults wanted to go for a ride around the lake, the kids had a fit, "Oh, this sucks! This is so boring." Grandma just looked at them and said, "Have you ever heard the expression, 'give and take?' " The kids reluctantly said, "Oh, okay."

You can be on your side and take care of your own needs by remembering the principle of give and take. One mother shared how it saved her sanity.

"My kids got into and car and wanted to listen to their music. I listened for about an hour before I was ready to go insane. I changed the station to listen to one song I like, and they got hysterical. Before, I would've lectured them and explained how wounded I was. This time I just said, 'Have you ever heard of the concept of give and take?' They knew. They got it right away."

Take Care of Yourself by Forgiving Yourself

It's impossible to grow and increase our awareness without discovering that many things we've done in the past were not effective and were possibly even damaging to our children. Teenagers do the best they can given their experience, knowledge, support systems, and developmental process. So do parents. It's to be hoped that we truly see mistakes as wonderful opportunities to learn and forgive ourselves for any and all past mistakes.

Don't Let Guilt Be a Barrier to Close Relationships

When we feel guilty, we may create all kinds of mischief by trying to keep our kids from making the same mistakes we did. Or we may be so busy trying to hide our feelings of guilt that we also hide our feelings of love and enjoyment.

Some parents try to make their children feel guilty to get them to behave "properly." If their children don't conform, the parents feel guilty about not being good-enough parents.

There are many ways for guilt to take form, but they all get in the way of relationships. Forgiving ourselves is essential to being on our own side, so we can get on with our lives and have close relationships with our loved ones.

When we get rid of guilt in our own lives we won't feel the need to make your kids feel guilty. When we realize we are doing the best we can, we can stop taking our teenagers' behavior personally and stop trying to make them feel guilty.

Don't Take Your Teen's Behavior Personally

Teenagers don't do what they do just to hurt their parents. The truth is that teenagers usually aren't even thinking about their parents.

When we take our teen's behavior personally, we are reacting to our children as if we were children. We save ourselves much grief when we see that, rather than doing something "to us" or against us", they are unique individuals who are going through the process of individuation.

Remember that teen concerns are very different than those of their parents. Teenagers think things like "How will I get enough money to party? How am I going to get my studying done? What will I do if my friend won't talk to me after school? What am I going to do about drugs, drinking, and sex?" Their parents run around thinking things like "They're not doing their chores to get even with me" or "How can they be so irresponsible and inconsiderate?" Instead, parents might think about whether they are understanding their teens' world, respecting the individuation process, and having faith in their teens' ultimate goodness.

In addition to understanding our teens, as we've said throughout this chapter, we can be of great service and influence to our kids when we focus on being on own side and taking care of our own issues. Being on our own side is ultimately the best way to be on our teenagers' side. Modeling self-respect teaches our teens to take care of themselves in a respectful manner and gives them many skills to help them in life.

▼
Chapter 6

"Don't Use Psychology on Me!"

(But It Sure Helps)

All of thirteen-year-old Kevin's behavior shouted: "No one can make me do anything! I'm unlovable! I'm awful to be around! I hate everything and everybody!" His teachers tried to get him to comply by using rewards, punishments, removal from class, transfers, and calls to his parents. His parents tried to help him by using patience, anger, threats, praise, ignoring, and shaming. Nothing seemed to work. Everyone dealt with Kevin based on *their* perceptions of him, but no one thought to find out about Kevin's perceptions—how he thought and how he felt.

One day in a therapy session, Kevin's therapist asked Kevin to share some memories from his childhood. His most vivid memory was when he was about four years old. He was playing with his sister, who was about ten at the time, and one of the kids in the neighborhood. The neighbor kid put some cleaning solution in a glass and tried to get Kevin to drink it. Kevin's sister knew the solution was poisonous and could hurt him, so she screamed and knocked the glass out of the kid's hand.

When asked how he felt about this memory, Kevin said he was angry. Surprised, the therapist asked him why he was angry that his sister tried to save his life. Kevin responded that nothing ever happened to the kid who tried to kill him, so he decided (at age four) that nobody really cared about him and that he would be better off dead. This perception became the underlying theme in Kevin's life motivating most of his behavior.

It is important to understand that, when dealing with human behavior, the "truth" or commonsense logic of a situation does not matter. Rather, all behavior is motivated by each individual's *perception* about what is true. Most often, we make the mistake of dealing exclusively with the behavior of our teens and not with the underlying beliefs that inspire their behavior.

In that same session, when his therapist asked what kind of animal would Kevin like to be and why, he said, "I wish I were a dog because everybody would like having me around and they'd pet me and play with me." This information made a big difference to Kevin's parents. Instead of feeling angered, challenged by, or disgusted with him, they were able to tap into his feelings of isolation, hurt, and abandonment. They began to cuddle him, to spend fun time with him, and to listen to his complaints of injustice. This certainly wasn't the end of the story, but it was an important beginning for Kevin and his parents.

Life-Style Analysis

Adlerian therapists use early memories and other techniques to help them understand the private logic of their clients. This is referred to as a *life-style analysis* because the focus is on understanding the perceptions, beliefs, private logic, or separate reality that inspires the behavior or life-style of each individual. As parents, we don't have to be trained psychologists but it does help to know how to tap into the separate realities of our teens. In fact, without this information, all we have are assumptions about why our teens do what they do. When we act on those assumptions, they may have nothing to do with why our teens behave the way they do.

Following is another example of how understanding private logic can help parents deal more effectively with their teens.

Two Different Realities

One of my friends has a thirteen-year-old daughter, Monica, who decided to run away from home because all her friends had; she wanted to see what it was like. She created an elaborate plan, telling her parents: "I've never had a room of my own, and I've always wondered what it would be like. I've talked with my teacher and the school counselor and they thought it would be a good idea for me to experiment. What I would like to do is take some food and go into my room and close the door. I'd like my sister to spend time somewhere else and sleep somewhere else, too. Then, in the morning, I'll come out for breakfast, and I'll have had a chance to see what it's like to have my own room."

Often, parents wonder why kids concoct such outlandish tales, but imagine how it would sound if this teen really told the truth. That would have been the end of her experiment. So her parents, being encouraging, kind, and understanding, said okay. They made arrangements for no one to disturb her, and off Monica went to her room with enough food to last a week.

But around 10:00 P.M., Mom noticed that Monica hadn't come out of her room even to go to the bathroom. Mom knocked on the door and got no answer. When she tried to open the door, she found it had been barricaded. Her daughter was gone!

When Mom called a friend of Monica's and found out what the girls were really doing, she panicked. "My daughter could be picked up, kidnapped, raped, murdered." But her teen had a whole different set of perceptions. All her friends had tried staying out all night, and she wanted to be cool and part of the group. She also didn't want to hurt or upset her parents. Her dilemma was how to do what she wanted without hurting or upsetting her parents.

By the time Monica crawled back in through her window at 2:00 A.M., her mother worried sick, said, "I'm so glad you're home! I'm so glad you're *alive*! I thought for sure you'd be dead by now."

Her daughter looked at her in complete disbelief and said, "Why? All we did was go to the school, but nobody was there. Usually kids go around stealing signs, TPing houses, or throwing eggs, but we didn't feel like doing any of that. We couldn't find any other kids, so we walked to the doughnut shop. Then we went back to the school, but there still wasn't anyone there. We got bored and came home. We knew we were perfectly safe." In her own mind, Monica had completed the experiment quite successfully and had learned something for herself.

At that point, her mother could have lectured her daughter and then punished her—and Monica would gain nothing but resentment. Instead, Mom said, "Well, I can understand this was important to you. I just have to say . . . I don't even know what to say! I'm so upset I can't even speak." She went into her room and closed the door, because that was how she felt. She wasn't trying to teach her daughter a lesson or trying to punish her. Later, her daughter knocked on the door and asked to come in and talk to her. She said, "I'm so sorry. I didn't mean to cause you any pain. I really didn't want to hurt you."

In this instance, both mother and daughter glimpsed the separate reality of the other. The mother realized that her daughter had only been thinking about being like her friends and having an adventure—and not about hurting her mother. And the daughter saw that by "running away," she had really worried her mother—even though she had no intention of doing so.

We often see our teens' behavior in terms of a power struggle or revenge when in reality it has nothing to do with us. Understanding their private logic can help us quit taking everything personally.

Parents, Take Heart!

When I do life-style analysis with teens, I ask them for four or five adjectives to describe their parents. Their choices are usually incredibly encouraging. Parents who have been convinced that their kids "hate" them, often hear themselves described as nice, friendly, helpful, and fair, even though their kids have been fighting with them morning, noon, and night. One stepparent, upon hearing her stepson list her as part of the family, said, "Don't put me in." He said, "Why? You *are* part of the family." Although she thought of him that way, she had no idea he felt the same about her.

Learning about Your Teens' Reality

"Mike, what was going on when you stole that spray

paint?" Mike looks sullen and replies sarcastically, "I just wanted to redecorate my room." "But, Mike," says Mom, "there must've been something else going on. Were you by yourself or with your friends? Were you guys pretending you were going shopping without any money?" Now in her amateur-psychologist mode, Mom asks questions that imply she knows why Mike does what he does. Like any normal teenager on the chopping block, Mike responds to these questions with sarcasm and disgust. "Mom, get off my back!"

Mom persists, believing that she really *is* trying to understand how Mike thinks and feels. "Are you telling me that if you want something, that however you can get it is okay with you?"

▼ *Listen instead of lecture.*

"Yeah," says Mike, "that's exactly how it was!" His angry and belligerent tone gets stronger, but still Mom persists with her "lecture."

"Okay. I hear you. I'm just thinking about what if my house was 'redecorated' with spray paint? Or what if it was your car that was painted? How would you like that? I have trouble with it, but I appreciate your telling me where you're coming from. Can I tell you what's going on for me?"

"I *know* what's going on for you. Don't take things that don't belong to you. Don't have fun at other people's expense. Work for what you get." Mike says all this in a sing-song, mocking tone.

"I know, I *am* pretty moralistic. I grew up in a church where I was taught stealing was wrong. Also, I know that if you steal and you get caught you may end up with a record, and that really scares me. I've never had a record, so I don't know for sure what it means, but my picture is that it might make it harder for you to get a job."

As Mom looks up she sees Mike rolling his eyes; he then waits for her to finish with a blank stare on his face. Suddenly, Mom realizes that she isn't learning anything about Mike's separate reality and is losing him as she tries to get him to listen to her. She says, "Well, the way you're responding to me now means something else is going on. . . . I just feel real hurt right now, and when I feel that way I *know* something's wrong."

Your Teen's Logic Emerges. "Can I go now? My friends are waiting." But Mike's eyes are filled with tears, and he blurts out, "I've heard it all, and I'm always wrong! I never do it right! I never live up to your expectations. I'm tired of hearing about it. And . . . I probably should listen. I'm probably a terrible person."

Now Mike's mom has something to work on, because she heard his underlying beliefs and can begin to see how he thinks abut himself. He feels he is always disappointing her and that he is a bad person.

After getting into our teens' world to find out what is really going on for them, we can let them know that we understand and then we can attempt to deal with their hurt feelings.

However, when you do understand your teens' world, you may find that they have different values than you, or that they are exploring different values. This can be very frightening to parents.

Whose Values? If being honest is one of Mom's values and her child thinks stealing is okay, obviously he didn't get his value from her. However, he may be rebelling by doing exactly the opposite of what his mother wishes, simply to prove that he's his own person. He may also be reacting to the pain of believing that his mother doesn't approve of him and that he can't do anything to please her. Or he may feel so hurt that he unconsciously seeks revenge by hurting everyone important to him.

After giving these ideas some thought, Mom said, "You know what, Mike, I figured out something about that spray paint. I know you're bored with the whole thing, but this is new information. I've been cramming my values down your throat, wanting you to think about everything the way I do and be just like me. I'm sorry.

That's not right. I hope you can forgive me. I don't want to act like that, it's very disrespectful. If you ever catch me doing that again, I wish you'd tell me." Even though Mike may not be able to help her with this, he may feel much better when Mom admits her part of the problem and lets him know she understands his hurt feelings.

At this point Mike's mom could see that it was more important to work on their relationship for long-term results than to try to control Mike's behavior for short-term results.

Many parents believe that understanding a child's perceptions and private logic is not enough—especially if a teenager does something as drastic as stealing. These parents feel they must do something to "control" this kind of behavior. While it's true that there are some things you can do (see the next section), control is not one of them.

Our purpose at this point is to emphasize how effective it can be to understand our teen's perceptions and how necessary to avoid doing things to increase their discouragement. Remember that perceptions and the level of encouragement or discouragement are the primary motivators of behavior, and that too often we deal with the behavior rather than its motivation.

Thoughts, Feelings, and Actions

Our unconscious thoughts drive our actions by creating feelings that give us the fuel to act. The following, from interviews with a group of teens, shows their separate realities and their resulting feelings and actions.

Teen One: Sixteen-year-old Boy

Event: Parents' sudden divorce.

Teen's Decision or Thought: My parents aren't the perfect people I thought they were. I had them on a pedestal and they both disappointed me. I can't count on them now. I can only count on myself.

Teen's Feelings: Anger, betrayal, loss, fear.

Teen's Behavior: He decided to stop living like a beer-drinking airhead and took charge of his life.

Teen Two: Thirteen-year-old Girl

Event: Parents' attempt to set up a financial reward system for good grades to motivate daughter to stop getting Ds and Fs.

Teen's Decision or Thought: All my parents care about is whether I go to college. They don't like me unless I'm how they want me to be. They don't even know or care about the things that are important to me.

Teen's Feelings: Anger, hurt.

Teen's Behavior: She decided to get revenge on her parents by running away and doing other things to hurt them, including hurting herself by cutting into her arms with a knife.

Teen Three: Fifteen-year-old Boy

Event: Childhood friend's death from illness.

Teen's Decision or Thought: I'll never make another friend because I don't ever want to feel this kind of pain again.

Teens' Feelings: Grief, despair, hopelessness.

Teen's Behavior: When his family moved to a new community shortly after the death of his friend, he decided the only way he could keep his commitment to himself was not to make any new friends and to flunk out of school. With all the intensity that a fifteen-year-old boy can muster, he succeeded in his campaign to get all Fs.

Teen Four: Thirteen-year-old Girl

Event: Parents' constant fighting and cold war.

Teen's Decision or Thought: My parents are probably going to get a divorce because they're so mean to each other. If they do, they'll probably split up the family, and one parent will take me and the other will keep my brother. They'll probably move far away from each other, and I'll never get to see my brother again.

Teen's Feelings: Hurt, fear.

Teen's Behavior: Noticing that her brother could make his mother really angry by refusing to do chores, this girl decided that if she copied him her mother would let both kids live with their father, and brother and sister wouldn't be separated. She refused to do any of the chores she had agreed to do.

Teen Five: Fourteen-year-old Girl

Event: Attempt by brother-in-law to molest her.

Teen's Decision or Thought: My brother did this to me when I was little. This must be how I have to be to get boys to love me. This must be how boys know you love them and how you show them they are important members of the family.

Teen's Feelings: Shame, guilt, fear.

Teen's Behavior: In order not to lose the "close family" she always wanted, she let her brother-in-law molest her and kept it a secret.

Behavior always makes sense when you understand your teen's perceptions and private logic. It was impossible to work effectively with these teens before understanding the beliefs and feelings motivating their behavior.

Understanding how our kids really think and feel takes a nonjudgmental attitude and the ability to keep our own perceptions separate. Teenagers place a tremendous amount of trust in the people to whom they confide their private thoughts and feelings. Sometimes the help of a therapist is the only way to get at a teen's innermost beliefs. But whoever elicits a teen's confidence must treat it with the utmost respect and seriousness, so that the child will not be hurt as a result of sharing their private world.

The Family Pie

The primary goal of every human being is to find belonging and significance. Every child in a family uses their own private logic to decide what they need to do to achieve this goal. In our families, our personalities are most influenced by the sibling we see as our chief competitor—although we don't consciously realize this. (For information on the importance of birth order, see

Chapter Three in *Positive Discipline* by Jane Nelsen.) Children seem to believe that only one sibling can be special in a certain way; if one sibling has already decided to find belonging and significance by being the "good" child, another may decide to be the "social" child, the "athletic" child, the "shy" child, or the "rebel." We call these choices "slices of the family pie."

The family pie consists of the children in the family, but not the parents. If a child is an only child, he or she may compete with the same-sex parent, a kid in the neighborhood, a cousin, or a sibling who has died. When asked who their chief competitor was, most only children are quick to name a specific person.

Many of the problems that we deal with in teen years have their origin in the family pie. We can better understand the private logic of our teenagers when we know what slice of the family pie they have chosen.

The No-Problem Kid

A family came to a therapist because one of their kids constantly created problems, driving the mother crazy. Each session, the therapist asked everyone if they had anything they wanted help with. The eldest boy consistently stated that he didn't have any problems, and he never lost the opportunity to point out that his sister was the problem child in their family. The slice of the family pie he had chosen was to be perfect. He was trying to find his way of being special and different in the family by "having no problems." Convinced that if he revealed a problem it would make him the "bad, sick" boy, he found it hard to get help with anything. He was also trapped in the cycle of trying to be perfect at all times—and if that failed, at the least he would find a way to show everyone how imperfect his sister was.

The Good-Kid/Bad-Kid Scenario

In many families, one of the kids has the label (or slice of the family pie) of being "good" and another "bad." In one family, the oldest boy played out the role of the bad kid. His teenage individuation process was painful and rebellious. His younger, "good-kid" sibling did all her rebelling behind her parents' backs so she could keep her place in the family pie of being "good."

In another family, the pie was divided by Mom's favorite and Dad's favorite. When the family split up, the kids went to live with the parent who they thought liked them best and then worked overtime—unconsciously, of course— to continually point out their sibling's negative qualities. This was their insurance policy on their special place in the family.

Many oldest children feel they must always be first; they become competitive overachievers. Second children often become the "we try harder" kids, peacemakers, or the rebels. The youngest become the adorable ones, used to having things done for them; they often develop skills for manipulating others to take care of them. Other youngest children become competitive, wanting the same things that their older siblings have; often these youngest feel they aren't good enough or smart enough because they can't do what the big kids can. Only children like to be special and often compare themselves to adults; sometimes this leads to feelings of inadequacy, since everyone else seems more capable than they.

Negative self-perceptions often lead children to negative activities, especially when children mistakenly believe that the only way to find belonging and significance is through what Rudolph Dreikurs called "the mistaken goals."

The Mistaken Goals

Whenever kids feel discouraged or insecure, they choose a mistaken goal—a goal that never takes them where they want to go—as a vehicle to belonging and significance. Instead, they find alienation from those closest to them, and deeper discouragement. It becomes a vicious cycle: the more discouraged they become, the more they escalate their efforts through the mistaken goal. Becoming aware of mistaken goals can help us change to behavior which takes us where we want to go and build closer relationships and self-confidence.

Behind every mistaken goal is mistaken private logic. Parents who deal with their teens' behavior without understanding and addressing the underlying beliefs will be frustrated in their efforts to effect change.

The Four Mistaken Goals and Their Underlying Beliefs

1. *Recognition:* I am significant when you notice me and treat me as special.
2. *Power:* I am significant when I do what I want—or at least don't do what you want.
3. *Justice:* I feel hurt when you don't treat me as though I were significant. I feel my only choice is to hurt you back.
4. *Adequacy:* I feel like giving up because I don't know what to do. I don't feel significant at all.

▾ *Have faith in your teens.*

Part of having faith in your teens is understanding that whatever they do they do because it makes sense to them. Just because parents don't know their logic doesn't mean it's not there. Teens are not doing things "to us" or "against us" (except in the sense of the mistaken goal of justice, when a teen seeks to hurt in revenge for being hurt).

▼ *It takes two.*

Parents need to know that it takes two to fuel mistaken-goal behavior. We have never seen a power-drunk teenager without a power-drunk adult close by. If your teens hurt you, they probably feel hurt by you. Awareness of mistaken goals is the first step toward change. The second step is to change your own behavior in a positive way. If you are in a power struggle, you need to give up trying to control your teenager. Your teen is then compelled to change his or her behavior in a positive way. (See Chapter Twelve on letting go.)

Identifying a Mistaken Goal

The easiest way to understand which mistaken goal our teen operates from is to tap into our own feelings. If you're irritated, annoyed, feeling sorry for your child, worried, or exhausted from giving undue attention or special service, the goal is probably a need for undue recognition. Feelings of anger, challenge, or frustration let you know the mistaken goal is power. If you are hurt, disgusted, or disbelieving, the mistaken goal is probably justice (revenge). And finally, if you feel a sense of despair and hopelessness, and think nothing will ever change, the mistaken goal is adequacy, (your child assumes his or her skills are inadequate or nonexistent).

Nine Steps for Changing from Mistaken Goals to Closeness and Trust

1. Look for the mistaken goal by recognizing patterns of behaviors for both you and your teen and how the behavior makes you feel.
2. Acknowledge your part in creating the mistaken goal. (This may involve looking at issues based on your own mistaken beliefs.)
3. Decide to change your own behavior. (Awareness of your own issues, your own mistaken goals and your own ineffective behaviors is the impetus for changing your behavior.)
4. Acknowledge your mistakes to your teen.
5. Show an attitude of faith in the basic goodness of your teen. (When you have this faith, it will show.)
6. Let your teen know specifically what you do appreciate about him or her.
7. Try to understand your teen's reality by making some guesses about what it might be.
8. Really listen. Be curious. Keep inviting more information.
9. Be open to what comes next. It might be problem-solving, a hug, or simply the good feelings that come from understanding.

This process gives others the feeling of being truly listened to and understood. Teens will be more likely to listen to us *after* they feel listened to. When teens feel their reality has been understood and respected, they are more open to hearing our reality.

Here are some case histories involving the mistaken goals.

Recognition

As a single parent, Mom was exhausted; she felt she could never do enough for her two kids. One was constantly in trouble, the other constantly demanding special help and time to talk about her feelings. No matter how much time Mom put in, nothing changed. She was convinced that the problems were caused by her working and the divorce.

When she learned about mistaken goals, it occured to her that her two kids were keeping her busy as a way of being assured that she loved them. She could see that the competition between them to be Mom's favorite was fierce and destructive.

One of Mom's first improvements was to stop listening to the tattling of the younger and then siding with her to get the older sibling in trouble. Mom would listen, then assure the youngest that she could work it out with her sibling. Mom also let her youngest know how much she was loved and spent a lot of planned special time with her doing things they both enjoyed. With her older daughter, Mom found ways to listen to her without her younger sister around. They found that they really enjoyed each other's company.

Another improvement was Mom's refusal to get involved in the fights between her two children, even when they got physical. This was very frightening at first, since the older child was quite a bit larger than the younger. At one point, out of desperation and fear for the safety of the younger child, Mom decided that the two kids couldn't be alone together; every time Mom went somewhere, one of the kids had to go with her. This soon wore thin, and the children decided they could stay home together even when their mother wasn't around. And over time, they fought less and less.

Power

One mother said, "I can see that my issues with my daughter involve power, because I'm always feeling angry with her, challenged, and overpowered. I can't open my mouth without her walking away or yelling at me. I don't feel that I've got a chance.

"One day, I decided that I'd been pushed around long enough. The next time she became angry, yelling hysterically and throwing things, I didn't wimp out. Every other time she has done that, I've said, "You've got to get out of here." If she refused to leave, I'd lock myself in the bathroom, go to my room, or get in the car and drive away. But by doing that I realized I was treating her like an out-of-control criminal. This time, I sat in the chair and said, 'Honey, you're out of control. You're really angry. I want to hear everything you're angry about, but I can't hear you when you scream at me and throw things. Sit down and tell me. I'll listen to every single thing you have to say.' She kept screaming and throwing things. Again I said, "Honey, I'm here. I care about you. I want to hear what you have to say. It's obvious that you're angry. It's okay that you're angry. But I can't hear anything when you sceam at me.

"Finally, she stood still and began talking. Two minutes later, she sat down and we talked for over an hour.

"Later, I realized that I'd switched from the power struggle to wanting to find out what was going on for her. It was a switch on my part from blame and defense to support and interest."

▼ *Redirect a power struggle.*

Dirk was in a serious power struggle with his mother over school grades. Even though his poor school performance was jeopardizing his participation in sports, he wouldn't study or do any homework. Although he didn't really want to fail in school, it was more important to him to show his mother that she couldn't make him do the things she thought were important. When he did things that were important to *him*, his mother would step in and take over. Dirk would then go on total standstill, copying his father's method of dealing with anger and frustration.

Luckily, with help from a friend and his parents, Dirk was able to turn his life around. He became an important athlete at his school and raised his grades from Fs to Bs. What caused these dramatic changes?

▼ *Validate your teen's feelings.*

The first step in this process involved validation of Dirk's feelings. His friend told him, "Yes, you're angry. You have a right to be angry. What your mother is doing is inappropriate."

▼ *Encourage and support your teen.*

The second step involved Dirk's parents. They took the advice of a friend, and began to look for ways to get out of power struggles and to raise Dirk's self-esteem. They began to listen to what was important to *him*, instead of telling him what was important to them. They became supportive of Dirk's individuation process and interested in teaching skills that would help him grow into a self-reliant and confident person.

Revenge

Chrissie is in terrible pain because her parents refuse to acknowledge who Chrissie really is and focus instead on who they want her to be. They want so desperately for her to be an athlete that they are willing to bribe her to get her to comply. They have good intentions: they honestly believe that if she's successful in a sport it will raise her self-esteem, which will be to her greater good and happiness. In reality, Chrissie—who wants to be a rock star—would feel better about herself if she felt validated for who she is and who she wants to be.

Chrissie feels that her parents don't love her for herself. They never bother to find out what really interests her and what she would like to do with her life. This hurts Chrissie so badly that she's caught in a revenge cycle, wanting her folks to hurt as much as she does. Fortunately, Chrissie's parents became aware—by tuning into their own hurt feelings—that Chrissie's mistaken goal was justice. They were able to put their hopes for Chrissie aside while showing genuine interest in hers. By supportively listening to their daughter, they were able to break the revenge cycle and promote her feelings of self-worth.

When kids get into a revenge cycle, they usually hurt themselves in the process of trying to hurt their parents. Some will even destroy their lives through drug abuse or suicide just to get even. Many parents have no idea how upset their children are, because the kids do not—or cannot—tell them and employ destructive behavior instead.

It doesn't do any good to tell kids that they are in a revenge cycle and are hurting themselves in the process. What helps is to find out *why* they are in pain by showing loving interest and support, so that they can reveal their true feelings.

Adequacy

Adam was feeling depressed and kept telling his parents how unhappy he was because he didn't have a girlfriend. He was the only kid in his circle of friends who hadn't invited someone to homecoming. No matter what his parents said to help him cheer him up or empathize with him, Adam insisted that that no matter what he did, no girl would ever go out with him. Adam's folks were so concerned about him that they suggested he talk to the family counselor.

When Adam came in to share his story the counselor realized that Adam had made a mistaken decision that no matter what he did, he would fail so it was better not to try at all. Adam was convinced that girls didn't like him because he was shy, and that if he even attempted to talk to a girl, she would be bored and tell all her friends what a jerk he was. When the counselor asked where he got this idea, Adam mentioned that he had overheard some of the girls at school talking about a guy who had called them the night before. The girls laughed and shared stories of how they would get rid of this guy if he called any of them. Adam knew he didn't want to make a fool of himself like this guy.

When a teen is that discouraged, the counselor or the parent's job is to help them get their courage back by showing how they can take small steps. The small steps have to make sense to the person, however, or they won't take them.

Adam's counselor asked him if he would be willing to look at the situation another way and Adam said, "Yes." She then asked Adam if he had ever purchased any clothing for himself? With a puzzled look he replied that he had just purchased a new ski jacket. "Did you just grab the first jacket you saw on the rack?" asked the counselor.

Adam said, "Of course not! I must have tried on about twenty to thirty jackets before I found the right one."

"Well, Adam," said the counselor, "do you think picking a girl to go to homecoming with should be any easier?"

"I never thought of it that way," said Adam. "But what if I call someone and she tells her friends what a jerk I am?"

"You could tell yourself how grateful you are that a girl that rude decided not to go out with you."

Adam thought about all this and said, "It makes a lot of sense, but I still feel scared to talk to a girl. What if I can't think of anything to say?"

Adam and the counselor practiced calling girls, letting Adam say "Hi, this is Adam," and then letting the silence remain and see what the girl would do. Adam realized that if a girl answering the phone would be just a little enthusiastic, it was easy to think of things to talk about. If a girl was quiet and uncomfortable, she might not be the right person for Adam to spend his first date with.

Adam was almost ready to go home and call someone, but he got cold feet one more time. The counselor noticed how scared he was and asked Adam if he had ever pushed through his fear anywhere in his life. Adam thought for a few minutes and then replied, "I used to be afraid to ski down real steep hills that had moguls on them, but now I love to."

"How did you manage to overcome your fear?"

"I stood at the top of the hill with my knees shaking and said to myself, 'Go for it!,' and I did. It was wonderful."

"Well, Adam," said the counselor, "go for it!"

Adam grinned.

Adam was able to make steps toward correcting his perception of inadequacy because no one said to him, "It's silly to feel that way." Instead his parents listened deeply enough to know he needed help. His counselor listened, empathized, and explored the basis for his perception. She then helped him work on skills, based on his own success experiences, to help him overcome his fears.

There are many ways to encourage our teen and improve a situation once we understand the mistaken goal. Then we must actively attempt to make things better, rather than merely reacting to our child's behavior.

Breaking the Mistaken-Goal Cycle

There are five steps for breaking this cycle.

Step One: Be willing to admit you might be part of the problem.

Step Two: Find out how you might be part of the problem by:

A. Talking with an objective friend or therapist.

B. Writing in a journal. You often gain insight when you go over what actually happens between you and your teen.

C. Askng your teen. Let your teenager know you are not a mind reader. Admit that you might not have been a good listener in the past, but you want to listen now. You may suggest that you contributed to the problem. (Even little kids, when told "I think I did something to hurt your feelings," can tell you what you did.)

Step Three: Make some guesses about your teenager's perceptions of what is going on. This is appropriate when kids aren't consciously aware of their reasons. If your guess is correct, you'll hit a responsive chord; your child will feel understood and will acknowledge the accurateness of the guess. On the other hand, it's okay if your guess is not correct.

Your aim here is not to be right but to get information. If you're wrong, you've still learned something.

Step Four: When you understand your teen's perception, validate him or her. Let your child know that you can see how he or she might have come to that conclusion.

Step Five: Plan together to make changes that are supportive of both of you.

▼ *Your disapproval hurts your teen.*

Often, parents don't say "I'm disappointed about what you did," but say, either directly or by implication, "I disapprove of who you are." Without meaning to, they can hurt their teens—and if the parents don't change the way they express their feelings, they can seriously damage their children's self-esteem.

Tammi's mom was excited about the nice new clothes she bought for her daughter. But Tammi slept in one of the outfits and threw the other two on the floor where the dog slept on them. Mom became hysterical: "How could you do this? What kind of a person are you? Don't you care about anything?"

Tammi interpreted this to mean "She's disappointed in me. She thinks I'm a bad person. She didn't even ask me why this happened. She didn't try to understand how it is for me. She just thinks I'm bad. I'm going to get revenge."

In this case, Tammi was so hurt by her mother's disapproval that she wanted revenge. Instead of focusing specifically on what Tammi *did* that made her angry, Mom focused on who Tammi *was*. Neither mother nor daughter came close to understanding one another—and Tammi's self-esteem was injured.

If we buy clothing for our teens it becomes their

business what they do with them. It can be quite effective to put teens on a clothing allowance and give them money in amounts we can afford. It is then up to them how they choose, how they care for, and who they loan their clothes to. The lessons they learn from their choices can serve them the rest of their lives.

▼ *Your fear can discourage your teen.*

Sometimes parents' fears can encourage children to lose faith in themselves. As a result, kids may decide that no matter what they do, they can never do it well enough, so they may as well not even try. This is the attitude of extremely discouraged teens that prevents them from gaining life skills by practicing and making mistakes.

Lindy's mother discouraged her from going on the senior-class trip. Mom told Lindy how awful the trip was—that no one had any fun unless they got drunk and slept around. Since Lindy didn't want to get drunk and sleep around—and since she had no reason to doubt her mother—she felt she couldn't go.

When questioned, Mom said, "I've heard a lot of stories about this trip. I'm not sure if they're true—but if they are, I don't want my daughter to go. She can find some other way to celebrate graduation."

One thing Mom seemed to be ignoring was that in a year or so Lindy would probably be living on her own at college. Not only would she lack the self-confidence that comes from handling difficult situations, she'd also lack the necessary skills—including decision-making—because her mother made so many decisions for her. The more we talked about it, the more obvious it was that Lindy, unnerved by her mother's fear, was scared to go out on her own. She readily believed her mother's version of the senior-class trip because she herself was afraid of what might happen there.

Many teenagers want their parents to place lots of controls on them and to do things for them because they're afraid to grow up. If parents feed their teens' fears with fears of their own, their teenagers *won't* develop the skills necessary to become successful adults.

▾ *Build your teen's courage.*

You can help your teens build courage by showing your enthusiasm for their growth process: "Won't it be exciting when you grow up and are old enough to leave home? Won't it be exciting when you get your first apartment? Aren't you looking forward to having a phone of your own, and a phone bill of your own? Isn't it going to be fun?" Your enthusiasm will be contagious and will help them look foward to being grown-ups in the world. More important, you can help them be courageous by giving them the chance to learn from you and then giving them the opportunity to use what they've learned. For instance, parents who give their teens a clothing allowance and the freedom to choose what to buy, also give them a valuable experience in responsibility. What you teach them now *is* useful to them later in life.

One mom who had conscientiously tried to provide her son with life skills asked him if he thought all the shopping he did as a kid helped him as an adult. He replied, "Are you kidding? I don't know how I would be able to live like I do if I hadn't had all that help. I know how to shop for bargains, how to stretch my money, how to plan ahead. I know how to do menus! I know a lot of stuff."

We need to realize that our kids were not born with the skills they need to go out into the world on their own. It's our job to help them get these skills. Parents with the long-range goal of helping their children grow into self-reliant adults provide the kind of parenting that teaches the necessary skills and instills confidence and self-reliance.

In this chapter, we've introduced several tools parents can use to help understand their teens' perceptions. Even if you don't feel completely comfortable using these tools, it's helpful to know that they exist—and that there are reasons, not always easily understood, why teenagers behave the way they do.

Remember that the perceptions teens have and the decisions they make about their experiences color their pictures of themselves and help explain some of their behavior. It's also helpful to remember that their reality may be different from yours. In addition, keep in mind that teenagers have not yet become adults—their current values, which many parents find disturbing, are not necessarily those they will hold as grown-ups.

It is not the purpose of this chapter to turn parents into amateur therapists. But introducing some of the tools of the therapist gives parents an opportunity to widen their perspective and look a little deeper into their kids' behaviors. This in turn allows them to be less judgmental, less reactive, and more able to have faith in the growth process.

SECTION 2

Nonpunitive Parenting

▼
Chapter 7

The Teen Within You

Finding Your Unresolved Issues

Unresolved Issues from Your Teen Years

Raising a teenager brings up a lot of unresolved issues from your own adolescence. Even though these issues may be unconscious, they influence how you parent your teen. Going through adolescence with our teens gives us another chance to work through some of these issues. In doing so, we also become more effective parents.

The following activity can help parents identify their unresolved issues. Some issues that parents discover concern body image, personal power, romantic love, relationships with parents, and independence. Anything that didn't get worked out when we were teens still lurks in the shadows of our unconscious, waiting for another chance.

Besides the opportunity of working on unresolved issues, the activity below can also put us in touch with our teen's world. Instead of thinking like a parent, by going back to your own teen years you will be able to recall how you thought, felt, and behaved. As much as possible, you will remember what it's like to be a teenager. This can give you a better understanding of your teen's perceptions, and show you that you may be taking some of his or her behavior much too personally.

Activity—Part One: Discovering Your Unresolved Teen Issues

1. Think of a situation that occurs with you and your teen that you wish were different. Write it out; be specific.
2. How do you feel when the situation occurs? Be sure to use "feeling" words and not words like *as if, like,* or *that.*
3. What is it that you, the parent, are doing in the problem situation?
4. What is your teen's response to your behavior?
5. What is your decision about that?

Sample Answers for Activity—Part One

1. *Think of a situation that occurs with you and your teen that you wish were different. Write it out; be specific.* Whenever I schedule an activity with my son, he backs out at the last minute. The chance of us doing a planned activity together is about 2%.
2. *How do you feel when the situation occurs? Be sure to use "feeling" words and not words like 'as if,' 'like,' or 'that.'* I feel sad because I don't get to spend the time with him, and I feel angry because he says yes but acts no.
3. *What is it that you, the parent, are doing in the problem situation?* I say, "No problem. We can try again another time."

4. *What is your teen's response to your behavior?* He says, "I'm really sorry, but something else came up and I just can't keep our date."
5. *How do you feel about your behavior and your teen's response?* I tell myself it's really okay because it's my job to be there for my son.

Activity—Part Two: Remember a Time from Your Own Teen Years

1. Think of a time when you were a teen and things weren't working out the way you wanted them to. Write it out; be specific.
2. How did you feel about the situation?
3. How did you behave in the situation?
4. How did the adults or parents behave in the situation?
5. What was your response to their behavior?
6. What did you decide about the situation?

Sample Answers for Activity—Part Two

1. *Think of a time when you were a teen and things weren't working out the way you wanted them to. Write it out; be specific.* It was my senior year and I didn't have a date for the prom. I finally asked a friend if he could get me a date.
2. *How were you feeling about the situation?* I felt embarrassed, scared and inadequate.
3. *How did you behave in the situation?* I asked a friend for help.
4. *How did the adults or parents behave in the situation?* There were no adults involved.
5. *What was your response to their behavior?* I didn't share anything with the adults, and I never

thought of doing that. My mother was my only parent, and we didn't have that kind of relationship.

6. *What did you decide about the situation?* I wasn't capable of attracting female companionship.

Activity – Part Three: Interpreting and Using the Information from Parts One and Two

1. After writing down both a current problem situation and one from your own teen years, *ask yourself how you would describe an issue that remains unresolved for you from the incident when you were a teenager.* This father said, "I feel unloved and unattractive."
2. *Then ask yourself what information, if any, you got from your teen memory that could help you deal more effectively with your current problem situation.* Dad then said that feeling unloved is a theme running through his whole life. If he didn't feel that way, he'd probably handle the situation with his son very differently.
3. *Now see how these insights could help with your parenting in your current problem.* Dad said, "I'd confront my son. 'If we're going to schedule something, let's do it. If it falls through after we've planned it, I'm going to be upset.'" He then realized that he hadn't had an emotionally honest relationship with his mother growing up and that he was parenting his son in the same way. He clearly would like to, and *could*, change by being more honest about his true feelings instead of saying no problem.

   He also realized that his son might be switching activities without even thinking of talking over his plans with his dad. He remembered how he never discussed his plans with his own mother as a kid.

How Your Fears Can Reveal Unresolved Issues

What are your fears? How many of your parenting methods are based on fear . . . fear of what the neighbors will think, fear that your kids will ruin their lives with their choices, fear that you aren't being a good enough parent?

A mother in one of our classes decided to explore her fears to find out what some of her unresolved issues were. She began with activity one, describing a problem with her teenage son. She wanted her son to be home more, saying that she missed him even though he wasn't very pleasant when he was there.

"Maybe I want him home so he can do his chores. I feel used when he wants to receive but not to give. And I'm afraid he won't be a responsible person and won't be happy later if he doesn't show responsibility now. Mostly, I'm afraid I'm not being a good mother if he doesn't do his chores.

"First, I need to take care of my issues about being a good-enough mother. What would happen if I accepted that I'm good enough, just by being who I am —and worked on feeling better about who I am? The trouble is, I can't convince myself I'm a good mother if my son isn't responsible and considerate."

During the part two activity, this mother revealed that she was raised in a strict religious home where all behavior was gauged by what the church and the neighbors would think. As a teen, she wasn't allowed to do many activities, including dating, considered by most to be normal for a developing girl, because they were forbidden by the church. When it came to dating, she was rebellious and sneaky. Her need to individuate and to honor her biological clock was stronger than her need to comply with the church.

The guilt, shame, and fear she felt at getting caught are the very issues that get in the way today when parenting her teenage son, especially because he is doing things society disapproves of out in the open.

"I can't stop worrying about my son's drinking and smoking and stealing. Not only am I worried about how it will affect his life, but I'm worried about what people will say about me. And I'm worried that he'll want me to support him when he should be supporting himself. I'm afraid that some of his habits might cause him unhappiness later in life—and that it will be my fault. So, what can I do about all my worries?"

With help from her group and with insights gained in the part three activity, Mom was able to get some new perspectives on the situation. She came up with the following alternatives to her previous behavior:

1. I can offer my son information about smoking and drinking. I can become a source of information for him.
2. I can quit providing him with unnecessary material things. I need to decide what I'm willing to provide—what makes sense to me—that I can give willingly, without any resentment or strings. I can prepare myself for the temper tantrums that will probably come when I quit indulging him—because I've been the biggest perpetuator of the belief that he should be indulged. I can help him plan to get things he wants—when he wants my help.
3. I can realize that the habits that will cause him

unhappiness are no worse than the habits that have caused me unhappiness; and that I can't rob him of the opportunity to learn what he needs to learn in this life. I've been a perfectionist, feared rejection, had an inordinate need to please, feared what others would think, been a workaholic, been judgmental, had unrealistic expectations, held grudges for supposed wrongs to myself and others, felt dissatisfied because I hadn't accomplished all that I felt I should. What right do I have to worry about his habits when I still have so many of my own?

4. I can let go of my fear that his habits might kill him. True, adolescence is a dangerous time. But my adolescent cousin was killed by a hay baler in the course of doing his normal chores. In other words, there are no guarantees. I'm quite sure my habits have caused just as much damage to my body as his do to his body. So the key is to work on my own healing.

It can be more difficult to eliminate ineffective behaviors when we don't have an understanding of our own unresolved issues and how they are the basis of our ineffective behaviors.

How Our Unresolved Issues Obstruct Parenting

A mother told us that her sixteen-year-old son's economics teacher called to say her son had been tardy or absent six days out of ten. The teacher wanted to know what Mom was going to do. Without a second thought, Mom said she would come in for a parent-teacher conference with the son.

When asked why she responded that way, Mom said she wanted to look good to the teacher. Upon further exploration, she realized she was automatically intimidated upon hearing the teacher's voice and immediately felt she had done something wrong. Immobilized, she turned her power over to the teacher.

Mom also realized, with help from her group, that she felt disappointment. When she thinks she's done something wrong, she's sure she's disappointed the other person and is thus disappointed in herself. In addition, Mom believes that to be worthy of love or friendship, she can *never* be wrong, otherwise no one will like her. So when she feels she's made a mistake, she immediately tries to fix the situation to the other person's satisfaction. So intent on doing what is "right," Mom can't see what is most effective or helpful. In this case, she was more intent on staying out of trouble with the teacher than in helping her son.

▼ *Deal with the needs of the situation instead of reacting to your fears.*

Rather than accepting what the teacher says at face value, it would be more helpful for Mom to talk to her son and find out what he feels is going on and what he wants to do about it. Or Mom could ask the teacher if he's discussed this problem with her son. She could also let the teacher know that she doesn't approve of her son's behavior but feels it is up to them to work it out. She could ask her son if he wants her to come to school with him to discuss the situation with the teacher or if he would like to handle it himself.

▼ *Let go by not taking it personally.*

Many parents feel that their kids won't talk to them because of something the parent has done. But teenagers need to figure things out for themselves. That is part of the individuation process. Often they won't talk to their parents because they see themselves as grown-ups and see their parent's help as being treated like little kids.

Once we get our personal issues out of the way, including the feeling that our teens are trying to hurt us, we can stop feeling guilty about our kids' problems. We can also be available to help our kids if they need us, instead of interfering to save face for ourselves.

▼ *Use a magic wand to deal with your unresolved teen issues.*

Mrs. Andersen shared that when she was thirteen, her mother read her diary and found out all about her first "going steady" experience. After reading that her daughter had kissed her boyfriend twelve times, Mrs. Andersens' mother wouldn't speak to her for several days. Not only did her mother not respect her privacy, but when Mrs. Andersen tried to say she was sorry, her mother replied scornfully, "You should be."

Mrs. Andersen imagined how she would change that memory if she had a magic wand and could redo it any way she liked. She said, "If my mother did find out about my boyfriend by reading the diary, she would sit down and talk to me. She might tell me she is scared and why. She might tell me what it was like for her at my age. And she would ask me if I would like to tell her what is going on for me. Then she would encourage me to use my best judgment—and tell me that even if I made a mistake, she was sure I could handle it. She'd let me know that if I ever wanted to talk to her, I could do that without being judged—and that if she ever did seem critical, it was just because she was bothered by her own issues."

When we have the parent rewrite their memory, stating what they wish *their* parent had done, it's probably very close to what their kid would like them to do. In addition to healing an old hurt, this procedure can also provide information that the parent might want to use with their own teen.

Dealing With a Child Who Is Addicted to Drugs

The following conversation took place with a parent who came to therapy to deal with her own issues around her twenty-two-year-old daughter's drug use.

Parent: I don't want my child to be a drug addict.

Therapist: I know you've done a lot to help your daughter get treatment and that she's still deciding to use chemicals. You can't make her stop using drugs, but you can help yourself let go. Let's explore some of your issues about letting go by going back to an early memory from your teenage years.

Parent: The one that comes to me is when I was a little older.

Therapist: How old?

Parent: Twenty-one.

Therapist: That's interesting. It's close to your daughter's age now.

Parent: I was divorced. I had custody of my two young children. Their father had the kids every Wednesday night and every weekend. But the kids were constantly upset about being shifted back and forth. One Wednesday night when their father hadn't brought them back on time, I was so upset I called my father and asked if he could come help me get the kids. Well, my Dad got real upset. All the time we were out looking for the kids, my dad was griping and complaining. I said to him, "You never did love me." He said,

"What do you mean? I always loved you more than all the rest put together." But I totally could not believe that.

Therapist: What were you thinking?

Parent: I have created this total mess of my life. My kids don't have a father. My Dad is mad at me. My kids are always upset.

Therapist: What were your feelings?

Parent: I was feeling hurt, inadequate, stupid, defensive.

Therapist: What are you doing in the memory?

Parent: I'm crying, lashing out at my Dad, accusing him of never loving me. I'm depending on him to help me and paying a big price for it.

Therapist: What is the price you are paying?

Parent: I have to listen to him yell at me and put me down.

Therapist: So what he is doing is yelling at you, scolding you, and putting you down. Anything else that the others are doing?

Parent: The kids' father is angry at me. That's why he's not bringing the kids home on time—not keeping his commitments. And when I picked up my father to look for the kids, my mother met me at the door with a disapproving look.

Therapist: Now let's go back to the situation with your daughter.

Parent: Good grief! She's messed up her life, and I'm scolding her and putting her down and giving her self-righteous, disapproving looks and messages.

Therapist: What are you telling yourself?

Parent: That she's messed up her life. That she's not doing the things that will make her happy. She's hurting me. She's not keepng her commitments.

Therapist: How are you feeling?

Parent: Unappreciated. Guilty. Self-righteous.

Good grief, I'm feeling every one of those feelings from my own memory. I'm feeling disapproving, guilty and blaming . . . and inadequate about how to handle it.

Therapist: What are you doing?

Parent: Lecturing and putting her down. Disapproving. Trying to fix it and take care of it. Trying to control her and make her do the right thing.

Therapist: Do you realize that in addition to all those things you're also seeking help and learning about your co-dependency? Part of your struggle is that you are half in and half out of being a co-dependent. Even though you are doing many of the things to her that made you feel worse, you are also working on changing old patterns. That takes time and practice. Just the awareness of some of your discouraging behaviors can help you stop doing them when you catch yourself in the act.

Healing the Teen in You While Parenting Your Teen

Two mothers were talking about how their divorces affected their relationships with their kids.

Mom A said she left her husband and children when the children were small. She felt very guilty about this. She asked the other mother, "When you left, did you feel you'd done something wrong?"

Mom B said, "No. When I left, I felt I deserved what I got in terms of happiness in my new life. I felt that I had suffered long enough and that I had a right to be happy. My kids had no right to deny me some happiness."

Both mothers were unable to help their children deal with the issues that troubled them until the mothers were able to get beyond their *own* issues. Mom A's issues centered around inadequacy and self-worth, Mom B's around justice. And both moms were playing out unresolved issues from their own teen years. As a teen Mom A never believed she measured up to her beautiful, big sister. Mom B thought it wasn't fair that boys had more freedom and girls were more restricted.

As soon as Mom A stopped feeling wrong, guilty, and defensive, she was able to enjoy her kids more and spend more time with them. Before, it had been too painful to be around them. Now, she was able to listen to her children explain how it felt for them to be left. As painful as this was to hear, at least both mom and children could experience the love and closeness they did feel for each other without the wall of guilt between them.

Mom B, with her justice issue, felt the need to defend herself. As soon as she stopped defending herself, she found it easy to be curious and listen to her children, who were very angry about and disapproving of her new marriage. She was able to say, "This is right for me to do, but you have totally different issues. How it's affecting me is very different from how it's affecting you. I want to understand how it feels for you." Her kids could open up when they felt she cared more about them than about justifying her own position.

The old baggage we carry around with us for our teen years gets in our way of living full, rich lives. It can also create stumbling blocks when dealing with our own teens. If we can use these precious years with our teens to go back and do some reparenting of the teen within us, the time is well spent. Not only do we feel better, but our teens benefit, too. Sharing some of these early experiences and what we learn from reviewing them with our own teens can lead to greater friendship and compassion between parent and child.

▼

Chapter

8

Control and Punishment

Fueling the Fires Of Rebellion and Revenge

Many parents think it's their responsibility to control their kids. They think it's part of their job as parents. If they don't make their kids do what they *should* do for "their own good," these parents worry about being permissive.

Most parents use some form of punishment as the primary method of control. With teenagers, the most popular punishments are grounding, withdrawing privileges, taking away allowances, and withdrawing love and approval.

We know most parents won't want to hear this, but *any* form of control or punishment is very disrespectful to teenagers and extremely ineffective for the goals of long-range parenting. Sometimes it's appropriate to withdraw privileges from children under twelve or thirteen when it is related to their misbehavior, is respectfully enforced, and seems reasonable by advance agreement to both parent and child. However, by the time kids reach adolescence, and see themselves as adults rather than children, they won't see grounding or removal of privileges as respectful or reasonable.

Long-Range Results of Control and Punishment

Alienation

Kids who finally get away from parental control often cannot stand to have a relationship with their parents after they become adults because they felt smothered, judged, and obliterated for being who they are. Their parents are very hurt, especially because they know they were trying to do what they thought was good for their children. It's hard for these parents to understand why their children now have such anger and hatred or simply withhold closeness.

Permanent Apron Strings

Other kids never escape the control of their parents. Their whole lives revolve around doing what they think their mother or father would want. They often grow up to become approval junkies who choose other people to continue the job of controlling them. This can be devastating to marriages, parenting, friendships, and jobs.

Late Bloomers

Some kids who were raised in a controlling environment later get into therapy, where they find support in learning to grow, because their parents never helped them grow up. It takes awhile to convince these people that it's okay to be separate people from their parents.

Letting Go of Control

The first step is to acknowledge that letting go of control is scary. Yes, your kids will make mistakes. Yes, it will be hard to watch them make mistakes, especially big ones. But remember, the freedom to make mistakes and learn from them is essential to individuation and growth. Try to find one person you really admire who has not made some big mistakes in his or her life, and you'll find that you can't! Knowing that making mistakes is an essential part of living, it's incredible how much wasted time and energy parents spend trying to save their children from making them.

Many parents develop the mistaken belief that if they use *positive discipline* principles with their kids when they are young, their kids won't make mistakes as teenagers. On the contrary, children who were raised democratically and respectfully are more self-confident about risking, rebelling, and learning.

The Rebellion of Positive Discipline *Children*

Mrs. Shaffer found her children used all the skills she had taught them about being self-reliant to rebel against everything she had taught them about healthy eating—at least for a while. She felt she had done a good job of teaching her kids about good nutrition. They discussed nutrition during family meetings, and the kids helped with the shopping and made their own nutritional lunches. But when the kids became teenagers, they seemed to throw everything they knew about nutrition out the window and went for junk food.

Mrs. Shaffer shared with her parent study group, "I didn't want to be nagging and wasting energy doing something that wasn't going to work anyway as soon as I turned my back. I didn't want to destroy my relationship with my kids, because I thought there were other places where they would really need me, and I didn't want to mess it up by yelling about potato chips. It wasn't always easy. I felt like a failure when they started eating junk food. At times I thought, 'Oh, they haven't learned anything. I tried so hard. It's obvious that all my parenting skills are worthless!' I felt disappointed, disillusioned, unhappy, scared, and worried. It was very uncomfortable, but I kept my long-term goals in sight. It was a rational process. If I'd acted on my feelings, I would've driven my kids and myself nuts. Thank goodness for all I've learned! I maintained faith in them and in myself. Now that they're grown-ups, my son is a health food nut and my daughter eats well because she's very conscious of her body."

Being a good parent does not mean saving our kids from living. It does not mean saving them from all pain, from all mistakes, from life. If we could manage to save them from all these things, they wouldn't be able to function as adults in the real world.

Teens' Resistance to Your Letting Go

Parents are not the only ones who resist letting go of control. Often, our kids don't want us to let go. Even when they've complained and rebelled against our control, they're afraid when we give it up.

Mrs. Forman had tried to control her son by attaching strings to having his own car. She told Kent he could use his car so long as he got As and Bs on his report card, had a job, came home on time, and didn't drink. Kent rebelled, got a few Ds and an F, came home late, and drank anyway. Although he kept his job, the other areas were a constant battleground. Mrs. Forman took Kent's car away from him, and he only got more rebellious.

It took an outspoken member of her parent study group to help Mrs. Forman see the folly of her efforts. "You had a whole bunch of rules that were ridiculous. When someone makes a rule, I'm either going to comply without thinking it through for myself—which isn't helpful to me—or I'm going to rebel—which isn't helpful to anybody. Making rules with teenagers is futile. Rules are arbitrary. They belong to kings. You're acting like a king or a queen, and that doesn't cut it with our kids."

Mrs. Forman had to admit that giving her son a car with strings attached did not produce the results she wanted. She decided to give up punishment, since it wasn't working anyway, and try something different.

Giving Up Punishment

When you decide to give up punishment, let your teenager know. Acknowledge that you made a mistake, that punishment doesn't work, and that you want to change.

Since Mrs. Forman didn't know how to do this, she volunteered to participate in a role-play with a member of her parent study group. The following dialogue is a transcription of that role-play. The dialogue in parentheses represents what the person later shared they were thinking and feeling in the role, rather that what they thought a teenager would actually say.

Mom: Kent, I made a mistake when I took the car away from you.

Kent: What was the mistake? Do you think you made a mistake buying the car? I don't think that was a mistake.

Mom: The mistake is all the strings I've attached to it—which just shows how much I've been trying to control your life.

(Kent: I'm trying not to drop dead here. I'm hoping this is as good as it seems.)

Mom: I've been doing this in the name of "for your own good."

Kent: Oh, don't be so hard on yourself, Mom.

Mom: Thanks. It's probably going to be hard for me, but I want to learn not to do that.

Kent: It's okay. I don't mind.

Mom: What don't you mind?

Kent: It's okay. You have to do that. You're a parent. (I'm starting to get scared. What if I make a mistake? As long as you control me, I can blame you. But if you let go and I make a mistake, it's my fault. Then I'm a bad person. I don't know how to handle this. You go ahead and take control. Being grounded is a very small price to pay for the benefits of not being responsible.)

Mom: But I don't feel good about it anymore. I don't want to do it anymore. I want to relieve you of having to live up to my expectations so that you can get on with figuring out what is right for you.

Kent: So what does this mean exactly?

Mom: It means that I'm removing the strings from the car.

Kent: But I might have an accident.

Mom: I'm scared about that, too. If you want some information about how to prevent accidents, I can help whenever you want. Actually, I know you're smart enough to figure that out by yourself.

Kent: (I'm feeling really nervous about this. If you

don't tell me not to drink, I might go ahead and drink and drive!)

Mom: I've finally learned that you're going to do what you're going to do. It's time for me to let go and let you figure out what's right for you in your life. It's scary for me, but I'm going to back off.

Kent: (This is feeling like a miracle. I'm afraid you got hit over the head or something.)

Mrs. Forman said that what she did in the role-play felt much better than her usual attempts at control and her tirades when control didn't work. She also felt she'd gained enough skills, and courage, through this exercise to try it out with her son.

The following week she shared with her group that she could hardly believe how similar the real thing was to the role-play. "When I told Kent I wanted to remove the strings from the car he said, 'But I could have an accident.'

"I said, 'I'd be glad to talk to you about things you could do to minimize the chances of an accident.'

"I got off track for awhile going right back into my good-mother bit by talking about what I thought he should do. But then I caught myself and went back to being curious about Kent's world. 'You're afraid you might have an accident if I remove the strings? What do you mean by that?'

"Kent said, 'Well, it's your job to get me to do the right thing. Moms are supposed to ground their kids.'

"I remembered to be curious. 'You mean you want me to keep trying to control you because if I don't you might get into more trouble and even an accident?'

"Kent grinned sheepishly and said, 'Yeah.'

"I continued, 'So you hate my nagging but you also feel like I might be helping you if I do it?' Kent agreed.

And it scares you what you might do if I stop nagging you?' Again Kent agreed.

"Finally, I asked 'Would you like to know how I feel about that?' Warily, Kent said, 'I guess.' So I told him. 'It scares me, too. For a long time, I've felt that it was my job to control you to keep you from getting into trouble. Now I know it's not my job. I *do* know it's important for both of us to grow beyond that, and I'm scared because I'm not sure how to do it. But you know what? I have faith in you and in myself that we can figure it out, even though it's scary.' "

Control As a Crutch

Another mother in the same parent study group had a son, Stan, who had been jailed twice for stealing. When she told him she would no longer get him out of juvenile hall, he panicked, saying angrily, "That sucks!"

Mom asked him, "Are you saying you want me to let you have the freedom to choose to steal, but if you get caught you don't want me to let you have the freedom to experience the consequences of your choice?" Stan, as creative as Kent, said with a sheepish grin, "Yeah."

Teenagers are often afraid—their lack of confidence leads them to look for a crutch. Their parents can provide this if they don't allow their teens to be responsible for the consequences of their choices and their behavior. Stan is a good example of this. He wants his mother to save him from the consequences of his choices. His behavior says, "I want to be as bad as I can be, and do everything I want to do, and never have to think about the consequences. If anything goes bad, I want to know *you* will be the responsible one." This role is perfect for a mother who wants to be a "good" parent. Actually, she's being a cruel parent by buffering him, because his behavior and the subsequent consequences will only get worse.

If you ask, many kids will say they want their parents to protect them. They want to be grounded and monitored. But what kind of people will their parents create? People who don't grow up until they are forty or fifty years old—if then. People who spend too much money, can't pay their bills on time, can't hold jobs, become addicts, become materialistic—because they were buffered all the time.

▼ *Don't buffer and don't abandon.*

Many parents buffer until they can't stand it anymore, then they abandon. They kick their kids out of the house, telling them they can't come back until they learn to "behave." This puts kids in a real dilemma. They're being asked to learn how to "behave" without any support system to teach them the necessary skills.

▼ *Support your teen.*

Supporting means allowing teens to learn from their mistakes. What they learn will eventually allow them to control their own lives.

It's easy to support our kids when they're making decisions that we like. It's harder when the decisions seem to be poor choices for their future.

Shelly was flunking several classes. She was refusing to do homework assignments because she thought they were busy work and that her teachers were "stupid" to insist that kids had to do homework even if they could pass the tests without doing it.

Shelly's parents listened to her ideas about homework and asked her if she could do it anyway because it might be even more "stupid" to miss out on going to college because of the Fs. Shelly insisted that she would not work for teachers who didn't respect kids and she didn't care if she lost credits because she could always make them up.

When Shelly's teacher called her parents to come in and talk about her poor performance, they said, "Shelly, you've decided how you want to handle these classes. We wish you could make a different choice because we think it would be better for you in the long run, but we honor your right to decide what is right for you. We have faith that if college is important, you'll find a way to make up the credits. We appeciate your willingness to share what is happening in school with us. We also feel this is between you and your teacher. We would be happy to come in with you to see your teacher if the two of you can't work this out, but it's up to you to talk to your teacher first. If you haven't worked this out with your teacher by next week, we'll call to set up an appointment so we can all go in."

Shelly made an appointment the next day to talk to her teacher. She explained her feelings about homework to the teacher and also said that her parents were completely informed about what was going on. She shared honestly that her parents were unhappy with her choices, but believed it was up to her to make her life work and that school work was her responsibility. Shelly said that her parents would come in if necessary, but would prefer that she work things out with the teacher if that was possible. The teacher responded that his policy on homework stood and that if Shelly chose not to turn in homework assignments, she would fail the class.

Shelly told her teacher, "It's up to me to pass or fail. If I fail, it's not your fault and it's not my parents' fault. I'm sorry we can't work this out, but I'm glad we could talk about it.'

Trying to control our teens does not support them

in learning skills and feeling good about who they are. Instead of control we can teach, have faith, model our values, work on our own motives for needing to control, learn to say no when appropriate without lecturing or criticizing, and work on our own growth. Following are examples of all these support skills.

▾ *Teach your teen.*

Some parents say things like, "If you don't keep the insurance payments up, I'll take the car away." This approach doesn't teach their teen much in the way of life skills.

Parents could use another approach, one that *would* teach their teen something. "I've noticed that when insurance bills come they're really expensive. Then I get scared because I don't have big hunks of money like that. So, when you get this car I have an idea about how you can deal with that. Do you want to hear what it is?" (It's important to get permission before you attempt to teach something. Otherwise, it sounds too much like a lecture. A friendly attitude and tone of voice are also important.)

A typical father and son might continue the conversation in the following way:

Son: Won't you pay for the insurance?

Father: No, I'm not paying for the insurance.

Son: Oh, come on.

Father: No. And you probably don't want to know why because it'll sound like a lecture—but do you want to hear my ideas of how you can deal with insurance? Because you can't drive a car without insurance. That's one thing you can't do. If your insurance expires, then I can't let you drive the car.

Son: Oh, okay.

Father: First, we sit down and figure out how

much the insurance will be. We'll probably have to call the insurance company to find out for sure. But suppose we find out it's about $600 every six months. How much would you have to save each month to pay that bill when it comes?

Son: Wow! That's $100 a month!

Father: Right. So how much would you have to put away each week from your paycheck?

Son: I only make fifty dollars a week. That means I have to save half just for insurance.

Father: Right. What kinds of things will you have to sacrifice to do that?

Son: That really sucks! I'll have only twenty-five dollars a week for gas, hamburgers, dates, tapes, and everything.

Father: Maybe it isn't worth it to drive a car. What are your other options?

Son: Oh, I'll do it, but it sure sucks.

Father: I understand that feeling. I've had it many times.

This father had faith in himself to teach and in his son to learn an essential life skill. Faith is an essential ingredient for being effective parents with long-range goals.

▼ *Have faith in yourself and your kids.*

At camp, nine-year-old Billy got too close to the edge of a fifty-foot waterall and fell over. Campers at the top of the waterfall watched aghast as Billy fell head-first. But as he fell he pushed himself off the side of the rockface, righted himself, and landed bottom first into a small pool of water. He turned death into a stunt. When his father heard about Billy's fall, he said, "All I could think was, thank God for all those times when I didn't rush in and rescue him. I kept having faith in him even when I was scared to death, so he had faith in himself. I gave him opportunities to figure out problems as he went along instead of doing it for him. The long-range results of not controlling and rescuing probably saved his life. Not that I saved his life, but he saved his life because I could give him those gifts." This kind of faith in our children can be carried into their teen years.

Mrs. Borden gave her study group an example of how easy it is to understand the importance of having faith in our kids after the crisis is over. "Stewart graduated from a church university, is now married with two children, and has a successful business. When he tells me the things he did as a teenager—even sold pot—I can't believe it!

"Now that it's over, it's easy to see that it would have made sense to have faith in him all along. But I'm not so sure I would've maintained faith in him at the time if I'd known what was going on. How do you have faith when you're in the middle of a problem?"

Part of having faith is *knowing* that you *are* in the middle of a transition, rather than at the end of a story. In addition, we tend to focus on the ten kids who have overdosed instead of the ten thousand who haven't, so we base our parenting on silly odds. Another way to maintain faith is to support our teens for being who they are.

However, many parents are afraid that faith will not teach their kids values, so they try cramming their values down their kids' throats.

▼ *Model your values.*

Modeling is the only way to teach values. If we cram them down our teens' throats, by lecturing and cajoling, our teens will resent it and rebel. If we model our values, our teens will be able to observe our behavior without feeling forced to behave the same way. We may not think our teens are absorbing our values because they don't immediately accept them—there *is* a time lag. But when our teens get older, they will probably adopt many of the values we modeled when they were growing up.

To avoid cramming our values down our teen's throat—and to allow us to model them instead—we need to look at the motives that underlie our desire to control our teen, to force him or her to agree with our values or else.

Motives Perpetuating Control

There are as many different issues behind the need to control as there are different parents, so we'll mention a few of the general categories and give a few examples.

1. *Fear of what others will think:* If they don't control their children, some parents feel others will see them as "bad" parents.
2. *Fear of loss:* If they don't control their children, some parents are afraid their children will do permanent damage to themselves, such as:

   Become pregnant

   Go to jail

   Drop out of school

   Not go to college

   Abuse drugs

   Die accidentally

   It's true that these things happen to many teenagers. But they happen to just as many kids (if not more) whose parents are controlling as to kids whose parents are not controlling.

3. *Fear of powerlessness:* Some parents feel they do not have belonging and significance unless they are in control.
4. *Fear of inadequacy:* Some parents feel inadequate if they are not in control.
5. *Overprotection:* If they don't control their children, some parents are afraid their teens might get hurt emotionally by others.
6. *Ignorance:* Some parents simply lack alternative parenting skills.
7. *Unresolved personal issues:* This usually underlies the need to control. When we feel stongly about something particular and attempt to control our teenager regarding it, it's probably an issue of our own that remains unresolved.

One mother was able to get past her need to control her daughter, Cindy, when she was able to understand her own unresolved personal issue.

During a counseling session, Cindy asked her mother whether she could go to a party. Upset that her daughter waited until the counseling session to ask, many issues came up for Mom. She was jealous because she felt Cindy thought the counselor was a better mother; she felt that Cindy and the counselor were ganging up on her; and she was angry because the counselor says what Cindy wants to hear.

Cindy explained that she doesn't ask at home because her mother always says "I'll have to think about it" and then doesn't get back to her. Mom wants to think about it because she worries about what her religion wants her to do; about her family being upset if she doesn't follow her religion; and about what her neighbors and friends will think. In addition, she's afraid that her husband—who isn't even the same religon as she—will call her a hypocrite if she doesn't follow her religion's dictates.

Cindy told her mother, "I'm not going to have you say 'I'll talk to you later' because I don't like being put off. I never know where I stand with you."

Mom finally said, "I'll let you go, but I have a lot of reservations." Helped by the counselor to get to the bottom of her reservations, Mom realized that her real issue was that she was afraid someone would break Cindy's heart. Her own heart had been broken when she was eighteen. By understanding her long-suppressed fear, Mom was able to begin supporting her daughter in living her own life rather than trying to control her and protect her.

Saying No Can Be Appropriate

Giving up control does not mean never saying no. No is very appropriate when we are controlling our own limits rather than trying to control our teenager's. It's important to know what our limits are as well as what our unresolved issues are.

However, often parents are not aware of their own issues. A parent who is a *chronic pleaser* may be afraid to say no for fear of rejection. A parent who is into *control* may say no too often for fear of being weak and humiliated. This no is seldom based on reasonable understanding of the teen's world or on parental wisdom and creates rebellious teens or approval junkies with low self-esteem. A parent into *significance* may be very unpredictable because no is based more on what others will think than on the issue at hand and the direct consequences to the teen. A parent into *comfort* may not say no when it would be appropriate to avoid the stress of following through with dignity and respect.

Although it's true that a teenager may very well reject a parent who says no, when the no is based on reason and wisdom and is said with confidence, the rejection usually doesn't last much longer than five minutes. In rare instances, the rejection may last longer but is hardly ever permanent.

Growing Together

Parents need to look at their part in creating problems in their relationships with their teens. If our kids don't want to talk to us, why not? If they are rebelling beyond what is normal for their age, why?

No matter how we look at it, we find that it's not only our teenagers who need to grow up, it's crucial for us to continue our own growth process as well. It's too easy to see the faults in others and yet be blind to our own.

One mother summed it up beautifully when she shared what she learned from another participant in one of our teen workshops:

"When working with Susan, it was so easy for me to see how uptight, rigid, and controlling she is and how suffocating that is to her daughter—and how miserable she makes things for herself. It was so easy for me to think, 'Why can't she lighten up and let go and trust the basic goodness of her daughter? So what if she even fails in school? Maybe that's exactly what she needs to learn to become the flower she is meant to be.' Then I realized how uptight, rigid, and controlling I am with my son because I'm afraid he might be making some mistakes that could ruin his life. It had seemed to me that to lighten up, let go, and trust his basic goodness would be permissive and irresponsible. Even though I know how devastating it was to me when my own mother was controlling with me, it's been easy for me to justify controlling my son because 'what he's doing is so much more dangerous than what I was doing.' I now see how easily I've justified hurting him deeply in my efforts to keep him from hurting himself.

"Having faith in my children's basic goodness is very difficult when I get uptight about how they seem to be growing—even though I *have* experienced the wonderful results of letting go and providing nothing more than nurturing."

We can't save our kids from all pain and all mistakes but we can teach them skills and nurture the strength that will help them live through pain. Control and punishment do not teach our teenagers the skills they need, but the following chapters include many effective methods that *will* help us teach life skills to our teenagers.

▼

Chapter

9

Long-Range Parenting

Nurturing Individuation

Someone once said that the teen years were created so that it would be easier for parents to let their kids go when they turned twenty. Sometimes that seems like an understatement. Teens can be very hard to love. They make promises that they forget to keep. They "know everything" and continually tell us how stupid we are. They hate to clean their rooms, they listen to music we can't stand, and they exaggerate everything. They even talk funny. Sometimes they talk so fast, only another teenager can understand what they're saying.

Often, we look at our teens and feel a sense of failure. We wonder how we could have created such a monster. We think we have to teach them lessons and have one last chance to mold them into decent human beings. We feel desperate and hopeless, angry and aggravated.

If we could simply relax and remember that these are the years when our kids are trying eveything in an attempt to find out what they think, we could enjoy them more. If we gave up trying to teach and control them and instead learned to be curious and amazed, we could appreciate their struggle. If we could relax, we could trust that who they are now is in no way a reflection on us or indicative of who they will be when they grow up. With these new attitudes, we could focus on long-range parenting.

▼ *Remember to see below the surface.*

When Sally became a teenager, her mother thought she had become a different person. But Sally was really the same person she always had been—she just looked different. She dressed differently, she had different friends, and she got into the world of rock (she played the guitar). Underneath, she was still Sally, but now she'd taken on a role (Sally the "rocker"). I asked her mother, "When she was little did she get into super heroes? Did she ask you to sew a *W* on her chest and let her be Wonderwoman? Did you think it was cute? Could you think of her that way now? Imagine that she's put on the suit of a rocker. That's what's going on; she's trying on an identity, but the identity is not who Sally really is."

Everytime we think this is who our teens have become, we get discouraged. We think we've failed as parents. Certain that this is who they will be forever, we think we should do something to get them back on track. Then we go crazy and do all the wrong things. Instead, if we can relax we can see they are still as beautiful as they always were.

In this chapter, you'll learn about the tools and steps for long-range parenting to help your kids build their inner resources and let them know they are loved just as they are. Long-range parenting empowers rather than enables our kids.

▼ *Helpful hints for empowering vs. enabling*

When we use the word *enable,* we are referring to

behavior that puts the parent between the child and life experience and that minimizes the consequences of the child's choices. Enabling behavior encourages an unhealthy dependence in our kids, and prevents them from learning to do things for themselves.

Here are some examples of typical enabling behaviors for parents of teenagers:

Wake kids up, do their laundry, fix their lunches, pick out their clothes

Loan money and give extra money after the kids have spent their allowance or used specially earmarked funds, such as a clothing allowance, on something else

Type papers, do research, deliver forgotten homework or lunches to school, lie to teachers when the kids cut classes or skip school

Feel sorry for kids who have a lot of homework or activities and excuse them from helping the family with household chores

Parents enable their teens when they engage in any of the following:

Doing too much for them
Giving them too much
Overprotecting/rescuing
Lying for them
Punishing/controlling
Living in denial about problem behaviors

Empowerment, on the other hand, helps them grow to be responsible young adults instead of dependent, rebellious people.

When we use the word **empower** we are referring to **turning control over to young people as soon as possible so they have power over their own lives.** Parents empower their teens when they engage in any of the following:

Doing nothing with love (listening and giving emotional support and validation without fixing or discounting).

Teaching life skills

Working on agreements through family meetings or the joint problem-solving process

Letting go (without abandoning)

Deciding what you will do with dignity and respect

Sharing what you think, how you feel, and what you want without lecturing, moralizing, insisting on agreement or demanding that anyone gives you what you want.

Sticking to the issue with dignity and respect

When most parents look at the lists for enabling behaviors and empowering behaviors, they become vividly aware of how skilled they are in enabling responses and unskilled in empowering responses. Since we believe the enabling responses are second-nature to most of us, we are going to leave those to your imagination while we concentrate on teaching the skills of empowerment. All of the following suggestions are empowering behaviors that can be used by parents when dealing with most problems with teenagers. We will use neglected homework as an example:

1. SHOWING FAITH: "I have faith in you. I trust you to figure out what you need. I know that when it is important to you, you'll know what to do."
2. RESPECTING PRIVACY: "I respect your privacy, and want you to know I'm available if you want to discuss this with me."

3. EXPRESSING YOUR LIMITS: "I'm not willing to go to school to bail you out. When your teacher calls, I'll hand the phone to you or tell her she'll need to discuss it with you." (A respectful attitude and tone of voice is essential.)
4. LISTEN WITHOUT FIXING OR JUDGING: "I would like to listen to what this means for you."
5. CONTROLLING YOUR OWN BEHAVIOR: "I'm willing to take you to the library when we get an agreement in advance for a convenient time, but I'm not willing to get involved at the last minute." "If you need my help with your homework, please let me know in advance."
6. LETTING GO OF THEIR ISSUES: "I hope you'll go to college, but I'm not sure it's important to you."
7. AGREEMENT, NOT RULES: "Could we sit down and see if we can work on a plan regarding homework that we both can live with?"
8. LOVING AND ENCOURAGING: "I love you just the way you are and respect you to choose what is right for you."
9. ASKING FOR HELP: "I need your help. Can you explain to me why it is not important to you to do your homework?"
10. SHARE YOUR FEELINGS: Share your truth by using the "I feel ____ because ____ and I wish ____" process without expecting anyone else to feel the same or to grant your wish. This is a great model for children to acknowledge their feelings and wishes without expectations. "I feel upset when you don't do your homework because I value education so much and think it could be very beneficial to you in your life, and I really wish you would do it."

11. JOINT PROBLEM SOLVING: "What is your picture of what is going on regarding your homework? Would you be willing to hear my concerns? Could we brainstorm together on some possible solutions?"
12. RESPECTFUL COMMUNICATION: "I'm feeling too upset to talk about this right now. Let's put it on the agenda for the family meeting so we can talk about it when I'm not so emotional."
13. INFORMATION VS. ORDERS: "I notice you spend a lot of time watching television and talking on the phone during the time you have set aside for homework." "I notice you often leave your homework until the last minute and then feel discouraged about getting it done."

These empowering statements and actions may not seem as powerful as they are to parents who are used to the short-range benefits of controlling, rescuing or abandoning.

These statements and actions *do* turn over control to our kids so they have power over their own lives. The difficult part of this for parents is that this power often leads to mistakes and failure. It is only when we understand that learning from mistakes and failure is an important part of a successful life process that we will also understand the importance of using these empowering statements and actions.

Empowerment: The Foundation of Long-Range Parenting

Empowerment is the process of developing courage, responsibility, cooperation, self-love, and social consciousness. As parents, we can help our teens develop and internalize these skills and attitudes. This internal strength can lead them to a healthy, happy, productive life whether we are there or not. Empowerment invites our kids to think for themselves, to think about their behavior, to make their own decisions, to live with their mistakes, and to have good memories of unconditional love.

Courage is the ability to hang in when the going gets tough. This is very important for teenagers because the going *does* get tough. They experience extremes in emotion, changes of loyalty from parents to friends, and a whole new world of temptations. Some kids go to the extreme of suicide because they lack the courage to see a problem through. They haven't learned to have faith in themselves, that there is always another day.

How do we help establish courage in our kids?

By having faith in them

By letting them know that mistakes are opportunities to learn

By giving them opportunities to try again, rather than punishing them

By working on agreements, solutions, and plans to overcome problems

By showing them that what happens now is now and that tomorrow is another day

Responsibility is the ability to face our mistakes and use them as opportunities to grow. How do we help establish responsibilty in our kids?

By not punishing them for mistakes

By teaching problem-solving skills for correcting mistakes

By not pampering them to help them avoid pain

By giving them opportunities for accountability in a supportive way

Cooperation is the ability to get along with other people. How do we help establish cooperation in our kids?

By holding family meetings

By holding problem-solving sessions

By working out agreements

By being nonjudgmental (fusing *we*, not *you* or *I* when solving problems)

Self-love is the ability to know our thoughts and feelings and accept them without judgment. Self-love includes the desire and skills to care for ourselves. How do we help our kids establish self-love?

By giving them unconditional love

By respecting their thoughts and feelings without having to agree with them

By modeling taking care of ourselves in respectful ways and supporting our kids in taking care of themselves in respectful ways

Courage, responsibility, cooperation, and self-love can all be used in negative situations unless they are combined with social consciousness. Gangs have courage, responsibility, cooperation, and self-love.

Social consciousness is the ability to understand that your behavior affects yourself and others; it includes the desire to find significance and belonging in a positive manner. How do we help our kids establish social consciousness?

By giving them opportunities to make a difference and to contribute

By letting them experience the consequences of their behavior

By sharing our honest thoughts and feelings about how their behavior affects us

By letting them know they are loved

All this will be harder for parents who have always had a tight rein on their kids than for parents who have encouraged independence. But it's never too late to take steps in the right direction. Taking one step at a time is a great way to start on long-range parenting. Over time, our kids will notice and respond to our changes. Since many of us have bounced from one new parenting manual to another, it will take some consistent effort on our part to convince our kids we really intend to parent differently. They've learned to listen more to our behavior than to our words and have developed a lot of bad habits in reaction to our old parenting styles.

The Ten Building Blocks of Long-Range Parenting

The following is a list of tips for long-range parenting. Implementing any of these steps will help our teens grow into responsible adults and will also invite a better relationship between parent and teen.

1. Use your parental authority wisely; save your no's for the really important things. With preadolescents, a no once a week is plenty. By the time kids are fourteen, once a month should do; and by the time they are seventeen once a year should be enough.
2. Encourage, or at least don't block, safe rebellion.

These are areas where your kids can experiment without hurting anyone. The areas include such things as music, hair, cosmetics, fashions, their own room, use of time, friends, and so on. Stay in the now and remember that what your kids do today is not what they'll do forever and is not a mark of their character—it's just part of their growing process.

3. Leave teens space to withdraw into their own private world, because they have a great need for privacy. Ignore their moods and don't get into their doldrums. Love them even when they're in a bad mood—it will probably get better soon.
4. Support your teens' roles, fantasies, ideas, and interests, even if you feel they aren't worthy of your teens' time. Your kids need you to be their cheerleaders and advocates. If they decide to try something and it fails, they'll learn more from that failure than if you discourage them from trying at all. Remember that you provided your toddlers with opportunities to explore. You need to do the same for your teens. These opportunities may include the use of cars, telephones, and computers, and attendance at concerts and lessons, and so on. This is not to say you should pay for everything, but you could help your kids figure out how to get the things they really want.
5. Say things to your kids with a smile. This isn't always easy, but your kids hear you better when you keep your sense of humor instead of getting uptight with them. Saying, "I notice" can be a lot gentler than "You never." Have faith in your kids to figure things out, to learn, and to grow.

This faith will help you maintain your sense of humor.

6. Let kids know you love them. This is easy. Simply tell them. Write them notes. Tell someone else when they can overhear you. Trust teenagers to be teenagers, and you'll find them easier to love. It's hard to feel loving when your expectations are crushed, but if you count on your teens to act like teens, you won't feel disappointed very often.
7. It's too late to force them to learn lessons, so give it up. It's not too late to teach, but only when your help is requested. You can ask your kids if they'd like to hear what you think or if they want or need your help. If they say no, then back off. Since kids this age think they know everything, don't argue. Let them have the last word. No one will remember the point in a week anyway, but a bruised relationship is remembered into adulthood. If you give information, give it without strings or demands that it be followed.
8. Count on teenagers to be obnoxious—step back and try to see it as cute. When they push you too far, set your own limits and follow through on them or ask them what they would like as an alternative. It's easier to do these things than to try to change a teen. Don't ever embarrass or correct your teens in front of their friends and *never* compare them to their friends or siblings.
9. Learn to listen without giving advice or trying to fix things. Just listen. Kids feel better when they feel heard. If you have something to say to teens, speak from your feelings and your ideas rather than lecturing them or trying to tell them

how to think. Watch out for judgment and blame. Use the word *we* when working things out. Finger-pointing with a teen leads either to a lack of faith in themselves or to revenge against you.

10. Validate your teens' biological clock. Eliminate the shame and guilt kids may have for doing what is normal at their stage of development. It's a great relief to your kids when you let them know it's okay to feel and think exactly the way they do.

Many teens feel they have no control over their lives and that their parents ultimately have all the power. Doing any of the above steps can help change that picture. We want our kids to feel power over their lives so they can also feel the responsibility that goes with it.

Three Families Switch to Long-Range Parenting

When we learn how to empower our kids, we can reverse some very discouraging situations with them. In the stories that follow, three different families implemented long-range parenting to help their children think for themselves, make their own decisions, and have good memories of unconditional love.

Patsy's Mom Exchanges Lecturing for Listening

Negative rumors about Patsy were being spread around school. She was so unhappy about this that she wrote poems about suicide. Around her friends, she pretended she didn't care—she acted flip and made a lot of jokes, but inside she was torn up.

When Patsy told her mother she wanted to change schools, Mom lectured her about how you can't run away from trouble (Mom was afraid that Patsy was trying to take the easy way out). These lectures made Patsy even more upset; she wondered why her mother couldn't simply support her.

When asked what it was about her mother's lectures that bothered her, she said, "What if she's right? If she *is*, then I'm wrong. If I'm wrong, what have I got left? I don't know if I can trust myself."

Patsy's mother decided to use some of the building blocks for long-range parenting. She said to her daughter, "Honey, I have faith in you to do the things that are right for you. If you need my help, let me know and I'll be there. If you still feel this way in a couple of weeks and want me to call the school, let me know."

By suggesting that Patsy see how she felt in a few weeks, Mom trusted Patsy to be a teenager, who can feel one way so strongly one minute and the next feel totally different.

Mom was also saying, "I have faith in you even when you're doing things I don't necessarily approve of or would do in the same way." This gives Patsy a chance to find out what she wants, who she is, and how she wants to live her life. Now she can learn from her mistakes instead of trying to please her mother or rebelling against her. In making her own decisions and her own mistakes, she can learn and perhaps even change her mind.

When Patsy's mother decided to really listen to Patsy instead of assuming how Patsy should think, she found that Patsy lives in a totally different world than her own. Patsy is not worried about her grades and how she does in school (but her mother is); instead, Patsy worries about whether she can handle going to school at all because of the name-calling and the way her friends treat her. She's concerned about one of her friends, who is afraid she might be pregnant. In addition, guys are trying to get Patsy to go to bed with them; she's trying to figure out how to be popular; and she's worried about what others think. On top of all this, she is trying to please her parents. Patsy is simply thinking and feeling like the sixteen-year-old that she is—and not like the grown-up that her mother expects.

Brandon's Dad Stops Interfering

Sixteen-year-old Brandon came in to see his counselor. He was feeling angry and depressed. His relationship with his father was at an all-time low. Brandon told his story, which is very typical for kids his age:

"I started off the first six weeks of school this year with fairly good grades for me. I got mostly Bs and Cs and a D in Spanish. My father had been staying off my back about school for the first time ever, because my grades were better. But then my grades started going down. When my dad checked up on me and found I was getting a 1.9, he said I wasn't keeping our 'agreement.' This agreement was that I couldn't drive unless I had a 2.0 or better. When I make an agreement with Dad he tells me what I have to agree to and I say yes. It doesn't feel like I have any choice.

"My dad decided I had to go to summer school to raise my grades. He didn't talk to me about this—he just signed me up and told me I was going. I don't ask him to do any of this stuff for me, he just does it. I don't like it at all, but I figure I have to do as he says. So, when I raised my average to 2.0 in summer school, I told Dad I was ready to start driving again. But then he said summer school didn't count and that what I needed was consistency. At that point he went too far. I decided he was unreasonable and unfair and I wouldn't do anything he wanted."

Brandon has decided that whatever his father says is the way it has to be and that he himself has no choice. Brandon says his father overreacts about everything, making simple things much harder than they need to be. This is stressful to Brandon, who feels angry and without control over his life. He's learned to go along with his father on the surface but gets revenge later by doing poorly in school.

In these circumstances, Brandon is unable to think about what is important to him or how he wants to do in school. Instead, school has become a big bargaining chip in the game of driving a car. When he feels he can't win the game, he no longer has any reason to do well in school.

Brandon also feels he can't tell his parents the truth. One night he went to a party but told his folks he was staying at a friend's. His counselor asked, "Why didn't you tell your folks you were going to a party and staying out all night?" Brandon replied, "You just don't say that to your parents. They don't know that I go out and do that. I figure I'm having fun and they're not hurt by it—they don't have anything to do with it. It would be like me asking them where they're going on vacation and telling them they have to call in every night. This is the way I have fun, and it's none of their business."

Brandon's counselor then asked, "Why do you go out and party when you know your parents wouldn't approve? Why not do activities that your parents would approve?" Brandon said, "They're older than me and have different interests than me. I like to be out, be with my friends and meet people." The counselor asked, "Do you think you like to party and drink because you see your folks do it?" Brandon said that the last thing he would ever do is anything his folks did.

Brandon then shared how bad it got when his dad found out that he wasn't where he said he would be. When Brandon tried to explain to his dad what had happened, he didn't believe him. Brandon then decided that he really didn't care anymore about anything he said. He always tries to get him to do things the way he would, and he tells him his friends are a bad influence on him. Brandon decided he can't relate to his Dad and he'll just have to put up with him until he can leave home for good.

Brandon's counselor asked him, "If you could give advice to your folks about how you wish they would treat you and what would help you, what would you tell them?" Brandon said he wished they would leave him alone and let him make his own decisions. He said he can't control how his folks think, but he wishes they could understand that he makes different decisions than they do and that he thinks differently. He said, "I'm not them."

Brandon's counselor then asked, "What do you think would happen if your folks really did back out of your life and stopped checking up on you?" Brandon replied, "I'd be less stressed. I wouldn't have to worry about so many things. If I made a mistake, I'd have to live with it myself—I wouldn't have to listen to them tell me I did wrong or I was ruining my life. I could decide what things were mistakes to me. If Dad stayed out of my school, I wouldn't have to use school as a way to get back at him. I wouldn't have to worry about how I acted or what I said in class."

Brandon's dad realized that he wasn't using his parental authority wisely; that, in fact, his methods were backfiring. He told Brandon, "You know I'd like you to do well in school, but I realize I've been trying to control something that is your business. I worry more about what others will think about me than about how all this is affecting you. I'm sorry. I intend to turn school over to you. If I forget, I hope you'll help me remember by telling me I have my nose back in your business."

Brandon's dad shared that it would probably never be okay with him for Brandon to party where alcohol was involved, but he wanted his son to know that he always loved him. He shared his fears about the parties and said he would work on having faith in him.

Brandon was relieved but suspicious. He knows his parents love him, and he knows he loves them, but his feelings have been badly bruised. It will take consistency on the part of both parents to convince Brandon that they mean what they say.

Philip's Parents Let Him Grow Up

Philip's folks had trusted him with the family car to take his first long-distance trip. Even though Philip felt ready, this was a big jump for his parents. The only thing they asked was that Philip drive straight through and not take any side trips. This statement is about the same as telling a three-year-old not to eat the cookies on the coffee table!

Philip intended to obey his parents—but, of course, something came up, so he decided he just had to take a side trip to another city 150 miles out of the way. While he was there, he used his parents' credit cards. Figuring his folks always caught him if he did something they didn't like, Philip saw no point in hiding any of this from them. But when his folks found out, they were very angry and felt betrayed. They did and said all the predictable things a parent would in this situation. They expressed their disappointment, punished him with grounding, and told him he didn't know his own feelings when he explained why he had done what he did. Then, when Philip got depressed, his worried parents called a counselor.

Philip shared his story with the counselor, saying he was afraid there was something wrong with him. He figured he was a bad person and questioned his own thoughts, feelings, and motives. It didn't occur to him that his parents might be having a hard time letting him grow up. He didn't think that he might be "misbehaving" as the only way to do what he thought was right.

When Philip's parents came in so that Philip could share his feelings and thoughts with them in a safe place, they weren't prepared for what they heard. Philip explained that he wanted to grow up, and he wished they would let him. He asked them to stop threatening him, because he didn't want to have that kind of relationship with them. He explained that he feels guilty and bad when he lies to them. Instead, he wants to share his thoughts and feelings without being told they are stupid or wrong.

Philip asked his folks to support his ideas with enthusiasm. He told them he could learn more from trying things out and making mistakes than from being protected by them. He said, "I want to taste the world for myself, not through you." He recognized that his parents were scared, but he wanted them to have faith in him.

Although Philip's parents were shocked, they were also proud. Many of the things he said they were simply unaware of. They wanted to be on his side and didn't realize how far off base they had been.

Staying in Denial or Seeing It Like It Is

Denial is the ability to go through life with a paper bag

over our head and earplugs in our ears, watching a screen inside our brain show a movie of how we wish it would be, instead of how it is. For many reasons, it seems easier for parents to stay in denial about their teens than to see them as they are—as going through a stage in their development toward adulthood.

When we treat our teens like incompetents—monitoring them, supervising them, controlling them—we stop them from growing up. Often, we are more controlling of teenagers than we are of a three-year-old at a playground. We give the three-year-old more room to learn how to use the playground equipment than we give a sixteen-year-old to learn how to use a car.

Small children will not try playground equipment if they think they can't handle it. Usually, we encourage them to try and maybe even teach them a few skills or offer support. Teenagers are no different. There are many things they won't do if they don't think they can handle them. They have as many fears as anyone else. They need the same kind of help from us that we give a three-year-old at the playground. They need our encouragement, our support, and our help in building skills.

The Challenge

Each of us has a challenge. We can decide whether to influence or control our teens, whether to raise their self-esteem or run their lives. We can either focus on building skills or focus on doing things for our teens to protect them. Parents often use the excuse that teens can make mistakes that could kill them or ruin their lives forever, but this is true at any age. Focusing on this fear encourages us to try to control our teens' lives rather than letting go so they can live their own lives.

We must always ask ourselves, "Am I coming from fear or trust?" Trust gives our kids room to make mistakes and to learn from them. As Rudolph Dreikurs said, "Better a bruised knee than bruised courage. A broken knee can mend, but broken courage lasts forever."

Chapter

10

Following Through

Many parents struggle with agreements that are broken, promises that go unkept, and consequences that turn into punishment and revenge. Once parents learn the art of follow-through, they will be able to help their kids learn skills, accept responsibility, and achieve real cooperation.

Many parents will not like hearing that logical consequences are usually not effective with teenagers, especially those who have learned how effective logical consequences can be with younger children. Even under the best of circumstances, using consequences effectively is a fine art, because it's so easy to cross the line between consequences and punishment. Consequences are helpful to the positive growth and development of our children, but punishment is not. Since the use of logical consequences has become one of the more popular parenting methods used today, it may be difficult to accept what we have to say about using logical consequences with teenagers.

In workshops and books on positive discipline, we've taught the Three Rs of Logical Consequences (related, respectful, reasonable). The Three Rs help parents understand the difference between punishment and consequences and are useful to parents of children before the teen years; however, they're little help afterward because teens usually see logical consequences as punishment.

Since the main life tasks for teens evolve around power, they see the use of logical consequences as a method to control them. Given that, the concept of follow-through is more applicable.

What Is Follow-through?

Follow-through is a respectful, four-step approach to parenting teens that teaches cooperation, life skills, and responsibility in spite of resistance from teens.

The Four Steps of Follow-through

1. Hold a friendly discussion to share information about what is going on for each regarding the problem. (Listen.)
2. Brainstorm solutions and choose one that both parent and teen can agree they are willing to do.
3. Agree on a date and time deadline.
4. At the deadline the parent simply follows through on the agreement by holding the teen accountable with dignity and respect.

The concept of follow-through is simple unless parents make it difficult by getting sidetracked into one or all of the following four traps:

Four Traps When Using Follow-through

1. Wanting teens to have the same priorities parents have and to be excited about keeping their

agreements to do the things that are important to parents. (Face it, they don't care what the neighbors think about their messy rooms.)

2. Criticizing, judging, and name-calling, instead of focusing only on the task or issue. ("How can you live like such a pig? What kind of irresponsible person are you? No one will ever want to hire you," instead of, "Our agreement was that you would clean your room at 6:00.")
3. Not getting specific agreements in advance.
4. Not maintaining dignity and respect for parent and teen.

Effective Follow-through

Thirteen-year-old James was not washing his clothes or changing the sheets on his bed as he'd agreed to do. Mom said, "I'd like to talk with you about your laundry. Let's meet after dinner." When they sat down, Mom asked James what his issues were about doing his laundry. She found out that he wasn't really sure how to run the machine and was afraid he would break it. Mom shared *her* issues, which were that she didn't like to see him wearing dirty clothes to school and sleeping on dirty sheets.

James said he was willing to do his laundry but he needed help with the machine. Mom agreed: "I'd like you to choose a day this week to meet me in the laundry room at 6:00 P.M. for a lesson. I'd also like you to choose which day of the week you'd like to set aside for doing your laundry and changing your sheets. With a family as large as ours, it would be best if we each have our own laundry day. I'll check back with you in an hour to see which days you've chosen."

An hour later, James said he guessed Tuesday

would be all right for the laundry lesson and also okay for his laundry day. Mom said, "Fine. I'll see you at 6:00 on Tuesday in the laundry room."

But on Tuesday when Mom went to the laundry room at the agreed time, James wasn't there. Mom found him parked in front of the TV and said, "Do you remember your decision about the best time for a laundry lesson?"

James said, "Aw, Mom, I don't want to do it now. I'm watching this."

Mom was very friendly but very persistent, "You agreed to do it at 6:00 tonight."

James responded, "I'll do it later, Mom."

Mom simply stood in front of him with a friendly but expectant look in her eye. James finally said, "Oh, all right! This is so stupid!"

Mom didn't respond to the dig but simply said, "Thank you for keeping your agreement."

Every Tuesday, they went through a similar routine. Mom would say, "Remember the day you chose to do your laundry and change your sheets?" No matter what kind of arguments or put-downs James came up with, Mom would simply follow-through in a friendly manner and avoided lectures and insults. She knew it would be absolutely abnormal for James to be excited about washing his clothes and changing his sheets. But it was important to her that he help around the house and also that he be equipped with these skills. She saved them both a lot of hassles by simply getting an agreement and then following through.

Mom gave up the notion that James would remember to do this job without being reminded. At thirteen, she realized James was thinking more about how to buy a new skateboard or how to tell his Dad that he got a poor grade on his report card rather than thinking about his laundry. Mom decided that follow-through once a week, as long as it didn't turn into a power struggle, was worth it to her. (She was pleasantly surprised when James started remembering to take care of his laundry without being reminded.)

This example illustrates how Mom decided to act as if James intended to keep his agreement by meeting him every Tuesday to do his laundry. Typical of a kid his age, his actions didn't match his good intentions. However, that didn't matter because Mom was in charge of her own behavior, not James's.

Mom took care of herself. She decided what her limits were and what she would do about them—not what she would make James do. She showed respect for her son and kept the lines of communication open by being curious about his views and by sharing her feelings. She and James worked out an agreement that was *related, respectful,* and *reasonable.* Mom then kept it simple by following through in a firm, kind, matter-of-fact way.

There Are Many Ways to Follow-through

Learning to follow-through is an important life skill for parents. An attitude of respect is the primary ingredient. It is also important to use as few words as possible to help stay focused on the task at hand rather than focusing on personalities. Try practicing the skill of follow-through by limiting yourself to one word.

One Word

Andrew had agreed to mow the lawn by 4:00 P.M. on Fridays. The first Friday after this agreement was reached, Andrew followed through and mowed the lawn. The second Friday, he forgot. Dad found him washing his car at five minutes after 4:00 and respectfully said, "Lawn."

Andrew said, "I'm in the middle of washing my car now, Dad. I'll do it later."

Dad maintained a respectful attitude and said, "Agreement."

Andrew said, "I know, but it won't hurt to do it a little later."

Dad repeated, "Agreement."

In total disgust, Andrew turned off the water and went to get the lawn mower, mumbling under his breath, "I can't believe you can't wait a few minutes!"

Most parents have experienced the results of waiting a few minutes. Next time, it's a few more minutes and then a few more; and then other manipulative postponement techniques are used. By following through with dignity and respect, Dad taught Andrew to keep his agreement even if he didn't like it.

Some parents say, "My son or daughter wouldn't give in that easily." This is usually not the case when they follow the Four Steps, and avoid the Four Traps. When kids know thay have made a specific agreement (to the minute) they are left with a feeling of fairness and responsibility when they are held accountable.

Other parents object to follow-through because they don't think they should have to remind kids to keep their agreements. They want their kids to be "responsible" without reminders. We have three questions for these parents. 1) When you don't take time to remind them with dignity and respect, do you spend time scolding, lecturing and punishing? 2) Have you noticed how responsible your kids are about keeping agreements that are important to them? 3) Do you really think mowing the lawn and other chores are important to them? (Even though chores aren't a high priority for teens, it is important that they do them.) Follow-through takes less energy and is much more fun and productive than scolding, lecturing and punishing.

▼ *Following up on follow-through helps.*

Later that night, Dad said to Andrew, "Thanks for keeping your agreement to mow the lawn even though it was inconvenient for you at the time."

Andrew said, "I don't see why you couldn't wait for me to finish washing my car."

Dad said, "I can see how that might seem unreasonable to you. But our agreements are very important to me. I really appreciate you keeping the agreement even when you were angry."

Dad did an excellent job of focusing on and reinforcing the positive aspects of the encounter.

The one-word method gets results while maintaining dignity and respect—an excellent model for our kids to fall back on when they get through individuating.

No Words

Sometimes a look, a smile, a raised eyebrow, a pointed finger, or hands on the hips can be more effective that any words at all. This kind of nonverbal communication is extremely effective when done with a friendly attitude and a twinkle in the eye to convey a sense of humor.

Mary left the vacuum in the middle of the family room floor. Her mother found Mary in her room, took her by the hand, led her to the family room, and pointed at the vacuum.

Mary said with exasperation, "Oh, Mom!" She then put the vacuum away and flounced back to her room.

Have confidence in yourself that helping your kids

keep their commitments, even when it's not a priority for them, is the kind of long-range parenting that teaches them skills that will serve throughout their lives.

The examples illustrate the following Four Hints For Effective Follow-through:

Four Hints for Effective Follow-through

1. Keep comments simple, concise and friendly. ("I notice you didn't mow the lawn. Would you please do that now?")
2. In response to objections, ask, "What was our agreement?"
3. In response to further objections, shut your mouth and use nonverbal communication. (Point to your watch after every argument. Smile knowingly. Give a hug and point to watch again.)
4. When your teen concedes (sometimes with great annoyance) say, "Thank you for keeping our agreement."

Appropriateness, Dignity, and Respect

There are three key concepts essential to the effectiveness of follow-through: appropriateness, dignity, and respect.

It will be easier to follow-through on what we say, if what we say is appropriate—appropriate to the developmental stage of our children and appropriate to the needs of the situation. Trying to maintain control over teenagers is not appropriate. Arriving at agreements through a problem-solving process involving our teenagers is appropriate. Once a consequence, solution, or plan has been mutually agreed upon, we do our teenagers a disservice by not following through with dignity and respect.

Meaningless threats of humiliation and punishment are not appropriate. There is no need for humiliation and punishment when we follow-through with dignity and respect.

There are two sides of the dignity-and-respect coin. We need to retain dignity and respect for ourselves as parents, which means carrying out our responsibilities to teach our teenagers certain life skills whether they want to learn them or not. This means respecting their right not to be excited about the things we are trying to teach them and understanding that, because of the individuation process, it is appropriate for them to resist. It also means focusing on what needs to be done rather than focusing on personalities. It means saying, "I understand that you don't want to do it now, but our agreement was that you would do it now," rather than, "What do you mean you don't want to do it now? You're being inconsiderate and irresponsible by not keeping our agreement. What kind of a person are you?"

Maintaining dignity and respect means understanding that normal teenagers resist our priorities. It also means avoiding manipulation.

Not Following Through

It is disrespectful to our kids and ourselves when we say we are going to do something and then we don't follow-through. By failing to follow-through, we teach our children negative life skills, such as:

1. They learn they don't have to keep agreements. If we don't, why should they?
2. They learn our word doesn't mean anything—that we're just "blowing in the wind." They may follow our example.

3. They learn to manipulate.
4. They learn that they can get away with all kinds of behavior because we don't allow them to be accountable by following through.
5. They may learn that love means getting people to "give in."

Avoiding Manipulation

Mrs. Haymore had fallen into a pattern of manipulation with her daughter Dani. Neither mother nor daughter knew how to deal with each other without trying to control the other's behavior.

Typically, Mrs. Haymore would make threats and pronouncements but would not follow-through. Dani understood this pattern well and knew she could talk her mother into or out of almost anything.

When Dani turned eighteen and wanted a car, Mom decided to follow the procedure for follow-through. She set up a time to discuss car shopping and purchasing with her daughter. Since Mom was concerned about succumbing to her daughter's manipulation, she did some advance preparation.

▾ *Prepare in advance.*

Since it was hard for Mrs. Haymore to be clear on her own limits once her daughter got involved, she decided to make a list before she sat down to talk with Dani.

1. I don't want us to take advantage of each other.
2. I want to give when it feels good to do so and to feel good about not giving when it doesn't feel good.
3. I want to give from desire, not from demands and manipulation.

4. When I give, it needs to be without strings.
5. I want each of us to feel free to pursue her own interests so long as it doesn't hurt anyone else.
6. I want to allow Dani to have whatever feelings she may have in response to my behavior without me trying to fix or change her feelings.
7. I want to feel free to give opinions and information without feeling that Dani must agree.
8. I want a plan that includes what Dani is willing to do as well as what I'm willing to do, so that we each pull our own weight.

With her limits clearly defined, Mom approached the conference with confidence. During the meeting, Dani told her mother she wanted her to cosign the loan for a new car and assured her Mom that she could make the payments. Before Mom agreed, she asked Dani to write up a budget. When the first budget didn't include insurance or car maintenance and repair, Mom asked for another one. Based on the new budget, Mom said she thought Dani could afford a car—but it would mean that Dani would have to work at least thirty hours a week, and most of her money would go toward the car. Dani agreed.

Mom and Dani found a car in Dani's price range, and Mom cosigned. For the first two months, Dani did fine. But then she began missing work regularly; and although she complained about her job she didn't look for another one. Eventually, she quit and then missed a car payment.

Before, Mom would have lectured and criticized—and made the payment, "Just this one time." Instead, Mom said, "Dani, please give me the keys to your car. As long as you're making the payments, the car is yours. But when I have to make the payments to maintain my good credit, the car is mine. When you catch up on the payments, you can try again."

Dani threw a fit. She begged for another chance, told Mom she hated her, tried shaming her with old stories about how unhappy she was when Mom divorced Dad, and, finally, refused to give up the keys.

Mrs. Haymore remained amazingly calm, saying, "I know how angry and upset you are. I'm not going to rip the keys out of your hands, but I'd appreciate your cooperation." Throwing the keys at her mother, Dani slammed out of the house.

▼ *Following through can be painful at first.*

When you're not used to following through with your teenager, it can be very painful. One way to be sure you're using follow-through is when you feel as bad or worse than your teenager does. In this case, Mom felt like a wicked witch. But even though she wanted to cave in to make Dani happy, in her heart, she knew that was how she had helped create the "monster" she was now parenting. Mom held firm.

When Dani could see that manipulation wasn't going to work, she quickly found another job and caught up on the car payments. Mom and Dani then made a new deal: Dani could have the keys as long as she agreed to give them to her mother anytime she missed a payment. After this, Dani seemed to have more respect for her mother and for herself. Increased self-esteem is one of the major benefits of following through.

Making Agreements

In another family, the mother of a seventeen-year-old boy shared the following:

"I remember the time Carl said he would be home

at 1:00 A.M. I said okay and went to bed at 10:00. For some magical reason, I woke up at 1:00 to use the bathroom. When I walked by Carl's room, I noticed his bed was empty. He wasn't home.

"Carl is the kind of kid who does what he says he will do, and I've always trusted him. So I started to worry that he'd been in a car accident. I sat on the couch waiting for the police to call. When Carl walked in at 2:30 A.M., I was still sitting on the couch. He was shocked. 'What are you doing up?'

"I said, 'I was waiting for the police. I thought you'd been in an accident.'

"Carl said, 'You're crazy.'

"I retorted, 'Why would I be crazy? Why would I have any reason not to believe you when you tell me something?'

" 'What am I supposed to do, call you at 1:00 A.M. if my plans change?'

" 'Sure.'

" 'But that would wake you.'

"I said, 'I don't care. It would be better than imagining you laying on a stretcher in an ambulance.'

"Carl responded, 'You always worry too much. Why don't you just worry less?"

" 'Well, I wish I could, but I can't. If you told me you were coming in at 3:00, and I went to the bathroom at 1:00 and you weren't home yet, I wouldn't worry. But if you weren't there at 3:00, I *would* start worrying. That's the way I am.'

"It was important to me to show him how his behavior affects me. Then it was up to him to decide what to do about it. And he did. He said, 'Since you're not going to stop worrying, why don't we have a range for my curfew? When I'm going out, I'll say I'll be home between 11:00 and 3:00.' I agreed. I found it interesting that he started coming in at midnight after our discussion!"

Mom and Carl made an informal verbal agreement that left Carl free to make his own decisions. At this point, many parents feel they have to get the agreement in writing as a "contract" with their kid. But these parents wouldn't act that way if they were dealing with a friend. It wouldn't be respectful or necessary. Anytime we do more or less than needs to be done in a situation we set up a mischief shuffle.

▾ *An agreement in writing is a reminder, not a contract.*

If an agreement is put in writing, it could be done in the form of a record, not a contract. Some families make decisions at family meetings and keep a record of their agreements in a notebook. Others put a note on a calendar or on the refrigerator, until the new arrangement becomes part of the normal schedule. Some written agreements take the form of a job chart. The emphasis on putting the agreement in writing is to help people remember their commitment—it's not the commitment itself since that's already been made verbally. Follow-through is the most effective way to help kids keep their commitments.

In the curfew example above, if Carl still doesn't come in when he said he would, Mom's response could be to continue sharing her feelings. She could let Carl know how his behavior affects her. But if Carl persists, Mom may decide that he is going to say one thing and do another. At this point, Mom can decide what *she* will do next. She may conclude that Carl feels disrespected when his mother worries about him. If this turned out to be true—and if Carl didn't think his mother would change—he might decide to come in whenever he felt like it. At this point, Mom would have to deal with her problem some other way. She might decide to reevaluate her own behavior and learn to go to sleep whether Carl is in or not.

What Works, What Doesn't

Some of our more useless parenting tools include lecturing, catastrophizing, fixing, rescuing, guilt-mongering, shaming, cramming morals down our kids' throats, and trying to make control look like it's for their own good. We all know these tactics don't work when an agreement isn't kept, but we often persist, thinking that if we just do them long enough our kids will get the message. Insanity once was described as doing the same thing over and over while expecting a different result!

When we practice follow-through we move in a positive and productive direction by communicating our feelings, sharing our values, listening to what our kids think and what is important to them, finding out what they want to do, and respecting their points of view. This means doing what needs to be done to achieve a goal, without expecting our kids to be as interested as we are.

Follow-through encourages us to have faith in our kids. We can step back to give them room to decide what they will do for themselves. Follow-through allows us to teach skills, to do with and not for, to focus on solutions, and to be curious and listen.

▼ *Think first.*

Kids complain about parents arbitrarily saying no all the time. But kids can be very demanding and persuasive when they insist they must have an answer immediately. They push their parents into a corner with all the intensity teenagers can muster. It's easy to react with an immediate no and then feel the need to back down later.

To avoid this problem, parents can buy some time. In a firm but kind manner, parents can tell their teen that they need to think for a few minutes before they answer.

Many kids resent this approach because their parents have used it in the past to avoid dealing with issues at all. So, to be respectful, parents need to give a deadline for their decision. Then they need to follow-through, giving their decision by the promised deadline. We need to practice follow-through with ourselves as well as with our teens.

Some Final Tips

It's easier to follow-through if we train ourselves and our kids in advance. By spending time working *with* our kids on the necessary steps to achieve the agreed goals, we can make follow-through much easier. But if we find ourselves negotiating a new agreement instead of following through on the original one, we *aren't* following through. We need to start and finish with the same plan.

Many times our kids don't follow-through because we don't give them a chance. Kids hate it when we don't show faith in them. It's much better to ask them if they *have* done something they agreed to rather than to assume they forgot.

Adults are not using their common sense when they expect kids to follow adult priorities. Follow-through is a respectful way to help teens live up to appropriate adult expectations and priorities.

Follow-through helps parents be proactive and thoughtful instead of reactive and inconsiderate. Once we understand that kids have their own priorities, and still need to follow some of our priorities, we can see their resistance as cute, adorable, and normal instead of lazy, inconsiderate, and irresponsible. Follow-through can make parenting pleasurable, magical, and fun.

Follow-through never involves threats. It allows us to keep our own power while letting our kids keep theirs. It feels good for everyone. Once we get in the habit of using follow-through, we can maintain a sense of humor when things don't go perfectly. It can be a wonderful way to enrich our relationships with teens.

Follow-through is an excellent alternative to authoritarian methods or permissiveness. With follow-through we can "meet the needs of the situation" while maintaining dignity and respect for all concerned. Follow-through is one way to help children learn the life skills they need to feel good about themselves while learning to be contributing members of society.

▼

Chapter

11

Teaching Life Skills

We have many opportunities to encourage our children to develop the life skills they need to enjoy success and satisfaction when they go out into the world on their own.

Usually, teenagers do not think ahead. And most parents say, "Since they don't think ahead, I have to take charge until they do think ahead." But that doesn't make sense. How will teens ever learn to think ahead if they aren't taught that skill and given opportunities to use it?

Long-range Consequences

Douglas stumbled onto the concept of long-range consequences by himself. He refused to get good grades because he thought his parents were pressuring him to; he felt they did this only because they didn't want to be embarrassed in front of his teachers, and not because they cared about him at all. So he messed around and got bad grades.

Then he joined the golf team, but his grades were so poor that his participation was jeopardized. The coach took him aside and said, "If you don't get your grades up, you'll get kicked off the team. I'm willing to talk to your teachers and help you find out what you need to do to catch up. But if golf is important to you you'll have to do the work."

Because golf was so important to him, Douglas went to all his teachers and found out exactly what he needed to do. He then brought all his grades up to stay on the team. It was the first time he could see any reason to do it for himself.

Essentials for Teaching Life Skills

Parents can help their children learn life skills (without taking over, rescuing, or criticizing) that will help them solve life problems. To do this, you must:

1. Maintain a friendly attitude
2. Know your teen's interests
3. Give information, not lectures (after getting permission from your teen)
4. Take time to train (work *with* your teen at first, rather that giving instructions)
5. Have faith in your teen
6. Allow for mistakes and appreciate their value

A Friendly Attitude

A friendly attitude invites closeness, trust, and cooperation. An unfriendly attitude creates distance, defensiveness, and resistance. We need to look at how often we create distance between ourselves and our teenagers with our disapproval, criticism, and lectures (and then wonder why they don't want to work with us on improvement).

A friendly attitude is essential if we want to have a positive influence with our teens. When we have created closeness they are more likely to listen and work on solutions. If you are wondering how to create a friendly attitude, ask yourself how you would treat a friend.

Know Your Teen's Interests

By being aware of what is going on in your teens' lives, you can determine what they need to learn. You can then become a resource for them. With patience, you can help your kids begin a growing process that may not come to fruition until they are young adults. But if you don't help them while they're still adolescents, it will be harder later, when low self-esteem and poor habits and perceptions are more firmly in place.

Long-range parents empower their kids with skills that will make their growing up a lot easier.

Give Information

Every teenager in the world knows that when an adult says, "I want your cooperation," they mean, "Do as I say"; an adult's "let's make an agreement" means the grown-up will issue a new mandate without any input from the teen. How can we give information so that our kids will hear us, instead of tuning us out and rebelling?

Many kids say they'd like to go to their parents for help but they don't because they're afraid to face their parents' disappointment, disapproval, lectures, or punishment. Even if that's not the case, some teens will discard any information from their parents, regardless of how good it is, just because it *is* from their parents (how can they individuate if they do what their parents want?). Other times, teens *will* hear the information but file it away until they're ready to use it—which is hardly ever as soon as their parents would like them to use it. Fortunately, there are several skills parents can learn in order to teach skills to their teenagers in a way that will diminish resistance and rebellion.

Take Time to Train

Often, teenagers are more willing to listen to someone else than they are to their parents. If this is the case with your teen, it's sometimes best to enlist the aid of a friend or relative to give the desired information. If you can keep your ego out of the way, you can be creative in helping your kids find other sources of learning.

▾ *Look for teaching moments.*

At this age, there are many opportunities for teaching life skills, such as those involving cars, money, clothing, shopping, family work, use of time, and attitudes toward learning and school. When teaching teens, look for these teaching moments rather than more formal teaching situations. The best moments can be found when you know what interests your teen. For instance, most teens are interested in cars, which offer many opportunities (besides the chance to teach them how to drive) to teach them about budgeting for insurance payments, repairs, car payments, and gas; about money-making opportunities; and about planning ahead.

Some parents believe kids should earn all the money for a car. Others want to help their kids by giving them a car. Either way, there are still many opportunities for teaching life skills.

One mother sat down with her son, Jack, and said,

"Now that you have a car, let's talk about what you need to do to be able to drive it."

Jack said, "All we have to do is put gas in and take off."

Realizing what a great opportunity she had for giving information, Mom figured out a way to do it without lecturing.

▼ *Avoid lecturing.*

Mom said, "That's part of it, but there's more. Let's make a list together. I'll start by putting gas at the top. Then, I'd like to add insurance and upkeep."

Jack said, "What about washing, waxing, and polishing?"

Mom added those to the list. When they were done, they had figured out how much money was needed each month for repairs, for insurance, for gas, and for minor upkeep. They had talked about where the car would be kept and how to minimize brake and clutch repairs. They had also worked out which parts Mom was willing to pay for and which parts Jack would pay for. He realized that most of the money he made at his part-time job would have to go for his car and that he was lucky not to have a car payment as well. This inspired a heartfelt thank-you to his mother.

Without going through this process, it would have been easy for Jack to take his new gift for granted and to be irresponsible because no one had helped him think through what it really means to own a car. Going through this process also saved Mom a lot of worry and frustration about how her son would afford driving a car, or the resentment she might feel if she "gave in" and paid for everything.

▼ *Use money to teach life skills.*

Money provides another opportunity to teach teens

life skills. Many people enter adulthood without ever being responsible for handling money or making decisions about it. They then turn over this responsibility to a partner who claims to be more capable, without ever becoming involved and aware themselves. If these adults ever have to assume responsibility for money, the transition will be much more painful than if they had been taught as teenagers.

▼ *Use allowances and chores to teach life skills.*

It's pretty hard to teach teens money skills if they don't have any money to use. We recommend that parents give their teens an allowance that is not connected to household chores. (Participation in household chores teaches responsibility, cooperation, and other life skills and allows teens to contribute as family members. For more specific information on chores, see Chapter Thirteen.) Allowances provide many opportunities for learning money management.

Payment could be offered to teens for jobs you would normally hire out, such as baby-sitting, car washing, painting, and so on. Not only is this respectful because these are jobs for hire, but it also provides more ways for kids to acquire money to manage. We recommend part-time work as yet another way to earn money and feel a sense of power.

Many parents want to limit the amount of money their kids have because they're afraid they'll use it to buy drugs. This is a very negative and disrespectful approach, and futile, too—if teens want to buy drugs, they'll find a way. Other parents use money to control their kids. Still others like to be the "benevolent dictator," and doling out money to show how generous they are. Some even use money to buy their kids' love.

None of these approaches empower kids. Instead, if you provide ways for your teens to acquire money, you'll be able to help them attain life skills while you still have some influence.

At sixteen, Dale had never really had an allowance. If he needed money, he either worked for it around the house or asked his parents for a handout. His parents decided to change this pattern and help him be more responsible about money. They asked him to make a list of his expenses, suggesting he be as thorough as he could about the things he normally spent money on. They would then use this list to help figure out a fair allowance so he wouldn't have to run to them every time he needed money.

Dale wasn't sure he liked this idea—he thought the old system worked just fine. Realizing that Dale needed to be reassured that this was a way to help him rather than to punish him or take things away from him, his parents asked if he would try the new system for one month. Dale reluctantly agreed.

After seeing Dale's list of expenses' his folks recommended that they give him $25 a month to cover general spending and another $40 a month for clothing. When Dale said he would need more money to get clothes for going back to school, his folks agreed to give him $150 to cover the basics; he could then use the $40 to supplement his wardrobe on a monthly basis.

Committed to treating Dale with respect and teaching him life skills, his parents said they'd be willing to share their cars with him if he found it too expensive to drive a car of his own. If he wanted to earn extra money for a car, they'd let him know about jobs for him around the house or would help him find a part-time job.

Dale found this new system gave him freedom and choices he never had before. He loved shopping for clothes and began watching the paper for sales. He opened his first bank account. He put his clothing money in a checking account and got his own instant-cash card. He felt very grown up. He used his parents as consultants to teach him how to go over his bank statement at the end of each month. It wasn't long before he decided to get a part-time job, because he was learning about and enjoying the power that comes from having and managing money.

▼ *Take the indirect route.*

Parents are so used to lecturing and criticizing, and teens to resisting and tuning out, that these patterns are difficult to break. One way to break them is to take the indirect route. The first road sign on this route reads, "Remember to maintain respect and a friendly attitude."

It seemed to Mom that Susan was too tense. She planned every minute and didn't seem to know how to relax. Mom could see that Susan would be less stressed if she could mellow out a bit, so Mom decided to look for opportunities to teach Susan the benefits of relaxing. When she tried talking about it directly, Susan became defensive. It was obvious that she felt attacked, unaccepted, and embarrassed. So Mom thought of ways to model relaxing rather than to discuss how to do it. She said, "Susan, you can do what you want, but I'm going to relax more. Since I really love to be with you, I'm going to ask you to join me. If you want to, terrific—if you don't, that's okay, too."

When Mom planned outings—sunning at the swimming pool, going to movies, shopping trips, picnics—she always invited Susan. When Susan chose to come, Mom said nothing—she simply focused on having a wonderful time with her daughter and letting her daughter experience for herself the joys of "mellowing out."

Have Faith in Your Teen

Shawn wanted to tell his dad something he had never shared before because he was afraid of getting in trouble or meeting with disapproval. Dad could see that Shawn wanted to tell him something but was having difficulty. Dad asked, "What's making you uncomfortable? What do you need from me?"

Shawn said, "I want your reassurance that you won't be disappointed in me if I tell you. And I have to work it out for myself before I'll tell you about it. Don't expect me to tell you first. I don't have the energy to deal with your stuff and mine. I'm not in touch with my own feelings. I can't be expected to be in touch with yours."

Dad listened without comment and then said, "I'm glad you shared this with me. I had no idea you felt this way. Whenever you're ready to tell me more, I'll be here. I can tell this was scary for you. I hope you'll feel more comfortable next time." Shawn's father demonstrated respect and trust. He had faith in Shawn even when Shawn didn't have faith in himself.

Allow for Mistakes

Many parents try to set everything up so their kids won't experience mistakes. As we've said many times before, parents must trust themselves and their children to be able to handle mistakes—that, in fact, mistakes are wonderful opportunities to learn. This kind of trust can change parenting.

Whenever you give directives to help prevent mistakes, you deprive yourself of an opportunity to teach and your kids of an opportunity to learn. This happens, for example, when you give something to your teens and then tell them how to use it.

In Paula's family, the kids received a clothing allowance twice a year. Paula decided to buy fewer but more expensive clothes. In her mind, she could always fill in her wardrobe by borrowing from friends and using her small monthly allowance.

Paula's mom insisted the new clothes were absolutely not to be loaned out or left on the floor. She was trying to prevent Paula from making mistakes, but then she remembered that she wanted to help Paula learn from her experience. Mom said, "Paula, I made a mistake. I wanted to protect you from losing these expensive clothes, but I'm sure you can figure out whether or not you want to loan your clothes. I know it's up to you to decide how you want to treat the clothes you have."

A few months later, Paula came to her mother in a rage. One of her friends had borrowed her designer jacket and lost it at a party. Mom bit her lip and skipped the "I told you so" lecture. She gave Paula a big hug and said, "I can see how upset you are. I'm so sorry." Paula looked at her mother and said, "I'll never let that friend borrow my clothes again."

Showing trust—having a little faith that when kids make mistakes they'll be able to learn from them—is one of the most effective ways to teach life skills. It's also comforting to have the same faith in ourselves.

Tips for Teaching Life Skills

Sometimes we box ourselves into a corner by giving our teens examples of what they shouldn't do without giving the alternatives. We constantly say, "Don't do this, don't do that, this is bad, I'll punish you if you do that." Threatening and ordering only invites problems, since teenagers are trying to have power over their own lives.

Instead, parents can teach skills by suggesting what *to* do rather than what not to do.

Suppose you are having a conflict with your teenager over study time. You've tried grounding ("You can't leave the house until you've done what I want you to do") and you've withdrawn privileges ("No more TV until you bring up your grades"). But you're still experiencing resistance, power struggles, and even revenge cycles. There *are* better ways of teaching your teens to take charge of their own lives.

Getting Permission

In the following example, notice how often Mom asks Kelly for her permission to teach her more. This is an important and respectful way to keep kids interested and motivated to learn. When you give information without asking permission, your teen tunes you out. But as soon as you ask their permission and they give it, you'll feel a difference.

Kelly's grades were suffering. Her mother asked Kelly if she'd like to learn some tricks about studying. Kelly, feeling suspicious because her mother usually tried to control her ideas and behavior about school, asked, "What kinds of tricks?"

Mom said, "I could teach you 'the handy-dandy four-step system' if you like." Kelly's interest was piqued, so Mom explained that when she had trouble getting things done she sometimes procrastinated or didn't even try. Then one of her friends suggested the four-step system, and it really helped. "Would you like to hear about it?"

Kelly said, "Okay:

"Step one is to decide what you want. Step two is to make time for it. Step three is to set up a deal or a trick to motivate yourself. Step four is to use lists."

When Kelly asked how the four steps could help her, Mom said she would go through the steps with her if she would like. Kelly agreed.

First, Mom asked Kelly to think of four things she really wanted to do each day. Kelly's list included time with friends, time to play her guitar, time to study, and time to watch TV.

Next, for step two, Mom suggested that Kelly think of when she could make time for each of her choices. Kelly wanted to be with her friends after school and then come home and play her guitar. She said she would have dinner with the family, then watch TV, and then study.

Mom didn't point out that saving studying for last was doomed to failure. Instead, she went on to explain step three, making "deals."

She pointed out that people often don't do their least favorite things unless they first make deals with themselves such as, "First I'll do what I don't like and get it over with," or, "First I'll do two things I like, one thing I don't like, and save the best for last." She said another trick is to make dates with someone to do the things you don't like. It can be more fun to study if you make a date to do it with someone else. In addition, you usually won't disappoint a friend, even if you might be willing to let yourself down.

Finally, Mom showed Kelly how to make a list of her four interests that included the amount of time for each and any deals she made with herself. They talked about how easy it is to go back to old habits and forget new plans when the plans weren't written down. Mom suggested that the list was a way to help Kelly remember the decisions she made for herself.

Kelly wanted to know if Mom planned to check up on her each day to see if she was following her list. Mom asked if that was what she wanted, and Kelly said, "No way!" Mom said "Good. My job is to help you learn. Your job is to decide if you want to use what you learn. I'll be happy to help if you ask me directly, but otherwise, it's up to you."

Friendly Bets Versus Bribery and Reward

A friendly challenge may help motivate teens to learn life skills. Deciding to try this method, Mrs. Wong said to her son, "I'll bet you can't get a *B* in that class."

Jon rose to the challenge, saying "How much?" Mrs. Wong said, "Ten dollars," and Jon said "You're on!"

We don't believe in bribes, rewards, negative expectations, or discouraging statements. You may wonder how a bet is different.

According to Dreikurs, a bet is like "spitting in the soup." Soup isn't very appetizing once someone has spit in it. A bet can be used when a teen has said, "I could do it if I wanted to." To be effective, the bet must be made with a friendly, respectful, playful attitude. "You're telling me you can, but I've got money that says you can't. Are you willing to put your money where your mouth is?"

You can make a bet with your teens without controlling them. But as soon as you hold out a bribe or reward, you *are* trying to control them. The trick is to learn how to be helpful while avoiding control.

Your Teens Can Teach You

One of the best ways to encourage and empower your kids is to let *them* teach *you*. They can teach you about their music, how to use digital watches, how to videotape a TV show, how to use a computer, and a million other things they're good at. If you're concerned about your teenagers' driving habits, ask them to help you improve *your* driving habits in as many ways as they can think of. They can share their hobbies with you, show you how to sand a car, or put on makeup so you can hardly see it's there. Your kids can be valuable resources if you give them the opportunity—and when you do, you not only demonstrate your respect for their abilities, you model the joys of learning as well.

Creative Teaching

Making a game out of things can be a great way to teach skills. By buying a dictionary calendar, you can challenge your kids to learn new words and use them in sentences. You can swap a joke a day with them, and you can play games like Scrabble and Pictionary. These are fun ways that also teach skills to your teens.

Other approaches include asking kids to survey other teens to find out how they and their families deal with money, curfews, allowances, and so on. You can help your kids plan a party or a picnic. Once you decide to be creative, you'll find there are many ways to teach skills.

Teens' Suggestions to Their Parents

Your teens can come up with approaches for teaching life skills to which they'd respond well. The following list provides a sample of solutions teenagers have come up with regarding areas of conflict:

> *Messy rooms:* It's my room, it's my part of the house. Close the door. When I get fed up with it, I'll clean it—but if I get nagged, I won't clean it for sure. Don't go in my room to put things away. Leave them by the door.

Forgotten or unfinished chores: Say it once. If I forget, tell me in a nice way that the chore isn't done. Give a time limit, like today or before tonight, rather than right now.

Telephones: Get a separate line and pay for it. I'll pay for my own long-distance calls. Having a phone of my own is like buying me a bicycle or a swing set when I was little.

Dating: There should be no age limit, because everyone matures at their own pace. And it depends upon what you mean by *dating*. Younger kids usually go in groups. Let me date when *I* feel ready.

Curfew: Let me use my own judgment. I *do* have enough sense to come in early if I have commitments the next day. If I blow it, I'll learn from my mistake.

Clothing: I want to wear what I want. It's up to me to decide about whether I want to loan my clothes or not. You don't know what the styles are or what I'll feel comfortable in at school.

Makeup: I should be allowed to wear makeup when most of the other kids do.

Pierced ears: I should be able to get my ears pierced whenever I'm ready. If you don't like certain kinds of earrings, like long dangly ones, let me know. I'll consider your feelings.

Parties: There should be no parents at parties. When parents try to monitor parties, kids lie about what they're doing. They'll party with or without your permission.

Friends: It's up to me to pick my own friends. I don't tell you who to be friends with and I don't appreciate it when you tell me. When you do, I sometimes end up being friends with people I don't like, just to rebel. You don't really understand what my relationships with my friends are like. You don't see or know my friends the way I do.

Cars: It's not okay to use grades against me, for instance, not letting me drive if my grades aren't good.

Many adults discount advice from teenagers, claiming they don't know what's best for them. That may be true. But—do *we* always know what's best for *us*? The real question is, "What's the best way for us and our teenagers to learn?" Do we learn when others control us, criticize us, and hammer away at our self-confidence? Or do we learn when our thoughts and ideas are listened to, respected, and taken seriously—and when we are encouraged to learn from our mistakes?

Empowering Teens

To increase your positive influence on teens, it's helpful to minimize any of your discouraging behavior, such as criticism, overambition, overindulgence, overprotection, lecturing, living in the future, punishment, and all forms of physical or emotional abuse.

The parenting skills we have taught in this chapter empower teenagers. Whether you use direct or indirect methods for teaching life skills, the six essentials for success are maintaining a friendly attitude, being aware of your teen's interests, giving information (not lectures) with your teen's permission, taking time for training, having faith in your side and your teen's, and appreciating the value of mistakes. If you want to help your kids grow up to be successful, you need to look at what you can do today rather than jumping into the future. Success builds success. If you think too much about how to get your kids into college or what they'll be like twenty years from now, you might miss out on how you can create a feeling of success in this moment and how you can teach the value of life skills to be used today.

When you're excited about learning new skills, you can help your kids see that learning benefits the learner —it isn't just about getting grades or praise. One teenager commented to her mother, "I just realized that the more I learn, the easier my life is." That's what raising teens is all about!

Chapter 12

Letting Go

Letting go is the essential step we must take in order to nurture our teens' individuation. Letting go is the foundation for having faith in our teenagers and an integral part of teaching the life skills so necessary for our teenagers to find success on their own. It's also often frightening for many parents, especially those who have been intent on controlling their children. For this reason, we present a step-by-step process that can make letting go more comfortable for both parents and teenagers.

The Letting-go Process

1. Describe the area where you are having difficulty letting go
2. Learn about your teens' issues (get into their world and respect their separate realities)
3. Look at your issues (usually unresolved fears)
4. Be committed to giving up control and letting go as an essential step toward growth for you and your teens

5. Decide on the smallest step you are willing to take and make a plan to implement this step

The Letting-go Process in Action

Describe the Difficult Area

On the morning of Tim's sixteenth birthday, he was first in line to get his driver's license. He passed both his written test (with a score of 97) and his driving test, which, in his mind, qualified him as an expert driver. He was ready to drive anything anywhere because the State of California said he could, and the state was bigger than his parents!

When he came home, he said, "Can I drive your car, Mom? I want to go to San Francisco."

Mom told her parent study group, "We live in a small, quiet town. If any of you have been to San Francisco, you know they have scary hills and heavy traffic. It's a very big city. I told Tim, 'No. You just got your license an hour ago.' "

Your Teen's Issues

He said, "But I've been waiting and dreaming of this moment. How can you ruin my life? The State of California says I'm ready to drive anywhere. They gave me a license. I got a 97 on the test. What's wrong with you? Do you hate me?"

Your Issues

Mom had to look at her fears. She continued, "I have to say this honestly. My car was my first fear. I have a really nice car, and I didn't want to see it all banged up. I was also concerned for Tim. I wanted to protect him. I was worried about him having trouble just getting on the ramp to the freeway! I pictured all kinds of disasters for him—on the freeway and on the San Francisco hills.

"But I really could see what his issues were. He felt like a grown-up now. He had a license, he had freedom, he had power, he had wheels. Also, he loves San Francisco, we've taken many trips there as a family. Now he could go on his own and take his friends. This was going to be great for him."

Your Commitment

"I want to be there to help my kids grow up. My goal is always to empower my kids. That's the bottom line. If I can't give them anything else, I can give them that. I can help them be strong and capable. But the only way that is going to happen is by me letting go."

▾ *Take small steps to begin the process of letting go.*

"Since I really wanted to let go for both of us, I had to decide what steps I could take. The smallest step for me was to dedicate the next two weekends to Tim, so he could take the whole family to San Francisco. We had him go places he would never go on his own, just to give him our own personal San Francisco driver's test, with many opportunities to park. He drove us everywhere—up and down hills, to North Beach, Fisherman's Wharf, Chinatown. After spending four days driving around San Francisco, I knew he could do it. I then gave him the keys to my car and he drove off. And, of course, I died—I was horribly scared. And he did fine. He did great! If he had any problems, I never heard about them. The car looks fine. And . . . somehow through that experience, he gained a tremendous amount of confidence in himself as a driver. The funny part is that since he's been going to college at San Francisco State, he's decided not to drive there because it's too much trouble. He would rather take public transportation!"

Letting Go Can Be Scary

The Petersons purchased a cabin just as their two children were becoming teens. The parents had fantasies of spending many hours of happy family time sitting around the fire, playing games, and telling stories. But over the next few years, reality set in when they found their teens didn't want to go to the cabin most of the time—they'd rather be with their friends. If they did go, they wanted to take several friends, be chauffeured around, or be left alone to enjoy their friends.

Seventeen-year-old Justin was especially resistant to family time. He wanted to use the cabin for parties with his friends when his parents weren't there. When they absolutely refused to let him do this, Justin did it anyway. He had a copy of the cabin's key made, lied about staying at a friend's house for the night, and then he and his friends would sneak off to the cabin.

Feeling angry and betrayed, his parents focused on the negative aspects of this situation rather than the positive ones—otherwise, they might have seen in what ways Justin had been responsible. He always left the cabin quite presentable. His parents really had to search for traces—maybe hairs left in the bathtub drain, a broken lid on a jar, ashes in the fireplace, or a few beer cans left in the woods. One time, when the hot water heater broke, Justin called a plumber, had it fixed, and paid for it. His parents found out when they noticed that a different tap had been used. When they confronted Justin, instead of acknowledging his responsible actions, they lectured him about his "criminal" behavior.

After attending a workshop on empowering teenagers, the Petersons decided to try something different. They used the Four Rs of Recovery to let Justin know they had made a mistake. They acknowledged that they had treated him badly, that they hadn't had faith in him to make mistakes and learn from them. In addition to fearing that he would use drugs and maybe do himself serious damage, his parents took his not wanting to be with the family personally, instead of remembering that teens prefer time with their friends. Their controlling behavior practically forced Justin to lie, rebel, and sneak so that he could try out the things that most teenagers try.

The Petersons decided that their relationship with Justin and allowing him to learn life skills were more important than trying to control him—especially since what they were doing wasn't working. After *recognizing* their mistakes and taking *responsibility* for their part in creating the situation, they tried a combination of *reconciliation* and faith. At this point, Justin was harboring such hurt and hostility that *resolution* was not yet appropriate (sometimes a resolution cannot be achieved until rapport has been built). The Petersons could see that they needed to establish rapport before Justin would feel enough closeness and trust to work on a resolution. In order to do this they simply gave Justin a key to the cabin and said, "We've been real jerks about how we've handled the cabin. We hope you can forgive us someday."

This threw Justin totally off guard. Incredulously, he said, "What do you mean?" Mrs. Peterson answered, "We mean we've made a mistake about your use of the cabin. We focused on everything you did wrong and didn't appreciate how responsible you were in leaving the cabin clean and fixing things that were broken. We hope you can forgive us."

Justin came to the rescue, "Oh, don't be so hard on yourself."

Mr. Peterson said, "We aren't being hard on ourselves. We're just admitting we made a mistake, and we hope you will forgive us someday. We don't expect that right now, because it'll probably take a while for you to believe we've changed. We're a little leery ourselves. This is a big step for us." The Petersons then found an excuse to leave the scene so Justin could have time to absorb this new approach.

Two weekends later, Justin went to the cabin and had a party. When the Petersons arrived, they found beer cans, cigarette butts, dirty sinks, ashes in the fireplace, and a few other minor messes. Justin had been less responsible when he could be open than when he had to sneak to avoid detection.

The Petersons decided it was time for *resolution* in the form of *follow-through*. The following dialogue occurred when Justin came home that evening.

Mrs. Peterson: I noticed you left some messes at the cabin. They'll need to be cleaned up before next Thursday when our company is coming. Would you like to go up by yourself and clean the things on this list, or would you like me to go with you?

Justin: Oh, can't you do it or hire someone to do it?

Mrs. Peterson: I'm not willing to do it by myself. I'm willing to help you. I'm also willing to hire someone if you want to pay for it.

Justin: How much would it cost?

Mrs. Peterson: The cleaning service charges ten dollars per hour. How long do you think it would take them to do it?

Justin: They'd probably take a lot longer than I would just so they could collect more money.

Mrs. Peterson: That's a possibility.

Justin: Well, can't I do it next weekend?

Mrs. Peterson: No, it has to be done before Thursday.

Justin: Well, I'm busy. I have other plans.

Mrs. Peterson: Me too, but it has to be done before Thursday. Do you want to do it by yourself, do you want to do it with my help, or do you want to hire it done? *(Notice her use of follow through.)*

Justin: You mean you would really go up with me to help?

Mrs. Peterson: Yes. I have a lot to do, but I'd actually enjoy spending time with you. I could cancel some of my other plans.

Justin: Okay.

Mrs. Peterson: Do you want it to be just you and me, or would you like to invite some of your friends to help?

Justin: I thought you didn't like my friends!

Mrs. Peterson: I know. I had too many fears and expectations. That was another mistake. Your friends are your friends, and I trust your judgment. Would you like to invite them, or would you like to go up with just me?

Justin: Well, I'll see if any of them want to come. They may be too busy.

Mrs. Peterson: You work it out. The best time for me would be tomorrow morning. How does that sound to you?

Justin: I have to be to work by noon.

Mrs. Peterson: How long do you think it will take us to get the things on that list done?

Justin: I'll bet we could get it done in an hour.

Mrs. Peterson: I wouldn't be surprised. It takes

three hours to drive up and back, so we'd better leave at 8:00 A.M.

The next morning, Justin was still sound asleep at 7:45. Mrs. Peterson continued with her follow-through skills and respectfully kept waking him up until he finally got up, complaining. Mrs. Peterson ignored this. She didn't expect him to like getting up, she just expected him to do it.

Since Mrs. Peterson suppressed her desire to lecture Justin for complaining about something he had agreed to do, Justin soon stopped. They had a nice experience driving up the mountain and cleaning the cabin together. Justin told his mother he was disgusted with his friends, who "wanted the privilege of using the cabin but weren't willing to go back and clean up their mess." He also talked more than he had in years. When he could see that his mother wasn't going to judge him, he told her about other times he had used the cabin. Once he'd forgotten his key and had to break a window to get in, but he paid for a new window to be installed. Mrs. Peterson acknowleged that he'd been even more responsible than she thought.

For Mrs. Peterson, the whole experience was like a new beginning in their relationship. She was amazed at how different her experience of Justin was when she stayed respectful and focused on what needed to be done rather than on fears of the future or what others might think.

Several people who heard Mrs. Peterson's story thought she was being permissive and condoning Justin's "drug parties" by giving him a key to the cabin. Mrs. Peterson responded "All I know is that what I was doing wasn't working. I finally realized that Justin is going to do many things that are contrary to my values. Trying to control him and make him conform to my values just increased his rebellion and my frustration. I still hope that Justin will someday adopt some of my values, but if he doesn't, I'll love him anyway. Meanwhile, I feel much better taking care of myself than trying to control him. I really want to get past my fears and my judgments. I really want to have faith in Justin to live his life as he sees fit—including the possibility of making some little mistakes and possibly some drastic ones. I really want to use these opportunities to do things that will help Justin learn some skills to serve him throughout life—rather than hammering away at his confidence through my judgments and disappointments. And . . . I really want to be as close to Justin as possible during his individuation process. This is new for me, and a little scary—but it feels much better than my old ways."

Mrs. Peterson wanted to support Justin by being "on his side." In the process, she found she was also being on her own side. She felt better, and her relationship with Justin improved. By focusing on opportunities to learn and to teach skills, she and Justin moved in a more productive and effective direction.

Letting Go Through Choices

Mrs. Farnsworth had her doubts about letting go. She was afraid her son would get totally out of control if she gave up trying to control him. But with encouragement from her parent study group, she decided to try.

Mrs. Farnsworth had been taking the responsibility to get Dan out of bed on Tuesday mornings for an early-morning class. She would wake him up, he would go back to sleep. This scenario would continue, with increasing anger on both sides, until Mrs. Farnsworth would yank the covers off. Dan would then stumble out of bed, saying "Get off my back," and finally leave about half an hour late.

Mrs. Farnsworth received a letter from the teacher saying that if Dan missed one more time he would fail the class.

One morning after Mrs. Farnsworth decided to "let go," she went into Dan's room and respectfully asked, "Do you want to go to class this morning, or do you want to miss it and fail the class?" Dan was quiet for a few seconds before saying, "I guess I'll go." Then his mother said, "Do you want me to help you get up, or do you want me to leave you alone?" He said "Leave me alone." She left, and he called out, "Thanks, Mom." (Quite a difference from "get off my back.") Five minutes later, he was in the shower and left on time. Mom thought he could feel the difference in her manner and tone of voice and sensed that she would not argue with him.

Mrs. Farnsworth told her parent study group, "It may have been better for me to stay out of it completely and let him experience the consequence of failing the class, but I wasn't quite ready for that. I *was* ready to accept negative answers to my questions. I *was* ready to have him consciously choose to sleep in and fail the class."

Mrs. Farnsworth empowered her teen to be responsible for his choices rather than inviting him to put all his energy into resisting. By letting go through offering choices, Dan could focus on his decisions rather than getting caught up in resisting what his mother was trying to "make" him do.

Getting Support for Letting Go

In one of our workshops, we asked for a volunteer who

has been afraid to let go, especially when faced with such issues as teenagers wanting to go to the mall with their friends, to pierce their ears, to have a clothing allowance, or to date. Mrs. Hopkins volunteered.

Facilitator: How old is your teen?
Mrs. Hopkins: Thirteen.
Facilitator: Her name?
Mrs. Hopkins: Meagan.
Facilitator: What grade?
Mrs. Hopkins: Seventh.

Facilitator: Any of you remember this magic age? It's tricky, because they still need a co-pilot in their lives —but they don't think they do. In fact, they'd like to throw you out of the plane! Kids this age want to do everything the older kids are doing. This is the age when they think they know more than you do—and you continue to become stupider as they get older, until they get old enough to learn that you aren't as stupid as they thought.

What is the problem you're having with Meagan?

Mrs. Hopkins: She wants to go steady.

Facilitator: How did you find out about this?

Mrs. Hopkins: She called me into her room and told me she wanted to speak with me. She said she'd been to a friend's house a couple of days ago and had met a young man. He was going to call her and ask her to go steady.

Facilitator: How old is he, eighteen?

Mrs. Hopkins: No, around her age.

Facilitator: And you said, "Of course, honey. That's fine"?

Mrs. Hopkins: No, what I said was, "I can't stop you. It's your decision, but I'd prefer you didn't."

Facilitator: And what did she say?

Mrs. Hopkins: "I'm going to do it anyway."

Facilitator: Are you willing to look at what your fears are around this?

Mrs. Hopkins: Yes.

Facilitator: It's common for us to have fears as our kids grow up. Sometimes it seems that they could make life-threatening mistakes. I remember when my son thought he was old enough to walk across the alley to play with his friends. He was so little, I was sure no car would ever see him. For a long time, I tried to control it. I made him stay in the house when he didn't come get me to walk across with him. Finally, when he kept doing it, I had to look at my fears. It's a process we're dealing with here. Our kids are growing. Our response to their growth is to say no, no, no and hold back. So what are your issues and fears around this?

Mrs. Hopkins: Well, I told her . . .

Facilitator: No, I don't want to know what you told her. I want to know your fears and issues. It's easy to stay in our heads and rationalize, explain our good intentions, and avoid our issues in any way we can. What are your real issues about going steady—from your heart and your gut? What do you have against people going steady? What is this about?

Mrs. Hopkins: At thirteen?

Facilitator: Now we're getting down to it! What are your issues about going steady at thirteen?

Mrs. Hopkins: That she'll redirect herself toward boys and not study.

Facilitator: Great. That's an issue. How many people would have a similar issue? Look at all those hands. Any other issues?

Mrs. Hopkins: Teenage pregnancy.

Facilitator: How many of you would have an issue over that? Look at all those hands. So these are both issues that come up for us when our kids start wanting to do these things.

The next question we want to ask is what are Meagan's issues. She's a seventh-grader. She knows this boy is going to call, because she's been told he is and has probably been asked what she'll say if he asks her to go steady. This boy has checked this out—because if she's going to say no he isn't going to call. So he has all his bases covered. At this age, they rarely speak to each other. It takes weeks of passing messages between intermediaries to set up any of this. They have a very complicated communication network. By the time the boy finally calls, this has been built up for a long time. So . . . what are her issues? Do you know?

Mrs. Hopkins: Her friend has a boyfriend.

Facilitator: I'll bet that's one of her issues. Her friend has a boyfriend and at this age she wants to fit in. Teens want to be like their friends. That's more important than pleasing their parents. They are often torn because they really want to please their parents, but if their friend has a boyfriend, *they* want a boyfriend. How many of you had friends who had a boyfriend or a girlfriend, and you didn't? How many of you felt happy about that? Some of us are *still* upset about that and are *still* trying to work it through. You can either help her work it through now, or she'll have to do it later.

What else might be an issue for her?

Mrs. Hopkins: It made her feel good to have a boy think she's cute.

Facilitator: Yes. She's not a liberated woman yet, right? She's only thirteen. Her worth is still somewhat defined externally. It feels good that someone on the outside, someone of the opposite sex, thinks she's cute. At our age, we don't care about that anymore, do we?

Okay, first you look at your issues and then you look at her issues and then you ask yourself, "Am I willing to let go just a little?"

Mrs. Hopkins: Yes.

Facilitator: What do you think is the smallest step you could do to let go? You did leave it up to her, but sometimes that feels like abandonment. It might feel like too big a step to her—it might feel too big because she knows you don't like it, she knows you won't be happy. She feels torn. At this age, kids need to do what they need to do, but they want to please their parents, too.

Can anyone help Mrs. Hopkins? What would be some small steps she could take? I'll write them down.

[In response to suggestions from the group, the facilitator compiled the list below.]

1. Say, "Gee, this is exciting. This is your first opportunity to go steady."
2. Join in her enthusiasm and say, "I'd really like to meet this guy."
3. Be curious. Try to learn everything you can about what this means to her.
4. Ask her for a definition of what it means to go steady. To my daughter, it's a status symbol (not her words), and all they do is talk on the phone every night.

Mrs. Hopkins: I'd like to try the third suggestion.

Facilitator: Okay, that will be your first small step. The other thing is to keep the doors of communication open and continue the dialogue.

What did you learn from this exercise?

Mrs. Hopkins: Well, I can see that I certainly was catastrophizing. I got right into my fears instead of finding out what was going on for her. I *do* know that going steady at this age is more a phone relationship than anything else, and I guess she can't get pregnant over the phone! I suppose if her grades go down, that would be the time to figure out what should be done. I feel that I can hardly wait to go home and be curious and find out what's going on for her. I can see that my fears really get in the way of a good relationship with my daughter.

Fear is usually at the bottom of not wanting to let go. In this chapter, we've tried to show you how to deal with your fear and to teach you how to let go. You'll find many things get better just by talking about them.

As parents, we do what we can—but during our children's adolescence, we have to let go, we have to realize that they must live their own lives. As long as we're respectful, we may have an influence. But when we try to control, we lose our influence and invite resistance or unhealthy pleasing and poor self-confidence. Letting go is essential to allow children to be what they can be.

Part of letting go is getting rid of the feeling that you have to do something for your kids. Just listen and have faith that they can figure out what to do. Be there to teach them life skills in ways that are effective. Then let go and let them grow.

▼

Chapter

13

Working With Your Teen

Instead of doing *to* our teens, ("This is what you will do!") or *for* our teens ("I'll take care of it for you"), it's important to learn to work *with* our teens. Whether we're making informal plans with our teens, holding family meetings, or using cooperative problem-solving steps, it helps to focus on coming up with agreements that both parent and teen can live with and can follow through on.

Planning With Our Teens

Life is filled with arrangements that need to be made around busy schedules. Many parents plan everything by themselves and simply inform their kids what they'll be doing. These kids have no idea from one minute to the next what is planned for them. This in turn trains them to expect their parents to do things for them, take them places, and even loan them their cars! They learn to be as inconsiderate as their parents when it comes to demanding things be done *right now*.

▾ *Plan ahead.*

Parents get better results, show respect and teach skills when they involve their kids in planning ahead. Place a calendar in a centrally located place so that everyone in the family can easily refer to it. Schedule a family meeting at a time when everyone can give their full attention to discussing upcoming activities and appointments. Everyone can then take part in planning ahead by noting what is happening, when it's happening, who needs to be involved, and who is responsible for what.

Chaos, hurt feelings, resentments, anger, and other frustrations can be avoided by making the time to formally plan ahead. Although many people complain they don't have the time, they don't seem to count the time spent in chaos and frustration! Good planning eliminates these problems—but it takes time, attention to details, and cooperation.

Annette was getting ready to go back to high school for her junior year. She had mentioned to her parents the things she needed to do to prepare for school. After dinner one day, they sat at the table and made a list of what needed to be done. They got out the family calendar to figure out when each thing could be accomplished and which parent would be available to assist if needed. Annette worked out a budget with her folks for school clothes and an allowance that would cover the rising costs for school activities and personal expenses.

The family also figured out ways Annette could get to school each day, as the school was too far to walk to and the bus didn't run at the right times. This allowed

Annette plenty of time to get on the phone and arrange car pools for the days when her folks couldn't take her.

Contrast this picture with many families where either the plans are made by the parents or no plans are made. Rick, Stephanie, and Sharon provide examples of the chaos and frustration resulting from not planning ahead.

▾ *Give your kids the help they need to make plans.*

Rick wanted to go to a rock concert in a city fifty miles away. Since he didn't have a car or a license, he needed his parents' help to make the arrangements. Every time he asked them, they said they were busy and would talk about it later. Rick was frustrated—he wanted to know if he should save money to buy a ticket, and he wanted to have enough time to ask friends to go with him. Since Rick's parents didn't take him seriously, they didn't get back to him in time, and he missed the concert. His parents didn't realize they were being rude; they just didn't see his plan as important as all the other things they were dealing with in their lives.

Rick's story isn't unusual. When Stephanie wanted to go to a dance, her parents weren't comfortable with her going out with a boy, so they kept putting off answering her questions about the dance. Stephanie couldn't make the arrangements all her friends were making—buying their dresses, planning where they would go to eat, arranging transportation—because her parents wouldn't respond, and she didn't know how to get through to them.

In another family, Sharon was angry because her mother kept making dates for her to baby-sit without checking with her first. Finally, Sharon told her mother that she refused to baby-sit any more unless she was in charge of her own arrangements. Although Mom couldn't understand why Sharon didn't appreciate her efforts to help, to Sharon, Mom's help was disrespectful and inconsiderate.

Too often, parents don't take their kids seriously or plan for their needs. Simply because we feel our schedule is more important, or that our kids shouldn't date, or that we can control their schedule, doesn't mean we can ignore our kids. Since they need our help, it's up to us to work out the details with them.

There are several ways to improve the situations just mentioned. One is to take your kids seriously and make time to plan informally with them when they or you have a need. Another way is to improve communications and work *with* your kids through formal family meetings.

Family Meetings

Families run more smoothly, work out problems better, experience working together, and provide many opportunities for training in life skills when they hold weekly family meetings. During these meetings, families can share mutual appreciation and discuss issues of concern to individuals or the whole family. They can plan menus, calendars, shopping trips, outings, and other joint activities.

Tips to Improve Family Meetings

1. It's important to hold family meetings at the same time each week, not only when there's a crisis.
2. Family members can take turns running the meeting or making notes of the decisions.
3. Having family meetings with older kids can be quite rewarding but difficult to arrange because

of busy schedules. In one family, the problem was solved by setting the next meeting date at the end of each meeting.

4. It's important that all members of the family have the opportunity to be present. Some family members may refuse to come, and younger kids may get restless and leave in the middle. The goal is progress, not perfection. Working together takes time and practice.
5. In family meetings, kids should feel they're taken seriously and treated as important, contributing members of their family. When people share at a family meeting, everyone should listen respectfully, without arguing or correcting.
6. Consensus is a key ingredient for successful family meetings. If everyone doesn't agree on a decision, dissenters will probably undermine any progress that could take place.
7. It helps to spend time talking about controversial subjects without trying to decide what to do in one meeting. For extremely controversial issues, it may take several meetings to reach any kind of consensus.
8. If a family can't reach agreement, they live with the results of indecision—which usually means keeping things the way they've been or doing as the parents say until the issue can be worked out at a future meeting.
9. Family meetings work best when there is a time limit. Thirty minutes is long enough for most families.
10. When families haven't been used to working this way, it takes time and patience to be

efficient and effective—but it's worth the effort.

11. If parents lecture or give orders, it will defeat the purpose of family meetings.
12. Focus on items that are less controversial, like time for fun, allowances, and so on, until the kids really start to believe their input is wanted and respected.

Many times when we counsel families, it's obvious to us that they could solve many of their problems themselves through family meetings. But families often don't spend time together. Instead, parents leave lists of orders for the kids—which the kids resist doing. And the kids can never find a good time to ask their parents for help, so they become demanding instead. A few family members feel responsible and do more than their share of work. They then feel resentful and nag and punish other family members for being lazy.

Although it may be more efficient to issue orders and plan for your kids without their input, it's less effective for the kind of long-range parenting that teaches your kids life skills.

Transcript of a Family Meeting

The Delano family was tired of trying to handle everything on the fly. They decided to learn the skills for family meetings by holding their first meeting in the counselor's office. The family consisted of Mom, Dad, Todd (seventeen), Laurie (fourteen), and Ann (fourteen), Dad's daughter from his first marriage. Ann spent weekends, holidays, and summers with the family and had just arrived for the summer.

Dad: I'd like to start our meeting with appreciations. I'd like to let Todd know I appreciate it that he cleaned the garage for me yesterday. Ann, I want you to know I appreciate you leaving your boyfriend behind so you could spend the summer with us.

Ann: I'd like to thank Todd for offering to drive me to the mall today. I appreciate Janet [Mom] for taking me miniature golfing.

Todd: I'd like to thank Mom for letting me sleep in the last few days.

Mom: I'd like to thank Mike [Dad] for cooking dinner last night.

Laurie: I'd like to pass.

Todd: Since I volunteered to be in charge of the meeting today, I'd like to make up the agenda. Who has something they'd like to put on the list?

Mom: I'd like to work out the transportation for Ann and Laurie's tennis lessons. I'd also like help with the shopping and cooking. And I've been emptying the dishwasher twice a day and I don't want to do that anymore.

Dad: I'd like to find a time this week that we could all go out to dinner together.

Laurie: I don't want to share my room with Ann. I don't think it's fair.

Ann: Maybe I should have stayed home this summer.

Todd: Ann, is that something you want on the agenda?

Ann: No, but I don't think Laurie likes having me here.

Todd: We can talk about that when it comes up. Right now, I'm just trying to make the agenda.

Ann: I'd like to talk about a baby-sitting job Mrs. Hansen wants me to do this summer.

Todd: I want to talk about our trip to Los Angeles.

Counselor: Todd, you've done a great job setting

up the agenda. Since your time is limited, perhaps you can start at the top and take the list of unfinished items home for your next family meeting. It's okay not to finish everything today. Your family has a lot to talk about.

Todd: I'd like to start with Laurie's complaint, since that seems like the most important.

Counselor: Why don't you check with the rest of the family and see if they agree?

[The family agreed and the meeting continued.]

Laurie: I don't think it's fair just because I'm the only girl in the family that I have to share my room when Ann comes. I like Ann, but nobody even asks me if it's okay. Ann gets up earlier than I do, and she makes so much noise that I can't sleep. And I don't like listening to Ann's music all the time.

Todd: Does anyone else want to say anything about this?

Mom: I'm sorry, Laurie. I had no idea you felt this way. You're right, we just assume Ann will stay with you and we never ask. I can't imagine where Ann would stay if she weren't welcome in your room.

Dad: Laurie, if you had more choice and could work out the wake-up and the music with Ann, would it be okay for her to say with you?

Ann: I could use my earphones when I listen to my music. I try to be quiet in the morning. Maybe I could leave my clothes in the bathroom and get ready in there.

Laurie: Now I feel like a real brat. [She starts to cry.]

Mom: Laurie, I'm glad we have a place we can say how we really feel about things, and I'm glad you had the courage to tell us how upset you were. We weren't being considerate of you, and we didn't realize it. Now we do. I know we can work this out.

Dad: I've been thinking of moving my office to my place of work. If I did that, it would give us another room. In the meantime Ann could use the pull-out bed there.

Laurie: I *want* Ann to stay with me! I just wanted to be *asked*. And Ann, you can get ready in our room in the morning. You're not really that noisy. But I would like it if you'd use your earphones when you listen to the stereo.

Ann: Thanks, Laurie. I'd much rather share a room with you than be alone in Dad's office.

Counselor: When do you think you will have a family meeting at home so you can finish the rest of your list? I'd also like to recommend that you keep a note pad somewhere handy so people can write down things that come up that they want to discuss at the family meetings. Your family shows us how much nicer it is to work together than to have to figure everything out alone. Thank you.

The rest of the session was spent trying to find a time everyone would be together for the next meeting —not an easy task in most busy families!

Using Family Meetings to Establish Cooperation

Relatively speaking, teenagers will be more motivated to participate in household chores if they have been involved in working on a plan. We say *relatively speaking* because, again, you need to remember that chores are not the priority of kids but of their parents. Your task as parents is not to make your teens like doing chores, but to gain as much cooperation as possible, which benefits you and your kids in the long run.

During a family meeting, have the family make a list of the household chores that need to be done. Next to each item, note the family consensus on how often that particular chore needs to be done and what the deadline should be for getting it done. Finally, allow family members to pick which chores they would be willing to do that week. Some of the more unpopular chores, such as cleaning toilets, may have to be placed in a hat for some lucky person to draw. It's good to have one person monitor the chore list each day to see whether chores have been completed by the deadline. If a chore didn't get done, the monitor finds the responsible person, lets them know they missed the deadline, and tells them it's time to do the chore. In many families, the youngest child likes this job and does it very well. Parents should avoid monitoring if they've been nagging the kids to get things done.

When families use this kind of chore routine, they find that deadlines work best if they are set for times when people would naturally be around the house, such as before bed, before breakfast, before TV, or before Sunday evening at 8:00. Follow-through (as discussed in Chapter Ten) is effective to hold people accountable for their agreements.

Some families find cooperation around chores increases when everyone works together. Setting aside an hour a week for housework usually succeeds better than hoping things will get done at different times during the week.

Some families are deeply involved in power struggles around chores. When this is the case, it may take steps smaller than a family meeting to progress toward cooperation, such as *follow through* or some of the following suggestions.

Handling Disagreements

At one of the empowering teens workshops, a parent wanted help on learning how to work with her son. She said he was uncooperative and defiant. When asked to demonstrate how it usually goes with her son, Mom and one of the workshop participants performed the following role-play.

Mom: Craig, please unload the dishwasher.

Craig: No. Stop telling me what to do. You're always on my back. I've had it.

Mom: I need your help because the Joneses are coming over.

Craig: I don't care. See this Sony Walkman you bought me for a lot of money? [He throws it on the ground and breaks it.]

Mom: I'm really angry! That cost $100!

Craig: So?

Mom: It really infuriates me to see that—to see you destroy property!

Craig: So?

Mom: Okay. There's nothing I can do to bring that back. It's gone. But I won't buy you another one.

Craig: I don't care.

In the discussion after the role-play, the facilitator asked how the participants felt, what they thought, and what they each learned from the interaction.

Craig: I'm not interested in what she says. I've had it with her demands. I know how to get to her.

Mom: I feel that I made a reasonable demand. I need help. We're having company. It's his chore to do.

Facilitator: That's what you *think*. How do you *feel?*

Mom: Infuriated. Frustrated. At the end of my wits. And really hurt.

In the above role-play, we saw a lot of revenge through punishment. Mom was angry and frustrated. Craig punished her by not doing his job and breaking his radio. Mom got even by threatening not to buy things anymore. Craig retaliated by saying, "I don't care." A power struggle had degenerated into a revenge cycle.

At this point, many parents try to use logical consequences. The idea behind logical consequences is that they are respectful, related, and reasonable. They are *not* punitive. Many of us learned to use logical consequences with our younger children. For example, clothes not put in the laundry by Monday didn't get washed. Children who made too much noise in the car had to wait while we pulled over to the side of the road until the car was quiet enough to drive safely. Many of our children came to breakfast to find their plate turned upside down because they had forgotten to clean their room or get dressed first when the family procedure was clean rooms and get dressed before breakfast.

Logical consequences do not work in a power struggle or revenge cycle. Most suggestions from parents, even if they seem logical to them, are seen as punitive by the teen. When you say things like, "If you come home late, you won't be able to go out for two weeks," you may feel it's logical but your teenager will say it's punishment. When you say, "If you don't get good grades, you won't be able to get your driver's licence" (knowing that insurance rates are lower when kids have higher grades), you feel it's logical. But what would your teenager say? "Unfair, punishment, spite."

Instead of trying to use logical consequences to get

out of power struggles and revenge cycles, families can use cooperative problem solving.

Using Cooperative Problem Solving

Cooperative problem solving is another way to deal with disagreements between parent and teen. The following role-play demonstrates how Mom and Craig came to an agreement.

Step One: Present the Problem

Mom: We're having problems with responsibility. Let's try to find something we can both live with. Are you willing to do that?

Craig: Okay.

Step Two: Look for Agreements That Lead to Solutions

At every point, parents should look for agreement. As the role-play continues, watch for times when the agreement changes from "let's work this out" to "let's fight."

Step Three: Gather Information on the Perceptions of Everyone Concerned

Mom: The other day when the Joneses were coming over for dinner, I asked you to unload the dishwasher, which was your chore, and you exploded. What are your thoughts and feelings about doing your chores?

Craig: I was busy. It wasn't a good time for me to do that.

Step Four: Stick to the Issue and Listen

This isn't the time to get sarcastic and say, "Well, I notice there never seems to be a 'good' time for you to do your chores." It's also not the time to say, "Well, I had a need, too. The Joneses were coming." A typical teen response would be, "Tough," and you're back in the fight.

When kids start sharing their feelings, parents need to listen carefully for the feelings underneath the words. Kids aren't used to using feeling words. And since they're used to parents responding with lectures and orders, they may be shocked and suspicious when you really want to know how they think and feel. You need to keep going for more feelings, to get as much information as you can by being as curious as you can. It helps to realize that all the things your kids tell you are their attempts to put you into their world, to let you know how they see things and how they feel about things.

If you watch your teenagers' faces, the boredom you see is a dead give-away that you're starting to tell them how it is for you before *they* really feel heard and understood. You need to find out all that's on their mind before telling them what's on yours. You need to be anthropologists in "teenland."

Mom: So you were busy at the time?

Craig: Yes, I hate it when you say, "Do it now"!

Mom: Oh, I didn't know you felt that way. Do you have any other feelings about it? What else is going on for you?

Craig: I was listening to my music. Then I got a phone call and was trying to figure out what I was going to do that night. I had to call my other friend and see what her plans were.

Mom: So you had a lot going on. You were listening to music and trying to formulate your plans for the rest of the day?

Craig: Right.

Mom: And it sounds like you didn't want to be bothered with anything else because you were thinking about that?

Craig: Right. I was busy.

Mom: Is there anything else you want to say about unloading the dishwasher or helping with chores around the house?

Step Five: Keep Asking, "Is There Anything Else?"

We can't emphasize enough how important it is to keep asking, "Is there anything else?" until it all comes out. Otherwise you'll probably be dealing with surface issues rather than the deeper ones.

Craig: Yeah. I hate unloading the dishwasher.

Mom: So that's your least favorite chore?

Craig: Yeah.

Mom: Well, I have to do lots of things I don't like to do, too.

Craig: Well, who cares?

Facilitator: See what caused the fight. This happens when we're too quick to let them know how it is for us. What's the question this parent needs to keep asking?

Mom: Is there anything else?

Craig: You told me you are never going to buy me anything again.

Mom: Anything else?

Craig: No.

Step Six: Reflect Your Understanding

Facilitator: Now see if you can reflect to your teen what he just told you.

Mom: So, you hate unloading the dishwasher. You were busy, and you hate it when I threaten you and say I'm not going to buy you anything? I'll bet you feel really angry when I threaten you?

Craig: Umhmm.

Mom: Anything else?

Craig: Yeah, I don't think you really care about me.

Mom: What makes you think I don't care about you?

Craig: I just don't think you care—when you say things like you aren't going to get me anything else.

Facilitator: What does the teen need to hear now?

Mom: You mean you feel loved when I get you things, so when I threaten not to get you things you feel unloved?

Facilitator: Isn't that the teen's logic? Now, aren't we tempted to teach teens a lesson and tell them how stupid their thinking is rather that just listening and trying to understand? A normal parental response at this point might be to say, "That's the most stupid thing I've ever heard! Why do you think I had you? You shouldn't feel that way. That's ridiculous!" This is how we train our kids, without realizing it, to be out of touch with their thoughts and feelings. How many of us got "trained" this way? And how many of us went on to marry people who were willing to continue that training by telling us what and how to think and feel? And how many of us are now going to Alcoholics Anonymous or Alanon meetings to break these bad habits so we can think for ourselves?

So, let's not discount their thoughts and feelings. Our teenagers think the way they think. They feel the way they feel. We need to let them know we understand. After we let them know we understand, we can say, "I have a slightly different picture. Would you be interested in hearing what it is?"

This is a lot of work. No wonder we resort to grounding! It's much easier.

Question from the audience: Shouldn't Mom respond to her sons' need to be told he is loved? Shouldn't she reassure him?

Facilitator: Absolutely not. Mom's job is to be an anthropologist in teenland—to be curious about how teens think and feel—not to fix it. Too many parents think it's their job to fix everything.

Which do you think will make Craig feel more loved, being told that he's loved, or listening to him and taking him seriously?

This process is not effective if you're just memorizing words and a technique. The important point is to be sincerely curious about how your teenagers think and feel; to sincerely want to keep asking, "Is there anything else?" before trying to explain your position; to sincerely take them seriously; to sincerely understand and validate their thoughts and feelings; to sincerely not need to lecture, correct, or fix; to sincerely share your thoughts and feelings as thoughts and feelings that are simply different rather than the "right" way to think and feel; to sincerely want to work for an agreement rather than to win an argument and be right; and to sincerely be more interested in the long-range skills you teach your child than in winning the short-term battle of getting the dishwasher unloaded.

Step Seven: Share Your Perceptions

One way to guarantee a nonreceptive teen audience is to share your perceptions with your kids before asking if they're willing to listen. There's something magical about getting their permission first that invites listening and cooperation. Asking if they're willing to listen demonstrates respect for them and also leaves room for you to ask for respect if they interrupt. If this happens, parents can say, "You agreed to listen to how it is for me. You don't have to agree with how it is for me, but I do appreciate your willingness to listen."

Facilitator: So, Mom gets Craig's agreement to listen. Let's continue from there.

Mom: I didn't see it quite the same way you did. I was feeling somewhat panic-stricken because the Joneses were arriving in half an hour and I had lots of things to get ready. I was exhausted. I'd been working all day. I didn't want to face a whole pile of dishes sitting in the sink. Also, I didn't realize you hated unloading the dishwasher so much. I thought it was just another job you traded off with your sister.

Step Eight: Ask Your Teens to Reflect Their Understanding

Mom: Can you tell me what you just heard me say?

Craig: That people were coming over. That you were panicked. That you didn't want to have dishes piled up because the dishwasher was full and you couldn't get the dirty ones in there. You didn't know I hated the job.

At this point typical teenagers feel that they've disappointed you. Feeling this way is painful, and they may try to avoid hearing more. They may respond:

"Yeah, but I was in a rush. Yeah, but I didn't know." If they respond this way, it really helps for a parent to say, "Honey, this is not a criticism. I'm not trying to tell you what to do. I just want to tell you what it was like for me and see if you can understand. I know it was real different for you, and I want to understand that, and it's okay that we don't agree." When you can say that to your kids, they'll have an easier time listening to you.

We don't recommend doing this very sophisticated problem-solving with younger children. You may want to, but it's usually more effective, for instance, to simply take them by the hand and walk them to the car, rather than finding out their issues about not wanting to get in the car.

Step Nine: Brainstorm for Solutions

Now that both teen and parent have said how they think and feel about the situation and both have had their thoughts and feelings validated (reflected without judgment or criticism), it's time to ask, "Could we see if we can come up with some ideas we can both live with?"

What do most kids do when we ask them to brainstorm? They say, "I don't know." And then what do most parents do? They provide answers, or think that their teens don't care, or that they're rebelling, or that they don't love their parents. But parents can use a different approach.

To get into the brainstorming mode, think of as many stupid ideas as you can until you engage your teens. For example, "Let's go to K-Mart and buy a six-year supply of paper plates. Let's all contribute money for a full-time maid. Let's throw out all our dishes and pans and buy things we can eat with our fingers straight from the box or can. Let's make Dad unload the dishwasher all the time." Using our sense of humor to give examples of wild and crazy ideas is one of the best ways to model brainstorming and help our kids get into the spirit of finding solutions.

Mom: Do you have any ideas?

Craig: Nope.

Mom: You don't have any ideas?

Craig: Nope.

Mom: How about if we agree never to use the dishwasher again? Maybe we could refinance the house and buy a lifetime supply of plastic utensils and paper supplies.

Craig: That's really dumb.

Mom: Well, it's just an idea. I'm going to write it down! Let's see if I can think of any more ideas or if you can.

Craig: Well, why doesn't my sister empty the dishwasher all the time?

Mom: Let's write it down.

Craig: We could hire a maid to do dishes.

Mom: We could switch jobs.

Craig: We could all fend for ourselves and do our own dishes.

Mom: We could let the dishes sit in the dishwasher until we run out.

Craig: You could give me more warning when you want my help and don't insist on "right now."

Step Ten: Agree on a Solution

At this point, the two have generated enough ideas to move to the next step, which is to see whether they've come up with an idea they both can live with for one week. In this role-play, the two decided to switch jobs for the week, and Mom agreed to give more time for a job to be completed. She agreed to ask Craig when he would be willing to do something and then to follow through with dignity and respect instead of saying "right now."

Step Eleven: Set a Date for Evaluation

Both Mom and Craig agreed to talk at the end of the week about how each thought it went. They also put chores on the agenda for the family meeting so the whole family could devise a system that was more up-to-date.

Step Twelve: Follow Through

Even though an agreement was made in a respectful manner, Mom needs to practice follow-through. She has several options. She can watch and see what happens during the week and then bring up any problems at the family meeting. She can also notice when her teen doesn't follow through on his part of the agreement; she can then say kindly, "Please keep your agreement," or, "Are you keeping your agreement?" or, "Remember what you agreed to do about the chores?" A friendly tone of voice and an attitude of respect are essential to prevent follow-through from becoming nagging.

With practice, most parents can execute the cooperative problem-solving steps. But when kids don't follow through on their part of the agreement, parents often resort to nagging, coaxing, or punishing. Or worse, they do everything themselves. To avoid this, refer to Chapter Ten, in which we discuss follow-through in detail.

Most parents fantasize a family in which the kids automatically do everything they said they would without any reminders. This is Disneyland—at least until new habits are firmly embedded in the family. But even though we won't ever reach such perfection, most of us will reap many benefits from working *with* our kids. The long-range benefits for our teens are that they will learn how to think things through and how to work in a more cooperative, responsible way with others.

Chapter

14

Communication That Really Works

Do your kids hear anything you say? Do you hear anything they say? What happens to all those words you use? Why won't your kids use more words and talk to you? Would your kids talk to you more if they thought they would be listened to, understood, and taken seriously? In this chapter, we will pull together all the concepts we've been writing about to show how to communicate so that both parent and teen felt listened to and understood.

Listening is the primary ingredient of communication and its least developed skill. So much has been written and said about listening that most people are aware of what it takes to listen well. However, most are not aware of why listening is so difficult to do. Simply put, it's difficult because issues keep getting in the way. People usually take everything they hear personally; they want to defend their position, explain, correct, retaliate, or tell a better story. Parents especially get extremely ego-involved with their kids; they take things even *more* personally, because they feel they may not be good-enough parents.

You interrupt the listening process when you:

1. Step in to fix or rescue so you can be a good parent, rather than listening to your teens as they try to figure things out for themselves
2. Try to talk teens out of their feelings or perceptions so they'll have the "right" perceptions and feelings
3. Give defensive explanations about your point of view
4. Interrupt to teach lessons on morality or values
5. Let your unresolved issues get in the way
6. Punish

By rearranging the letters in the word *listen,* you can find a primary key to good listening—*silent.* Be silent when listening. You can't talk and listen at the same time.

We know how hard it is to be silent while listening. It takes tremendous self-discipline. It means giving up the temptation to engage in any or all of the six points made above, especially the first one. It's very hard to realize that your kids often don't need solutions—they simply need to be listened to, understood, and taken seriously. That's all! As Archie Bunker would say, "Stifle yourself."

Of course, there are times when it's appropriate to work on solutions. Later in this chapter, we will give suggestions on communicating for solutions, but first we need to demonstrate the importance of simply listening to your teens in order to understand them.

Skills to Help Us Be Silent and Listen for Understanding

The following skills are effective only when you are sincerely interested in understanding the world of your teenagers and are willing to respect their reality.

1. The *feeling* behind what you do is more important than what you actually do. Being silent while "listening" because you are reading the paper or thinking about something else doesn't count. Effective listening requires that your body language be wide open to indicate interest.
2. Have respect for separate realities. Be open to fact that there is more than one way of seeing things.
3. Show empathy. "I can understand why you might feel that way or see it that way."
4. Be curious enough to try understanding your teen's point of view. Being curious means that if you do open your mouth, it's to ask questions that will invite more information from your teen, such as, "How did that make you feel? What about that was important to you? Could you give me an example of when I made you so angry? How often do I do that? Is there anything else that is bothering you?"

The last suggested question—"Is there anything else that is bothering you?"—is one that deserves more exploration. Many parents have shared with us that remembering to ask that particular question over and over has done more to help them get into their teen's world and understand core issues than anything else they do.

Anything Else?

A key skill for demonstrating curiosity is to keep asking, "Is there anything else?" Too often, parents react to the first bit of information they get, although it usually isn't even close to the key issue. You discover the core issues and feelings when you avoid the temptation to respond to the surface information and instead keep asking, "Is there anything else about that that bothered you? Is there anything else you want to say about that? Is there any other reason you can think of? Is there any other information you could give me to help me understand?" There are many ways to ask, "Is there anything else?" Use your creativity, but keep being curious enough to elicit more and more information. It may seem awkward and phoney at first, but keep practicing. Once you get over the awkward stage, you'll find yourself being truly curious and interested. Then ways to say, "Is there anything else?" become more spontaneous.

Communication by Example

It might be easier for parents to be silent and patient if they realized how much more effective it is to live what they believe than to preach what they believe. In the long run, your kids are much more likely to "hear" your actions than they are to "hear" your lectures. Although they may seem to rebel against your "example" for a short time, when you quietly and respectfully live what you believe, you'll be amazed at how many of your values your kids adopt when they grow up.

However, when you try to cram your values down your teens' throats, they have to either rebel against those values or pick them up as pleasers rather than thinking them through and making them their own. Instead, if you simply live your values, your kids can pick and choose from those that they "hear." In cases like this, teenage rebellion against your values is usually temporary.

In a family where education was a high value, Josh, a seventh-grader, decided it wasn't cool to be smart. He messed around in school until he realized that all his grades counted toward college—then he made sure he at least got *B*s. But he was careful to get nothing better because he didn't want anyone to think he was a nerd. In class, he cut up and occasionally "smart-mouthed" his teachers. But when Josh got to college, all he wanted to do was study, study, study and learn, learn, learn!

In another family, the fourteen-year-old daughter often complained about having to attend family meetings. But one day she came home and announced, "My friend's family is having a lot of problems. They should have family meetings."

Remember that how your teens act now is not who they will be forever. Keep this in mind and you can view your teens' behavior with perspective, hope, faith, and humor. Meanwhile, there are times when it's appropriate to communicate your feelings and desires directly, rather than by example, and to communicate to solve problems. You must call on different resources to be effective communicators in each of these areas. There are times when it's effective to communicate from your head, other times when coming from your heart or gut is more effective.

Head, Heart, or Gut

Lectures, judgments, arguments, rationalizations, distractions, catastrophizing, and futurizing all come from your head. Feelings of sadness, loneliness, love, compassion, empathy, and understanding come from your heart. Honesty, fear, anger, and courage come from your gut. One place is not better than the other. There are times when judgment and analysis from your head will serve best. Other times call for listening to the love, compassion, or sadness of your heart. And at others, you need to be gut-level honest or to listen to your fears, anger, or courage. The solution to so many communication problems is to find the appropriate balance.

After Mrs. Sanders' divorce, she realized that a big chasm had developed between herself and her daughter, Julia. But when Mrs. Sanders learned the skills of communicating from the head, heart, or gut, she was able to bridge that chasm. She shared the following excerpt from her journal:

"About six months ago Julia took me to a movie. Before the movie, we were talking, and I started to listen to what she was saying instead of arguing. I didn't realize I hadn't been listening until I started to listen. I could see how, in the past, I would go right to my head and would try to explain my point of view instead of listening to her from my heart.

"It took self-discipline to bite my tongue. When we were through, I had this uneasy feeling that nothing had been solved. I hadn't done any of my usual behaviors like giving her advice or telling her the "correct way" (my way) to see things. However, over the weeks I noticed our relationship got better, even though there was still some uneasiness. About a month after this first "listening" experience, I drove her home after a family dinner. She made it a point that she wanted me to drive her home. I could tell she wanted to say something to me, but was afraid. So I decided to share with her from my heart. I said, 'I feel so bad about the gap in our relationship. We have this kind of superficial relationship. I love you, and I think you love me, and when we spend time together it's very pleasant and cordial, but it feels so superficial. I just wish there was something we could do to close the gap.' Julia said, 'I'm not going to talk about this anymore. I've been through a lot, I'm not getting into this stuff again.'

"I kept saying, 'I think I'm a better listener now. I've learned a lot. I used to think I knew how to listen, but I didn't. Please give me another try, I want to know what you've gone through.' So Julia started talking to me. It was very painful to hear what she had to say. It was just breaking my heart to really listen to her, because she told me that she felt that the person who had always helped her deal with her pain had abandoned her when she was in the most pain of her life. She wondered how I could really love her and do that. She realized that many of the things she had believed were just myths; that her mother was just a person—and not the person Julia believed her to be.

"She said, 'In a way, I have to thank you because I'm a better person for going through this, because I was just going along in life and having a good time. All I thought about was where the next party was. I didn't really take anything seriously. I figured life is just a game. When this happened, I found out differently. Life is very serious and I'm in control of my life. Because of that, I made a lot of decisions about not abusing drugs, about how I'm going to spend my time, about what's important to me, how important school is to me. I don't think it's really bad, but it can never be the same now because you're different than I thought you were. You were my mother and now you're this person.

"I was sitting there crying hard because I really heard Julia with my heart. My heart was breaking, and I kept saying, 'I'm just so sorry that you had to go through this. I'm so sorry I couldn't listen to you. I heard everything you said as a criticism—I couldn't hear what was behind it. I was too defensive. I can imagine how invalidating that must have been. How insulting that must have been to you! You know, I love you so much, and it's so hard for me to see you go through pain. And to think that you went through all this! I just wish I would've known. I wish I would've understood. I wish I *could* have! You thought you saw me being happy, but I was going through incredible pain. But you didn't see the pain, you saw something else. And some day, when you're ready, I'd like to tell you about what was going on for me then. I don't think this would be a very good time, but there's a lot you don't know and a lot you don't understand. I hope some day you'll want to know.

"This was all happening in the car, in the driveway, and the two of us were just sobbing and I was holding her, and I said, 'I just love you so much, and I feel so bad.'

"She said, 'And I love you.'

"All of that big barrier got broken down between us. It was painful to listen from my heart, but it was worth it. I feel like I have my daughter back."

Communicating Gut Feelings

The heritage of our society is to discount or ignore feelings—especially those from the gut. We've been taught to not feel angry and to not be honest if it hurts someone else's feelings. (Isn't that an interesting paradox? It must be okay for other people to have feelings because we aren't supposed to hurt them, but we aren't supposed to have feelings of our own.) Although a lot of lip service is given to developing individuality, we are judged when we don't conform to the "norm," and the only way to conform is to discount the feelings that make us different.

If you don't learn to acknowledge your feelings, to listen to what they have to teach, and to express them in ways that are respectful to yourelf and others, your life will be superficial. And it helps if you are able to do these things for yourself in order to teach your children how to do them.

Part of long-range parenting is to help your kids know that they have feelings, to know what their feelings are called, to be comfortable expressing them in a respectful manner and as information, not as absolutes, and to stand up for themselves. Kids need to understand separate realities, to realize that people feel and think differently from one another. In addition, teenagers need to know that it's okay to have feelings, no matter what they are, and that they don't have to do anything about them. Having "bad" feelings does not make someone a bad person.

You teach your kids about communicating gut feelings when you hear their feelings and validate them, and when you share your feelings using the listening skills taught at the beginning of this chapter. You need to listen without thinking you must "fix" anything, without getting defensive, and without explaining your position. You are much more respectful when you simply listen or employ your curiosity skills.

Aside from listening, one of the best ways to encourage our kids to express their feelings is to model expressing your own feelings with complete honesty.

Honesty

We want to stress the importance of being honest with your teen about how you feel now and how you felt and what you did as a teenager. Often, parents are afraid to talk about what they did as kids because they think their kids will take it as encouragement to do the same things. But many teenagers have told us the opposite is true. Don't be afraid to be honest with your teen—it's an excellent way to encourage communication.

When her fourteen-year-old daughter, Erin, began going steady, Mrs. Sheldon decided to be honest with her. She said to Erin, "I want to share some things that happened to me as a teenager . . . but I have to tell you, it's scary for me! I did some things that weren't good for me, and some things I knew my parents wouldn't like one bit—and I'm scared that if you know I did these things you'll want to do them, too. But I'm not going to pay attention to my fears, because I think what I can tell you can be helpful." Mrs. Sheldon took a deep breath. "I was sexually active from the time I was in the tenth grade. I was *very* lucky that I didn't get pregnant. I was having sex because I was looking for love . . . I didn't know that wasn't the way to find it. It was also a real moral issue for me, because I was taught it was a very bad sin to engage in sex before marriage. So I felt like a sinner, I felt guilty, and then I did it anyway—which made me feel even worse. I could never ask anyone for information or ask about birth control. In fact, I kept promising myself I'd never do it again but then I would. Then I'd feel guilty all over again.

"I wonder what I would've done if I'd felt loved . . . if I had information and even permission to use birth control . . . if I knew I'd be accepted even if I did make those choices. I have a hunch I might've been much wiser in my decisions. I don't know if I would've abstained, but I *know* I would have loved myself much more, and I wouldn't have had to look for love and approval in that way. That's why I want to tell you what I wish my parents could have told me.

"I get scared that you'll get involved in sex before

you've developed enough judgment to understand long-range results like pregnancy, your reputation, and disease. I wonder if you respect yourself enough to feel good about saying no if you want to, rather than feeling like you have to give in to someone else's demands. I wish I could protect you from being hurt by any mistakes you might make, but I know you have to make your own mistakes and learn whatever you learn from living your life the way you choose. Just know that I'll always be here to love you and accept you unconditionally, and I'll be glad to give you information if you ever want it."

Mrs. Sheldon used a lot of words—which doesn't seem to matter when you're sharing feelings from the heart and gut. She was amazed at how effective her sharing was. Erin told her all about the kids at school who everyone knew were "doing it." Erin told her mother that she didn't have any trouble saying no because she'd noticed how it wasn't long before everyone in the school knew "everything"; she didn't want people to talk about her that way.

Mrs. Sheldon would not have known what was going on for Erin if she hadn't decided to be honest with her. Aware that Erin will probably change her mind about sex as she grows older, Mrs. Sheldon plans to keep the lines of communication open so Erin can feel free to use her mother as a resource any time.

It takes honesty to get in touch with your own feelings, the source of those feelings, and what you want to do about them. When communicating honest feelings, it's easy to get sidetracked into explanations, rationalizations, attacks, defensiveness, and other attitudes. Following the "I feel" formula—*I feel* ______ *because* ______, *and I wish* ______—helps keep us centered on our feelings, the reasons for our feelings, and possible solutions. Notice the word *possible*. Asking for what we wish doesn't mean anyone else has the responsibility to give it to us. Neither should we expect anyone else to agree with us or feel the same. Instead, the "I feel" formula is an effective procedure for honoring and respecting yourself and expressing yourself in a way that's respectful to others.

The "I Feel" Formula

"I *feel* upset about the dishes not being done *because* I like looking at a clean kitchen and cooking in a clean kitchen—and I *wish* you'd do them before I start cooking." (Note how the words italicized here are used in variations below.)

"I feel happy when you keep your agreement to do the dishes because the kitchen looks so nice. Now I can fix dinner in a good mood." As you can see, the last part of the forumla was changed from "I wish" to "now I can." This doesn't mean other people are responsible for your good or bad mood. Some people can fix dinner in a messy kitchen and still stay in a good mood. It *does* mean that you've expressed how you feel.

"I feel hurt when you put me down, and I wish you wouldn't do that." In this case, the "because (it hurts my feelings)" was omitted since it's clearly understood. The formula is flexible; it provides guidelines, not rules. When appropriate, it's helpful to include the "because" and the "I wish" since they help us stay in touch with the whole picture and to give others as much information as possible.

"I feel happy for you for getting that *A* on your report card because I know how hard you worked for it." This comment ends with the focus where it belongs—on the effort rather than the person. To say, "I'm so proud of you for getting an *A*," leaves your kids feeling you won't be so proud of them if they don't get *A*s.

Your kids need to feel that you're proud of them no matter what.

"I feel upset about that *F* on your report card because I'm afraid you might be missing out on something that could benefit you. I wish you'd take another look at what a good education could mean to you." Comments like this invite teens to look at how their behavior affects their life, rather than attacking a teen's character.

"I feel really angry when you hit your brother because I dislike violence. I'd like you to consider other ways to express your feelings and other ways to get what you want." This comment models for your child that it's okay to feel angry but not okay to be disrespectful to others. It also allows room for follow-up on the issue of violence, which could be discussed at a family meeting or at another time when parent and child are in a good mood. At that time, a list could be made of possibilities other than violence for dealing with anger and for getting what we want.

The "You Feel" Formula

In the rare instances when kids do open up to their parents and try to express their feelings (sometimes in disrespectful ways), parents often react negatively (with disrespectful parent responses). They tell their kids that they shouldn't feel that way or they should be more respectful—or they counterattack their kids in a variety of ways. No wonder so many kids grow up with the idea that it's not okay to have feelings.

You can help your children learn how to honor and express their feelings in respectful ways when you model for them the "I feel" formula; it then helps to validate their feelings with the "you feel" formula—whose key word *you* differentiates it from the "I feel" formula. Sometimes it's easy to reflect what they've said because it's very clear. In these instances, it's important that you don't sound like a parrot. Your intent will come through. If you really want to understand and validate your teenagers, they will *feel* understood and validated.

DJ was watching television when his father came into the room and asked him to take out the garbage. DJ ignored Dad. Five minutes later, Dad came back into the room and said, "Turn off that TV right now and take out the garbage."

DJ said, "How come I have to do everything you want right now? How would you like it if I told you to turn off the TV and do something for me right now?"

Dad could see that he'd created resistance and defensiveness with his demand. Fortunately, he remembered the "you feel" formula and said, "You hate it when I tell you to do something right now and feel angry because I'm not being respectful of your time and interests—and you wish I'd give you more warning or more choices about when it would be convenient to you?"

DJ said, "Yeah."

Dad said, "You're right. I was disrespectful. When would you be willing to empty the garbage?"

DJ said, "At the next commercial."

Dad said, "Good enough for me."

When Dad shared this example with his parent study group, he added, "Before, I would've escalated the problem by telling my son not to get disrespectful with me instead of realizing I had been disrespectful to him."

A mother in the same group shared, "When my daughter used to tell me about her fights with her friends I would say, 'Oh, honey, I'm sure it'll be okay tomorrow. You know you always have these fights, and they don't last long.' She would stomp off to her bedroom and slam the door. Now, I say something like, 'You feel really bad when you have had a fight with your friend because you aren't sure you'll be able to make up, and then you won't have a best friend?' I see the relief in her face from feeling listened to and understood. Then she says, 'Yes, but I'm sure we'll make up tomorrow.' It's actually a lot easier to reflect her feelings with understanding instead of trying to 'fix' them or make them go away. It's also comforting to know that she now feels validated rather than put down."

▼ *Reflecting your teens' feelings is not always easy.*

Sometimes your teens' feelings are not clear. This means listening with a "third ear" to what might be underneath an outburst and reflecting to them what you've heard. Your reflection may not be correct, but if you present it in a friendly manner, with real intent to understand, your teens will help you out by correcting your perception.

▼ *Get permission before giving advice.*

Most people who are sharing their feelings are not looking for advice. They just want someone to listen and to understand. On the other hand, most people who are in the listening position think it's their *job* to give advice. Teenagers don't want our advice unless they ask for it. Whenever you're tempted to give advice, first ask, "Would you like my advice?" They'll usually say no, but they might say yes!

Of course, there are other times when listening is not enough, when it's appropriate to work on solutions.

Communicating to Solve Problems

Listening is the first step in problem solving. One problem we often encounter during the problem-solving process is getting sidetracked into the blame game.

▾ *Avoid the blame game.*

One of the greatest barriers to effective communication is playing the blame game. If you're looking for blame, you will find it. And if you're looking for solutions, you will find them.

We saw a cartoon that beautifully illustrated the blame game. It depicted a father running after his child with a stick. The mother was calling, "Please give him another chance." The father shouted back, "But he might not ever do it again!"

How often are we more interested in making our kids "pay" for what they have done through punishment, or at least through feelings of guilt, than we are in communicating for solutions?

A nice motto for any family (or any organization) is, "We are interested in solutions—not in blame." However, we must warn you that if you adopt this family motto, your kids will hold you accountable. Every time you get into your blame routine, one of your kids will say, "Are you looking for blame, or are you looking for solutions?" That's when you must have enough humility to say, "Whoops. Thanks for reminding me."

The Needs of the Situation

Rudolph Dreikurs taught over and over how important it is to "stick to the needs of the situation." This simply means doing what is necessary to solve the problem at hand rather than futurizing and catastrophizing. If your two-year-old has eaten a forbidden cookie, this doesn't mean he's a thief. It means he's a normal two-year-old who will eat cookies that are available. The needs of the situation require that you figure out how to keep forbidden cookies out of your two-year-old's reach. It's going way past the needs of the situation to slap hands and say, "Bad boy."

▾ *Stick to issues rather than personalities.*

Sticking to issues rather than personalities is a close cousin to sticking to the needs of the situation. Parents who believe that the way their teenagers are acting is an indicator of their final personalities will find it very helpful to stick to the issue rather than the personality. Communication will then focus on what needs to be done rather than on personal attacks.

Mrs. Barton came home to find her daughter, Dionne, and four friends sitting on the couch watching television. The girls had left the kitchen in a mess after making brownies and popcorn. In the past, Mrs. Barton had attacked her daughter's personality under similar situations. She'd say, "Dionne, I can't believe you'd be so irresponsible and leave such a mess! I want your friends to go home right now, since you obviously can't control what happens when they're here."

This time, she decided to stick to the issue rather than focusing on personalities. She said, "Girls, it's a rule in our house that we clean up after ourselves. When do you plan to clean up, during commercials or as soon as the program is over?"

Dionne said, "Oh, Mom, we'll do it."

Mom said, "I know you will, honey. I'd just like to know what your plan is for when you'll do it."

Dionne asked her friends, "Should we do it during commercials or after the program?" Her friends got into the spirit of the task, deciding they could all work fast during commercials to get the mess cleaned up.

Sticking to the issue and getting a commitment increases your chances of getting results. If the girls did not keep their commitment, Mom could use follow-through.

Keep It Simple

We've talked a great deal about understanding and expressing feelings and understanding our own and our teen's world. But watch out—it's very easy to go overboard and become engaged in "the paralysis of analysis." Again, it comes back to appropriateness and balance. There are times when the communication process *is* intricate because truths are buried. But there are other times when the situation is straightforward.

One Word. We discussed the one-word method in Chapter Ten on follow-through, but it's worth repeating in the context of communication.

When your teenager has left his towel on the bathroom floor, this is not the time to "get into his world" and try to figure out what feelings might have been behind his action. His feelings are obvious. He's a teenager—he doesn't care if towels get left on the bathroom floor! *You're* the one who cares. What you now need to decide is whether you want the towel picked up or your teenager to feel bad, guilty, inconsiderate, and a failure.

If you want your teen to pick up the towel (with the hope that someday he might learn this life skill), the sum total of your communication should consist of one word, "Towel." If by some chance he doesn't get it you can add one more word, "Bathroom." Since towels on bathroom floors are so low on his priority list, it's within the realm of possibility that he still won't get it. At this point, you might use two words, but only if you run them together, "Bathroomfloor."

We hope you get the point that using only one word is more to help you learn self-discipline and respect than to help you teenager learn self-discipline and respect. It's ironic how often we try to teach our teenagers to be self-disciplined and respectful by using disrespectful, unself-disciplined methods.

The one-word method gets results. Are you looking for blame or are you looking for solutions? One word can be very effective communication and an important way to follow through.

Ten Words or Less. Another variation of the less-is-more school of communication is learning to use ten words or less—another exercise for parents in self-discipline and respect.

In the Kenrick family, every time Mom opened her mouth to speak, other family members would walk away, roll their eyes, start reading the paper, or give her a blank stare while they thought about something else. She had trained everyone to tune her out, because they couldn't stand listening to her go on and on about what she thought and felt. Her daughter, Kerry, was the most blatantly disgusted with her verbosity.

When Mom heard about using ten words or less, she knew she was a good candidate. She wanted to break the tune-out pattern so that her family would listen to her and take her seriously.

That night at dinner, she said to her family, "I sure go on and on when I talk to you guys." (Twelve words, but an improvement from before.) No one spoke because they were used to hearing another paragraph or two. Mom just waited quietly.

Kerry said, "Were you talking to us?"

Mom said, "Yes." (One word.)

"What do you want?" asked Kerry, feeling confused and uncomfortable.

Mom answered, "To let you know I'm practicing saying less." (Eight words.)

"About what, Mom?"

"About everything, Kerry, and I'd like your help." (Eight words.)

Now Kerry felt more at home—she got ready for Mom to give her no-one-ever-helps-me lecture. But after tuning out for a few minutes, Kerry realized no one was talking. She was shocked. Kerry said, "Mom, what are you talking about? What kind of help do you want?"

"If I go on and on, tell me to stop." (Ten words.)

Kerry said, "Sure, Mom, whatever you say."

If Mrs. Kenrick keeps working on the skill of using ten words or less, she'll learn to organize her thoughts clearly before she starts talking. She'll also get more attention from her family, as she has already discovered. Most importantly, she'll create opportunities to experience the real joy of conversation with the give and take that comes when people are truly engaged in effective communication.

No Words. Using no words as discussed in the chapter on follow-through is worth repeating as an effective way to communicate. We've all heard that a picture is worth a thousand words. You can communicate very effectively by facial expression or body language.

Steve had promised to mow the lawn before noon on Saturday. At 11:30 A.M., his friends came by and wanted him to go to the lake. He said to his mother, "Can I go to the lake? I promise I'll mow the lawn tomorrow." Mom put her hands on her hips and looked at him with a disbelieving smile on her face.

Steve said, "Come on, Mom. I promise."

Mom just continued to look at him, adding raised eyebrows to the smile.

Steve gave up. He said to his friends, "Come help me mow the lawn. Then I can go."

It takes confidence and the ability to focus on the needs of the situation for nonverbal communication to be effective. Don't bite the bait that your teens will throw at you in the form of disgust or coaxing. Keep long-range parenting in mind and your own issues out of the way. This takes maturity and self-discipline—characteristics we hope our teens will learn someday. What better way to teach than to model?

Communicating in Family Meetings

Family meetings can be used to explore family members' feelings and discover their separate realities. The same skills employed in interpersonal relationships can be used during the meetings.

In the O'Brien family, Dad felt that everyone should sit down together for their meals. He came from a family where everyone ate three meals together. He subconsciously felt that this is how it should be—that this is how a family shows love—and that he feels loved when people sit down and eat with him.

Mom came from a family whose father was gone most of the time working in other towns. Her mother gave up trying to deal with fussy appetites and allowed the kids to fix their own food, except on Sundays when they would have a roast or chicken. So, Mom decided mealtimes didn't matter, except for special occasions. To her, mealtimes mean the freedom to eat what you want, when you want, and how you want. Her definition of a family is where everyone has the freedom to pretty much come and go as they please and do their own thing. But she also had the vague feeling that this was not how it "should" be done. Since it didn't fit her image of the ideal family, she was subconsciously confused about actually liking it the way it was but feeling it should be different.

The two teenagers in this family, David and Cindy, are more interested in doing their own thing than sitting together for family meals.

Dad decided he wanted to discuss his concern about mealtimes at a family meeting. The O'Briens invited their counselor to act as a moderator.

Dad: I feel really disappointed that I can't get more cooperation for something as simple as getting people to have at least two meals together a week. [Dad's tone of voice was more expressive of judgments than of sharing a feeling.]

David [defensively]: Ah, you get more than two meals a week.

Cindy: Yeah, Dad.

David: Okay, you've got it two days a week!

Counselor: How about listening without interrupting and trying to find out how and why people feel the way they feel? David, see if you can find out why this is important to your dad.

David: I don't care why.

Counselor: You don't have to care. This is just an assignment.

David: I *know* why.

Counselor: Let's see if you can give three reasons why.

David: He wants to spend more time with his family.

Dad: Yes.

David: Because he loves us.

Dad: Yes.

David: Because he wants us to have a good meal.

Dad: Yes.

David: Because he wants to talk to us.

Cindy: Because he wants us to learn manners!

Dad: No. I want you to sit with me because I want to know you love me.

Cindy: Oh, you know we love you.

Dad: How would I know that?

Counselor: Find out why that makes your dad feel loved.

Dad: Because when I grew up my family did that three times a day. That's why I got the perception that people who love each other do that.

Counselor: Did you picture that's how it would be in your family?

Dad: Not consciously, but yes.

Counselor: So that gives you a feeling of love?

Dad: Yes.

Counselor: David, what does mealtime mean to you?

David: A time to get fed.

Cindy: I just hate it that when we're done eating we have to just sit there!

Mom: It doesn't matter to me. My mother gave up on mealtime. Everyone fixed what they wanted except on Sundays.

Counselor: Is there any way to work this out so everyone can get their needs met?

David: I have a comment. I think we do eat together a lot.

Mom: So your perception is that you eat with us more than we think you do?

David: Yes.

Counselor: What would be a normal mealtime in your house?

Dad: Just me.

David: He's lying.

Cindy: I get so hungry because I don't eat breakfast or lunch, so I come home and eat something, and he has a cow!

Counselor: If you want your family to eat with you, one of the things you would have to give up is harping about what they eat. Have you guys ever had the system of taking turns picking out what you'll eat? When my kids were growing up, our family had a rule that you eat what you eat and you leave what you don't want to eat. Anyone could leave when they were ready to leave but we at least started together.

Mom: I think that's one of the reasons we don't want to eat with Jim [Dad]. He has so many rules about how it should be—what we should eat, how long we should sit there, and on and on.

Dad: I can see that I've done that. It just didn't occur to me that other people felt so differently about mealtime than I did. I'm willing to stop harping about what you eat, and I won't make you stay at the table when you are through. Under those circumstances, how many times would you be willing to sit down and eat with me?

David: I wouldn't mind starting dinner most of the time together, at least four times a week, if you wouldn't put us down so much.

Cindy: That sounds good to me.

Mom: I'm certainly willing to be more considerate about what's important to you. I just didn't know it was that important. I'd also appreciate it if you wouldn't be so critical when we *don't* sit down together—because other things are more important on some days.

Dad: That sounds reasonable to me. So when will we have our next meal together?

Mom: How about tomorrow night?

David: I'll be there.

Cindy: Me, too.

This family might have continued bickering for years if they hadn't learned to listen to each other's feelings and separate realities. Communication for understanding invites cooperation.

We have discussed several methods of communication between parents and teens. Some seem complicated because we need to dig beneath the surface to find the hidden truth. Others are obviously simple, like using one word or ten words or no words. The whole point is to listen, to understand from our teens' point of view, to validate, and to practice emotional honesty ourselves.

Chapter 15

Time That Counts

During their teenage years when your children spend less and less time with you, it's more important than ever to find ways to connect that really count. Unfortunately, there are several conditions that make quality time especially difficult to achieve: busy schedules, teenagers' preference to be with their friends, and parental time spent lecturing, judging, and punishing their teens.

Mr. Hall decided to try spending quality time with his son, Ted. His relationship with Ted had been damaged by trying to control Ted's experiments with drugs and alcohol. Dad and Mom had grounded Ted, taken his car away, and lectured ad infinitum ("How could you do such a thing? You'll ruin your life forever. What have we done wrong?"). All to no avail. Ted got more defiant and more rebellious, and the father-son relationship deteriorated badly.

Dad took off from work one day, showed up at Ted's school during his lunch period, and got permission to take his son to lunch. Dad had decided that his whole purpose was just to *be* with Ted and enjoy his company. When Ted saw his Dad, he asked belligerently, "What are you doing here?" Dad said, "I just wanted to have lunch with you." During lunch, Dad focused on his purpose, avoiding third-degree questions. He didn't even ask Ted how his day was. Ted was completely surprised and very suspicious all during lunch, waiting to be criticized or lectured. The entire lunch was spent in silence. Dad took Ted back to school and said, "Thanks for having lunch with me. I really enjoyed being with you."

Mr. Hall continued showing up at Ted's school for lunch every Wednesday. It took three weeks for Ted's suspicions to disappear. He then started telling his father small things about his day, and his father did the same. Ted even began asking questions about work and college. Dad was careful to answer his questions without lecturing.

Meanwhile, Dad had stopped trying to control Ted through punishment and withdrawing privileges. During this time, he noticed Ted showed up for dinner more often and sometimes brought his friends over to watch television.

One day, three months into the lunch routine, Mr. Hall got stuck in a meeting that lasted through the lunch period. That night, Ted said, "What happened to you today, Dad? I was expecting you for lunch."

Dad apologized, "I'm sorry, son. I didn't know you were expecting me. I guess the surprise factor has been eliminated and we've established a routine. I'd love to continue the routine, how about you?"

Nonchalantly, Ted said, "Sure."

Dad said, "I'll be sure to leave a message if I ever get tied up again."

Mr. Hall felt pleased and gratified about the effectiveness of spending quality time with his son. He didn't know if it made any difference in Ted's experimentation with drugs and alcohol—but he knew his control efforts hadn't had a positive effect. Now, at least, the damaged relationship was being repaired, and Mr. Hall was grateful that the importance of this had gotten through his thick skull. He felt satisfied that he was providing good memories for his son and letting him know from experience that his father loved him unconditionally.

Hanging Out

We were impressed with Mr. Hall's commitment to spending time that counts with his son. He demonstrated true dedication by being willing to take time off from work and making his son a priority.

We've found it can be equally effective just to "hang out," to be available at certain times when you know your kids will be around. The pitfall is expecting that your teens will overtly notice or care or that they will talk to you. Although it may seem that they don't notice or care, if you're really available your teen will know it on a feeling level. You create a different energy when you're truly available than when you're "there" but preoccupied with other concerns or too busy to be bothered.

In addition, kids can tell when you expect something from them—and with teens, expectations create resistance. We've heard many parents complain, "Well, I'm available but my teenager still won't talk to me." Hanging out means being available to listen *if* they want to talk. It means being a "closet" listener (not making it obvious that you're listening) and listening to who they are rather that focusing on their words.

Five helpful tips will increase your chances of making the time you spend hanging out with your teenager count as quality time. For at least five minutes a day, spend time with your teenager:

1. With your mouth shut (listening)
2. With your sense of humor intact (perspective)
3. With your ears open (listening)
4. With your heart emanating warmth and gratitude (love)
5. With a desire to understand your teen's world (listening)

Mouth Shut

For just five minutes a day, take Archie Bunker's advice and "stifle yourself." There are very good reasons for keeping your mouth shut. When your mouth is open, what are you usually saying? Can you resist the temptation to lecture, moralize, show disappointment, or try to teach lessons?

Can you imagine the impact on your teenager if he or she received five minutes a day without hearing your judgments, your lectures, or your disappointments? Work on *your stuff* another time (preferably with a good friend or therapist). We know you think it's your job to make sure your teenagers avoid all mistakes that could ruin their lives. We know you're especially concerned about the big mistakes like lying, stealing, cheating, sex, and drugs. We know you think it's your job to help them overcome the little mistakes like irresponsibility, inconsiderateness, self-centeredness, and lack of motivation. But remember that indirect methods sometimes have a greater impact than direct, and often misguided, methods.

In the book *Raising Self-Reliant Children in a Self-Indulgent World* (Prima Publishing & Communications,

1988), H. Stephen Glenn and Jane Nelsen list five barriers to good relationships: assuming, rescuing or explaining, directing, expecting, and adultisms ("How come you never? Why can't you ever? How many times do I have to tell you? When will you ever learn?"). Glenn and Nelsen claim that a relationship can improve 100% by simply eliminating these barriers. Where else can you get a 100% return by doing nothing on purpose!

Sense of Humor Intact

How does behavior affect you when you don't have a sense of humor? You lose perspective and objectivity. In this state of mind, it's easy to believe your teenager is a finished product. You catastrophize about all the worst things that could happen. But a sense of humor can help you realize that all your fears and insecurities are *your* stuff.

One way to put the teen years into perspective is to get together with a bunch of adults and tell each other stories about what you did as teenagers that you hoped your parents would never find out. If you "lighten up," we predict your teenagers will be more willing to hang out with you a little more often.

Ears Open

When your ears are not open, you miss knowing who your teenagers really are. You have to be a good listener to get into their world and learn about their reality.

Your ears and mouth cannot be open at the same time. With your mouth shut, you'll be surprised at how much you can hear, although sometimes what you hear is nonverbal, at the feeling level. Kids who are used to lectures, moralizations, judgments, expectations, and disappointments have done a lot of closing down. They've created defensive or offensive strategies for self-protection and self-preservation and may not open up right away.

Keep your ears open without expectations of what or how you will hear. One mother said "I kept my mouth shut and my ears open for a month, and my teenager still wouldn't talk to me." He could probably sense that her silence was full of expectations. Try to just hang out until your teens get the idea that it might be safe to share something—even nonverbally. When you're willing to hang out, you may find your teenagers more willing to hang out around you. Don't underestimate the value of them simply being around absorbing good feelings even when words are not used. Some teenagers never open up and tell all. Drop all agendas and just *be* with your teenagers with your mouth shut and your ears open.

Warmth and Gratitude Emanated

What do you emanate when you don't emanate warmth and gratitude? Self-righteousness and conditional love. But with your mouth shut, your sense of humor intact, and your ears open, your heart will naturally emanate loving warmth and gratitude. You have now reached a state of mind where compassion, wisdom, and gratitude are all you have left! From this state of mind, your teenager will look different to you. You'll also find this state of mind very inviting and nurturing. It creates energy that can be felt by anyone around you. You'll see possibilities and solutions with your teens rather than mistakes and problems. There's a catch, however. You won't see *anything* until you expect *nothing*. Possibilities don't appear until you have gratitude for what already *is*.

Open to Your Teen's World

What are you doing when you are not trying to understand your teen's world? You're probably trying to mold him or her into living up to your expectations—trying to make a petunia into a rose.

A desire to understand the world of your teenager is natural from a loving state of mind. Right and wrong become moot issues. Understanding and respecting separate realities becomes fascinating.

But what about all the lessons I have to teach my teenager?

Spending quality time with your teenager may sound like wonderful advice under normal circumstances, but what if your teenager is involved in drugs, has stolen your car, lied to you, or burned your house down? Think of all the things you're tempted to do, like grounding forever, or imprisoning. Will those methods solve anything? Or will those alternatives increase your stress and widen the gap between you and your teenager. Remember all the mistakes *you* made as a teenager. And if you didn't make any, remember the price you paid by becoming an approval junkie. You might be surprised at how many conflicts resolve themselves when you focus on spending quality time instead of spending time on the problem.

Ideas for Spending Time that Counts

Participants at your teen workshop brainstormed the

following wealth of ideas for spending time that counts with your teenagers.

Listen without judging
Validate their feelings
Stop nagging
Take extended trips
Go on day trips
Do activities planned by them
Tell stories about your own childhood
Watch their television programs
Look at photo albums of when they were little
Hang out with them
Work less, play more, be available
Go to concerts or ball games
Go to a flea market
Work on creative projects (arts and crafts)
Ask for their opinions
Cook together
Make home a comfortable place for their friends
Keep a sense of humor
Remember differences are okay
Avoid overreaction
Work on mutual respect
Invite them to see you at your job
Do activities with them of their choice
Support their activities and interests
Share about yourself if they're interested
Include them in your discussions
Work on joint problem solving

Schedule regular family meetings
Ask for their help
Give choices
Practice role reversal
Allow them to make their own mistakes
Show interest in their world
Backpack together
Take care of self and own issues
Go to a retreat together
Learn what's normal; don't take it personally
Treat them to activities they enjoy but can't afford
Take off time from work to be with teen
Eat together
Play games together
Spend special time alone with each child
Plan an event together
Plan vacations ("What do you want to do?")
Have faith
Have trust

We suggest you refer to this list often. It may inspire you to spend time that counts with your teenagers in ways you haven't thought of or that get lost in the shuffle of busy lives. End every family meeting by planning at least one family activity from this list or from a list that comes out of your own family brainstorming.

Short periods (even minutes) of quality time a day, a week, or even a month, can do wonders to improve our relationships with our teens. Focusing on spending quality time with our teens will help us remember to get into their world, see them with perspective, and bring back the joy of being the parents of teens.

SECTION 3

Normal and Dysfunctional Teen Behavior

▼

Chapter

16

Your Teen and Drugs

Fear of drug abuse is the number-one problem plaguing parents of teens today. Everyone knows drugs are dangerous. Everyone has heard the stories of ruined teenage lives and teenage deaths, from drug overdoses or drug- and alcohol-related accidents. Because of fear, parents tend to panic, to catastrophize, to try to control, and to use other disrespectful methods that rob their children of learning life skills and developing the confidence they need to be successful on their own. In efforts to control, parents punish through restrictions and withdrawal of privileges.

Advice from many well-meaning groups does not help. A lot of the current literature suggests that parents should know what is going on in their teens lives at all times. Parents are told to monitor their teens' friendships, supervise their relationships, communicate with other parents, supervise teen parties, and refuse to let teens go anywhere that they might encounter drugs. Parents are told that these methods will protect their kids from using or abusing drugs.

Some experts go even further, suggesting parents purchase their own home drug-testing kits, search their teens' rooms regularly, and do a breath test when teens come home from parties.

As we saw in Chapter Eight on control and punishment, such methods will make the situation worse, by increasing rebellion and giving our children messages that lower their confidence and rob them of developing their capabilities.

In this chapter, we offer a realistic approach to dealing with the drug problem (we include alcohol in our definition of drugs).

Most parental efforts we've seen have been based on fear and external control. But in this book, we've demonstrated over and over that external control doesn't work with teenagers—and usually leads to rebellion or approval junkies. The more we try to make our kids do what we want, the greater the risk of accidentally pushing them towards the things we most want them to avoid.

Often, teenagers themselves offer good advice on what their parents can do to help teens make wise decisions on issues like drug use. But many parents discount such advice, saying disrespectfully, "They don't know what's best for them." This simply isn't true. Humans of all ages have an infinite capacity to do what is best for themselves when given the freedom of choice, the safety of choice, and faith to learn from their own mistakes. It's true they will make mistakes while figuring things out—just like adults still do. Teens have to learn their own limits—and they eventually will, with or without our help. But while our kids are still living at home, we have the opportunity to influence them. We will lose that opportunity by using any of the controlling methods discussed earlier. Because the risks can be so great and the mistakes so frightening, it's more important than ever to look at alternatives to external control, finding ways to increase our influence instead.

In this chapter, we'll learn how to support our teens to do what is in their own best interest and for their own good. We'll learn how to look at the ways we might be inviting our kids to feel bad or ways we might be treating them like second-class citizens. We'll focus on ways to continue creating openness, honesty, and room for our teens to think for themselves.

We'll answer questions like, "How do I know if my kids are using drugs? What should I do if I think they are? What can I do to prevent my kids from becoming drug addicts?" And we'll talk about what to do if you realize your teen is already addicted to drugs.

Increasing Your Chances of Preventing Drug Abuse

The best thing that we can do to help our kids make intelligent decisions about drugs is to empower them in all the ways we've been suggesting in this book. When our teens have opportunities to contribute, when they feel listened to and taken seriously, and when we provide opportunities for them to learn skills and experience success, they are less likely to abuse drugs. We need to ask for their thoughts and feelings about drugs and have faith in their innate ability to do what is best for themselves.

We are amazed at the number of parents who object to having faith in the ability of their children to do what is best for them. They argue, "They don't have enough experience, enough judgment, or enough sense of the long-range consequences to know what is best for them." But isn't this all the more reason not to escalate rebellion by being overcontrolling? If we provide our children with opportunities to learn from their mistakes without feeling they are bad or a failure, they can gain experience, judgment, and an understanding of long-range consequences. When young people do not feel they have the courage and capability to solve life's challenges they often turn to drugs instead. Drugs provide a protection from the anxiety and fear of failure for kids who have not learned to glean insights and skills from life experiences. Overprotecting and overcontrolling parents often overestimate the danger inherent in most activities. We do not lower the risks inherent in life by protecting a child. Overprotection and overcontrol actually increase the chances of an unsuccessful passage through childhood.

We can't overemphasize the importance of allowing young people to develop competence to respond to challenges and believe in themselves. Our kids will not have faith in themselves if we do not have faith in them. Having faith does not mean expecting perfection. It means knowing they can learn from whatever experiences they have.

As parents, we would prefer that our kids never use any drugs at all. We're also realistic enough to know that many of them will. Since that is the state of the real world today, we want to be more careful than ever to help our kids learn the kinds of attitudes and skills that will keep them from abuse, even if they choose to experiment with or use drugs occasionally.

Warning Signs for Potential Drug Abuse

The attitude of a person who abuses drugs or is chemically dependent is very different from the attitude of a person who does not abuse chemicals.

The following checklist can help us determine if

our teen's attitude is healthy or potentially dysfunctional. If our teen's self-talk is fixed on these thoughts, drug abuse or some other dysfunctional behavior could be the outcome.

— I'm worthless, a nobody.

— Feeling good now is more important than anything else.

— It's everybody else's fault.

— Nobody cares and neither do I.

— I have to be perfect or I may as well give up.

— I'll show them who's boss.

— I've been hurt, so I'll hurt back, keep others at a distance, or cover up the pain.

— I must avoid responsibility at all cost because I can't do it right anyway.

It's normal to have some of these thoughts occasionally and still not be a drug abuser. However, a pattern of this kind of thinking invites the desire to numb feelings in one way or another—and drugs are often the choice.

People who are chemically dependent usually display other characteristics, such as an inability to express feelings of almost constant pain, shame, fear, and guilt; an ability to disassociate or leave one's body; a tendency to look for an external rather than an internal "feel good"; and a willingness to continue doing what doesn't work over and over and over. When we look at the family, we can understand how these characteristics develop.

Family Rules That Invite Chemical Dependency

One of the strongest themes discussed in the current drug-abuse literature is the unspoken rules in homes where someone is chemically dependent. These rules are: don't think, don't talk, don't feel. Parents create these rules when they attempt to control their teens' feelings, actions, and thoughts out of fear of what might happen if they don't—and sometimes out of fear of dealing with their own fears. Teens won't feel encouraged to express their thoughts and feelings when they know they won't be listened to, taken seriously, and respected—or when they know their parents will be disappointed in them.

Insisting that our teens not think, talk, or feel invites them to find external ways to cope with their thoughts and feelings. Unless we want to supervise our teens twenty-four hours a day, we're fooling ourselves in believing part-time control accomplishes anything more than encouraging them to secretly do what they want when we're not around—and to make their choices without the skills we can teach when we let go of control and give them the opportunity to live their own lives. It's most important that our teens be able to think for themselves and attain the skills to make good decisions about using drugs during this period of their lives, when peer influence is strong and drugs readily available.

Ten Suggestions for Dealing with Teens and Drugs

Given all this information about drug use, we're still left with the question, "What can we do?" As much as we may hate to admit it, in today's society we can't stop our teens from using drugs. What we *can do* is follow the ten suggestions below to decrease their chances of becoming drug abusers. We wish we could offer a simple solution, but the drug problems of our society are too complex. Many parents are involved in putting on drug-free dances, safe parties, safe-ride programs, and the just-say-no program. Even though it's unrealistic to think that these activities by themselves can tackle the drug problem, all efforts are important—and these programs *have* made a difference.

We don't know of any perfect solutions; however, any combination of the ten suggestions below will improve our teens' chances of dealing effectively with drugs.

1. Get and give information.
2. Share your values.
3. Give teens a safe space to learn from their mistakes.
4. Foster emotional honesty, both yours and theirs.
5. Use long-range parenting to develop internal control.
6. Don't remove or minimize consequences of your teen.
7. Allow for differences. You and your teens are not going to see things the same way.
8. Show love and unconditional acceptance for your teens; let them know they're special.
9. Know when to get help.
10. Have faith.

Empowering our teens to help them become adults who like themselves and have internal controls is a process that takes years. Practicing the ten suggestions above will help us do that job. We'll learn more about each suggestion in the remainder of this chapter.

Get and Give Information

We agree with many people in the field of drug-abuse prevention that we need to give our kids information on drugs beginning in kindergarten or even earlier. We must not leave this responsibility to the schools alone. As parents, we need to learn all we can about drug abuse so we can become sources of information for our kids. Bookstores are filled with books about chemical addiction and what it's like to grow up in a family in which someone is or was chemically dependent. We need to read books on co-dependency to become aware of how we may be contributing to the problem through enabling behaviors.

Rather than repeating the information found in these books, we've referenced the books in our bibliography. But we're including information on why kids use drugs, the continuum of drug abuse, and the progressive nature of chemical dependency because such information is more difficult to find.

Why Kids Use Drugs

Since drugs are readily accessible to our teens, they are confronted on a daily basis with the necessity of making choices regarding drugs. We need to be aware of the many reasons that motivate the choice to use drugs. Teens use drugs to feel good, to feel different, to avoid feeling at all; to fit in, to find excitement, to rebel; to relax, to solve interpersonal problems, to overcome shyness; to "be cool," to experiment, and to take risks. For some teens, using drugs is a sign that they are now "grown up." Since it's typical for teens to feel omnipotent, many are convinced that drugs can't hurt them. In addition, we cannot underestimate the impact of television. Our kids have grown up in a drug-culture mentality that emphasizes speedy relief and short-term "feel goods."

One teen told us he wished parents would tell their kids that drugs are dangerous, but that they can be fun if you don't overdo them (and the opposite of fun if you *do* overdo them). He said he would want his parents to tell him how they feel about drugs and then leave it up to him to work out whether to use them or not. We know very few parents who would feel comfortable giving this kind of information to their teens, but it's the kind they could hear and use to help them make decisions.

Sharing What You Know

Many kids think their parents don't know what they're talking about when it comes to drugs. Sometimes, that's because parents *don't* know what they're talking about! Other times, it's because parents feel afraid or embarrassed to share honestly their own personal experiences or problems with drugs. They're afraid this may encourage their kids to go out and do what they did—but the result is usually the opposite. Kids are relieved to find that their parents are human and that perhaps they really understand. It invites much more open communication between parent and child. Kids will listen more closely to someone who has had problems and has overcome them if that person shares without lecturing or judging.

When it comes to giving information to our teens, we need to remember that they won't want to talk to us unless they have a guarantee that we won't be disappointed or try to control their lives—and that we will still love them and won't punish them if we find out what's really going on. We need to look at the difference between what happens when we come from fear, anger, and overprotection, and what happens when we come from love, concern, and an interest in sharing honest feelings and information with examples from our own lives.

A good opening for sharing information is to find out what it means to our teens to be doing what they are doing. We can help them clarify their thoughts and feelings for themselves if necessary by resisting our temptation to lecture and instead using the communication skills we learned in Chapter Fourteen. An understanding of the continuum of use is especially helpful for clarification of whether or not someone has a drug use problem. Both parents and teens can benefit from such an understanding and can find it not only helpful but a huge relief.

The Continuum of Use

There are different kinds of drug use. People without information think of drug abuse as the only alternative to abstinence. The continuum of drug use moves from abstinence at one end to chemical dependency at the other, with experimentation, social use, regular use, and problem use in between.

- Chemical dependency
- Problem use
- Regular use
- Social use
- Experimental use
- Abstinence

Abstinence. Abstinence is a choice that may be made for many different reasons, including fear, religion, preference, recovery, and love of our body. This is the choice that most parents would prefer for their teens. It's not necessarily the choice that many teens prefer for themselves.

Experimental Use. Experimental use means: "I heard about it. I want to try it out. I want to know what it feels like. A bunch of us are going to get together and find out what happens when we get drunk, or what happens when we take pills." A teen experimenting may try a drug once and never again. But since there are some experimental things our teens could try that could kill them, experimentation can be real scary for parents. (With this argument, it might follow that we should never walk across the street because it could kill us!) Kids who party have often seen what happens when someone has a "bad trip"; these kids have their own limits to what they feel safe trying. And teens *can* be careful on their own; when we talk with them, we find they have a variety of ways to prevent taking something someone "slips" them just to be "funny."

Social Use. Some of our teens, just like some of us, use drugs socially. Many adults never drink unless they go to a party, or never buy wine unless having someone over for dinner. The same is true for many teens. Drinking or using other drugs may be a way of spending time with friends on the weekend. Drugs are strictly for social use.

Regular Use. Another kind of use is daily or regular. Regular use can have a lot of different faces, but it is use that has become ritualized. For instance, some adults have wine with dinner everyday or whenever they go to a restaurant. For some teens, regular use means getting stoned everyday or drinking every time they go out. As soon as anyone begins to use drugs regularly they've progressed further on the drug-use continuum. Although many who use drugs this way will never become chemically dependent, others will. By creating a habit and building tolerance to a drug by regular use, we are committing ourselves to some patterns that can be destructive down the road. Our teens need to know that.

An important characteristic of regular use (and a good way to tell whether you've become a regular user) is that you must have continual access to a supply of the drug. If you're an experimental or social user you won't notice a lack of supply.

Problem Use. Problem use has been reached when people use drugs so much that they begin having problems managing their life. They have problems with school, family, and work. With teens especially, the more they use, the less they develop their skills to meet challenges and develop competence. They use chemicals to repress their feelings instead of expressing them. They may even cause serious physical damage to themselves from prolonged use.

Somewhere between problem use and chemical dependency there is a line that is different for every person. Some people will never cross the line, others will. Some people become chemically dependent without going through all phases of the continuum. We need to know when our teens are at the chemically dependent end of the continuum.

Chemical Dependency. There are different definitions of chemical dependency. Some of the most common follow.

1. When use of chemicals creates problems for an individual, and he or she continues to use anyway.
2. When a person is afraid to talk about his or her chemical use, is hiding it, or is defensive when others bring up the subject.
3. When a person uses drugs to achieve a feeling of normal well-being.
4. When the chemical controls the person rather than the person controlling the chemical.
5. When a person craves alcohol or drugs for no good reason.
6. When a person is in love with a chemical and their primary relationship is with his or her drug of choice.

It is possible to use chemicals only once and become chemically dependent but that is extremely rare. It is also possible that someone could progress down the continuum without ever becoming chemically dependent. They might go from abstinence to social drinking and remain at that level throughout their lives. As we have already discussed, however, the risk factor increases as tolerance increases. Also, millions of people in recovery have gone from chemical dependency back to abstinence. The important point is to know that all drug use is not the same. Many teens fall into the experimental or social category, never going beyond that point, yet we panic and act as though any teen who uses any chemical will become chemically dependent.

We might offer to share information about the drug-use continuum with our teen by saying, "I don't think you have certain information. I'd feel better if you knew certain things so you could make up your own mind based on solid knowledge. I'd like to learn about this information with you or share it with you [if the parent has drug specific information to share]."

When our teens understand the continuum of drug use, they can evaluate their position for themselves. Understanding the progressive nature of chemical dependency can also help them beware of the dangers of drug use.

The Progressive Nature of Chemical Dependency. Many of us, including our teens, have the notion that people aren't chemically dependent unless they're falling down drunk, passing out, throwing up, or swaying down the street. Because of this misunderstanding, many teens don't realize they may already be in the early stages of chemical dependency. Some of the signs are subtle, such as occasional relief drinking, increase in tolerance, the onset of memory blackouts, and an urgency to use.

If a person continues to use at this point (once in the early stages of chemical dependency), what will happen is predictable and progressive. Some of the next symptoms include remorse, resolutions to quit everyday without success, constant thinking and planning for use, neglect of food, and decrease in tolerance.

▼ *Your kids can get off the down elevator.*

Chemical dependency is like being on an elevator going down. People don't need to hit bottom before getting off—they can get off on any floor. With very few exceptions, however, once a person is chemically dependent, the only choice for breaking the cycle is abstinence along with help (treatment, therapy, group help like Alcoholics Anonymous).

Even if we can't stop our kids from abusing drugs, we can give them chances to try again and learn from their mistakes by supporting them to get into treatment. Getting help through intervention is discussed in Chapter Seventeen.

Share Your Values

The second suggestion for dealing with teens and drugs is to share our values. Gut-level honesty is essential. Some of us may have problems with our teens using chemicals but are afraid to tell them for fear it will make them worse. However, sharing our values is not the same as trying to control what our teens do. It simply means being honest with them about what we believe without imposing our beliefs on them. It's okay to tell our kids that we don't approve of the use of chemicals and that we don't want them to use.

The interesting thing about values is that they are seldom learned by listening to what people say. They are much more apt to become internalized by listening to what people do. If both our words and our actions match, our kids will often adopt many of our values at some point in their lives, but only if the decision is theirs without pressure from us.

▼ *Do what makes sense under the circumstances.*

Some people believe *no one* should use chemicals, and especially not kids. These people feel that the safe-ride program gives adult approval to kids for the use of chemicals. Fortunately, there are many parents and other adults who have approached drug use more realistically. They might say, "I don't like it that my kids drink, I wish they'd never drink, and I'm sorry that they do. But . . . my kids *do* drink. One thing *I* can do about it is to find a way to get them home without killing themselves or someone else (and living the rest of their lives in guilt and shame). If I could change it so they'd never drink, I would. But the world is the world, and reality is reality. And me telling them not to drink is not going to stop them from drinking but I can provide a safe ride."

Give Teens a Safe Space to Learn from Their Mistakes

Sometimes we can improve a situation simply by stopping behavior of ours that invites problems. Monitoring, searching rooms, and refusing to let our kids go out are just a few of the things we can stop doing because they aren't working. Checking up on our kids and insisting we have to approve of their friends could also be added to the list.

Teens will make many mistakes as they grow up, and the area of drug use is no exception. They need the space to work out on their own how they feel about using drugs. For many parents, this is very scary; they operate under the illusion that they can stop their kids from using drugs by grounding, taking away the car, forbidding them to go to parties, or not giving them any money, thinking these actions will prevent them from being able to afford drugs.

We have heard parents object, "But my daughter doesn't make good choices! Am I supposed to stand by while she hurts herself?" We are not saying you should just stand by and do nothing. Rather, we're suggesting you do the things we have been advocating in this book that invite closeness rather than distance. One thing is to be honest about what you observe in a nonthreatening way. "I notice that you're using a lot of alcohol (or pot, or whatever). This is how I feel about it, and this is why I feel that way. It will be interesting to see if any of this information is useful to you. I'm telling you all this because I think what you're doing could hurt you, and I love you."

Mr. Addison told his teenage son, "I'm concerned about your drinking. I notice that you drink a lot and drink fast. Your grandfather is an alcoholic, and research has shown that kids who have one or more relative who is chemically dependent have an increased risk in becoming chemically dependent themselves. I hope you'll think about what I'm saying. I love you, and I wouldn't want you to go through the pain of addiction."

Mrs. Goodwin told her teenagers, "I know there will be times you may decide to use drugs. It's not okay with me to have drugs in our house or at any parties here. I realize that may create some problems for you, but I'm happy to help in any way to plan parties with you that can be fun without drugs. If you do decide to use drugs I want you to know that even though I prefer that you don't, I love you and I'm here to listen and not judge you if you'd like my help or want to talk to me about it."

Open or Hidden Behavior

When we don't invite our teens to be open with us, either by our words or actions, we invite them to go underground.

A group of teens was asked whether they thought it was helpful or effective for parents to sign agreements with other parents about providing safe parties. The kids looked completely confused—they wanted to know what safe parties were. When they were told that a parent agrees to be home if there's a party and that there will be no alcohol served, the kids laughed and said,

"Oh, that's not a party. That's a get-together. A party is a place where there are no parents."

Mrs. Jensen was driving home with her daughter and her daughter's friend. The friend asked the daughter why she was telling her mother about parties and other teenage activities. She replied, "Oh, my mom is cool, you can tell her anything."

Her friend asked, "But aren't you going to get into trouble?"

"Oh no, we've worked all that out. I don't get into trouble. She doesn't like it, but I can talk to her about it."

The friend was astounded. "You know, I'm listening to you talk to your mother, and I'm sitting here trying to figure out how I'm going to 'dog' my mother."

Mrs. Jensen asked "What does that mean, 'dog' your mother? I've never heard it before."

He said, "I'm trying to figure out what lie to tell my mother when she calls tonight, because she wants me to stay home, but I'm going to go to a party. She's out of town, and I don't want her to worry about me and I don't want her to be upset . . . but I'm not going to do what she wants. So I have to use all my energy to figure out how I'm going to 'dog' her."

Our kids will learn for themselves with or without our help. How much nicer to do the things that increase the possibility of our influence rather than inviting them to "dog" us.

Foster Emotional Honesty

Chapter Fourteen on communications is filled with information on emotional honesty. It would be useful to refer to that chapter and review heart- and gut-level communications.

Our teens' responses to us give us the best indicator we have of whether we are being emotionally honest. An activity from our workshop on empowering teens demonstrated this to the participants. We had people line up across the room from each other. One group played teenagers, using as many drug words they could think of while they walked toward the other group, who played parents.

The parents' instructions were to take an attitude of control and to tell themselves, "I'm the parent, so they should respect me. I'm the parent, so they should do what I say." In this simulation of parent-child communications, the parents lectured, ordered, yelled, and threatened as the teens got closer to them. When the parents were close enough, they made remarks such as, "You will not use drugs. I'll search your room. You'll be grounded. I'll take away your allowance."

After experiencing this interaction for a few minutes, the group was asked to share their feelings. Those who played the teenagers said they were feeling excited and challenged, and that they would think about sneakier ways of doing whatever their parents were saying not to do. They also felt that their parents didn't understand and were stupid.

The parents were feeling upset, stressed, angry, afraid, irritated, and panicky. Their thoughts were, "How am I ever going to be vigilant enough? How am I ever going to stop this kid? I have to stop her. I have to control him. How did I go wrong? What will people think?" During the discussion, they were able to see that control is not the road to emotional honesty but rather the road to frustration and despair.

Next, the parents were asked to turn their backs on the approaching teens to simulate denial. They were to stick their heads in the sand, pretending the problem didn't exist. This time, the teens felt panic-stricken, abandoned, unloved, uncared for, rejected, and scared; they wanted to run away from home. During the discussion, they said they preferred control to neglect.

Those who played the parents said they felt irresponsible (some felt relieved) and scared. For most of them, it was so uncomfortable they wanted to run away and make the denial complete. Again, it's often easier for us to ignore or to hide from a problem than to be emotionally honest. But denial doesn't make the problem go away, and it clearly doesn't help our kids deal effectively with their drug issues.

Finally, we directed the role-play to simulate an atmosphere where emotional honesty could take place. When the teens walked toward the parents saying drug words, the parents put their arms around the teens' shoulders and began walking in stride with them, saying, "Listen, I'm not into this. I don't really know much about it, and I don't really like it. I don't think I approve of it. But I want to know what it's like for you. I want you to tell me more about it. I want you to help me understand what it means to you."

Now, there was contact without control. The parents were curious to learn about and understand their kids' thoughts and feelings. They were also letting their kids know how it was for them. By making contact in this loving, nonjudgmental way, parents were beginning a relationship with their teens rather than ending one.

The parents felt relieved. The stress was gone. They felt curious, interested, nervous, uncomfortable—but close to their teens, part of their lives. They were thinking, "This is very scary, because I'm not sure I know how to handle this, but I'm glad I'm here."

The teens were thinking, "I'm going to be in trouble. I'm really not sure that what I'm doing is okay. I'm feeling very uncomfortable because my parents aren't giving me a hard time. When I think about my behavior, I feel bad about what I'm doing to myself." All the things parents want their kids to feel and think happened when they *walked in stride*.

The parents who participated in this activity invited closeness and emotional honesty. Relating to our teens in this way takes awareness, skill, and practice. Fear and lack of practice might tempt us to slip into our old, controlling or neglectful behavior, but faith in ourselves and our kids plus practice can help us make emotional honesty part of our lives.

Use Long-range Parenting

We have referred to long-range parenting throughout this book as the kind of parenting that helps our children learn the skills and attitudes that will serve them throughout their lives. Again, long-range parenting is a matter of awareness, skills, and practice. Once we are aware of the importance of long-range parenting and have learned the necessary skills, it's possible to make changes. We simply need courage to practice taking small steps one at a time. Each small step increases our courage to learn and grow more. We will make mistakes —just as our teenagers will make mistakes. We can use these mistakes to learn and to serve as gentle reminders to try again.

▾ *Enabling and co-dependency is short-range parenting.*

Many people reading this book will be familiar with the terms *enabler* and *co-dependent*—a person who gets in between another person and his or her life experience by rescuing or trying to control. A co-dependent or enabler is one who actually contributes to the problems experienced by his or her teen by rescuing instead of teaching life skills. Long-range parents do not control or abandon their teens. They empower their teens by teaching life skills, by having faith in the basic capabilities of their teens to learn from mistakes, and by giving unconditional love.

Empowering Versus Enabling

Enabling is a short-term parenting skill. The short-term benefits are a feeling of being loving and helpful. What is really going on rescuing, overprotecting, controlling, or in any way taking responsibility for the life of someone else. Although the enabling parent sometimes gets the satisfaction of being appreciated by the child whom they have rescued, that appreciation is temporary, because the child soon demands more and more and is verbally abusive when all his or her demands are not met.

Empowering is a long-term parenting skill because it allows children to learn the life skills that serve them throughout their lives in an atmosphere of love and support, which gives them a sense of self-confidence, self-esteem, and power over their own lives. Empowering is treating teens as adults-in-training.

Tim Jones is twenty-one years old and has been heavily into cocaine and marijuana. He went to a treatment center and did well for awhile. Then he started using drugs again. His mother enabled for quite awhile before she finally got the courage to tell Tim he could no longer live at home as long as he chose to abuse drugs. Tim left, vowing to never, ever, forgive his mother. One month later Tim wanted to come home and sleep on the couch for "just a few days" until he could find another place to live. Mom knows Tim is conning and manipulating but finds it very difficult to refuse such a reasonable request—for just a few days—

even though she knows she will be manipulated into more than just a few days. Mom has also learned enough about being a co-dependent and enabler to know she is not helping Tim by giving in to his manipulations. It is still hard for her to say no.

During an empowering teens workshop, Mrs. Jones was asked to role-play her son. Participants on one side of the room were asked to be enablers, and those on the other side were asked to be empowerers.

Mrs. Jones: Well I know who I am going to go to.

Mrs. Jones as Tim, going to the enablers: Hey guys, can I sleep on the couch tonight? I will be moving into an apartment real soon.

Enabler: Sure honey, I'll get your favorite pillow for you.

Mrs. Jones: I'm not that bad.

Empowerer: Sounds like you are making progress. Sounds like you have plans to find an apartment.

Mrs. Jones as Tim: Yes, I'm doing real good. I'm going to stay at my job, and as soon as I find a place I will move into an apartment. But, I've been staying with a friend and I'm getting tired of staying on his couch. Can I sleep on your couch?

Empowerer: Have you started a recovery program yet?

Mrs. Jones as Tim: Oh, you are so screwed up about that. I don't need a recovery program. Can I stay on your couch for just a couple of nights?

Enabler: Okay, but just for a few nights.

Empowerer: I love you Tim, but until you are back into a recovery program, you cannot stay here.

Tim: You mean I can't even sleep on your couch?

Empowerer: That's right.

Tim: Why not? I can't believe that! If you don't let

me stay here you can just write me out of your life forever.

Empowerer: I'm really glad you are getting it together. You are welcome here when you are in recovery, Tim. Do you miss staying at home?

Tim: Sure I miss it. It is nice being able to go to the refrigerator whenever I want, and to know someone cares. I don't miss you telling me what to do all the time, but I miss having a place where I'm safe.

Empowerer: I've really missed you.

Tim: You've missed me?

Empowerer: Yes. I wish so much that you would get into recovery so you could come back.

Facilitator: What are you learning?

Mrs. Jones: As Tim I'm aware that I can really manipulate the enablers. With the empowerers I really do feel empowered. It is scary, but the funny thing is that I don't feel good about myself when I can manipulate. Deep down I know it is not helpful for me. As myself, I'm learning that it always sounds so simple and so clean to just say no, but I'm so scared to do it. (Mrs. Jones started to cry.)

Facilitator: Can you talk about feeling scared? Can you talk about what is behind the tears?

Mrs. Jones: Behind the tears is what the one person said about, "I really do miss you." I get so mixed up in how to give my son loving messages from my heart without getting into enabling. When I heard, "I miss you and wish you would get into recovery," that is what I want. I want him to know that I love him without enabling.

Facilitator: Would someone volunteer to be Tim, so Mrs. Jones can practice this?

Volunteer as Tim: You really do miss me?

Mrs. Jones (through tears): I can't tell you how much I miss you. And I can't tell you how hard this is for me to do, but you really cannot stay here anymore until you get into recovery, if you ever decide to. I can't control you. I can't make you do that, but I worry about you every night—and you can't stay here.

Tim: You really do love me, don't you?

Mrs. Jones: I really do love you, and I can't support you in the lifestyle you are choosing anymore.

Tim: Maybe I will get into a recovery program.

Mrs. Jones: Let me know when you are ready.

Facilitator: What did you learn?

Mrs. Jones: That I can be loving and firm. I have always been loving and enabling or firm and angry. It feels so different to be honest with my love and firm at the same time. I also learned how different it feels to have tears from my heart. I have used tears in the past to produce guilt. Yuck. Tears from love feel clean. Tears used to produce guilt feel so yucky. That's a big one for me.

Person playing Tim: I could feel that your tears were from love. That and your firm stand did make me feel empowered, that maybe I could do something different. Your love gave me the courage to look at myself. There was no way I could get into my con game and manipulation in the face of such love and such firmness.

Facilitator: This is why it is hard for us to be empowerers. Look at the feeling. Look at the pain. Look at the struggle. Look at the issues that we all deal with to empower our teenagers. Mrs. Jones is dealing with a drug addiction. Some of us might be dealing with a thirteen-year-old wanting birth control pills, some of us are dealing with letting our kid go to the mall alone. It's very hard to empower in the places that are the toughest for us to let go.

If we want to make it easy on ourselves we can punish. This is short, sweet, to the point—You're grounded. We don't have to think, just attack in anger. We can bring in reward and try to bribe and manipulate and get into a power struggle. We can make it look like we are doing "good" while we are doing "bad." Or we can go for courage and empower. This takes guts.

Participant: As a mom, I want to show love. If my child came and wanted to spend the night, I would think I was showing love by letting him spend the night. But then I have to stop and think about what I am doing. Am I really showing love? What Mrs. Jones just did by saying, "I can't because I love you so much," was so powerful. That was really showing love.

▾ *Decide what you will do.*

Another long-range parenting skill worth reviewing is deciding what we will do about certain issues of importance to us. We need to be honest with our kids about our feelings and our wants—even though we recognize these may not seem reasonable or fair to our teens.

Mr. Daniels, father of a fourteen-year-old boy, was very clear with his son about having parties at their house. "I know you kids use alcohol and drugs at parties, and I know you don't have the same values I have; but I don't want you having a party here with people using marijuana or alcohol. If I see anyone using them, I'll ask them to go home. If that will embarrass you, you need to work it out to have a party without drugs, or you can boot out your friends who are using before I boot them out. I know you feel differently about it, and I understand that. I know you think I'm old-fashioned, but that's how I plan to handle it in this house. I'm concerned and scared about the possible short- and long-range effects of teens using drugs, and, although I know I can't stop you from using, I prefer that it doesn't happen in my home."

When we make a strong statement like the one Mr. Daniels made, it's important that our actions match our words and that our attitude is firm, kind, and nonpunitive. The motivation is caring for ourselves rather than controlling our kids.

▾ *You can get involved in drug-free activities.*

Getting involved in the many drug-free programs, like safe rides, is another way of deciding what *we* will do rather than what we will try to make our kids do.

Being involved in drug-free activities for teens gives many of us a sense that we're being helpful and doing something about potential problems. Since teens often listen to other people when they won't listen to their parents, it's possible that in such a program we might be helping someone else's kid, while someone else might reach ours.

▾ *Share your own experiences.*

Another part of long-range parenting is being honest about our own experiences. Most kids think we grew up perfect. Many have said, "I wish my parents would tell me stories about the affairs they had, the drinking they did, the drugs they used, the experimenting they did. It would help me, because sometimes I think I'm the only person who does those things and that I'm bad because of that." It really helps teens to find out that their parents have done those things, too; otherwise, when teens see their parents as perfect, they can feel a lot of shame for not being as good as their parents.

▾ *Example is the best teacher.*

We need to take a look at the messages we give kids about pills. We can open our medicine cabinets and ask,

"What is the message here?" Do we rush to get a pill to make the pain better everytime our kids get hurt? How often do we take pain-killers and other prescription drugs? How do we deal with pain? Are we always trying to fix pain, or do we allow pain to happen? Taking a look at the messages that we give about drugs in our own homes is another way to improve our long-range parenting skills by deciding what we will do.

Television is often the "drug of choice" in many of our homes. Sitting for hours in front of TV and allowing our kids to do the same allows our minds to get used to and to tolerate an altered state. Altered states are part of the appeal of drugs, and, without realizing, we have programed our kids to feel comfortable in such a space for years and years by letting them watch too much TV.

There is a wonderful story about Gandhi. A mother came to him and said, "Please tell my child to stop eating sugar." Gandhi said, "Would you come back in three days?" The mother came back in three days with her child, and Gandhi said to the child, "Stop eating sugar." The mother asked, "Why did you have to wait three days to tell him that?" Gandhi said, "Well, I had to stop myself before I could tell him to stop."

Don't Remove or Minimize Consequences

It is common practice among many parents to vacillate between trying to control and trying to rescue their children. Neither tactic empowers teenagers.

When Mrs. Carter realized the mistake of her controlling and rescuing behaviors, she decided to give them up. She sat down with her son and said, "Cal, I want to stop trying to control what you do, but I also plan to stop rescuing you when you get into trouble. I have faith in you to make decisions for yourself, to learn from your mistakes, and to figure out how to solve problems that come to you or that you create. Specifically, this means that I'll no longer write excuses for you if you choose to cut classes. It also means I won't badger you about doing your homework, and I won't type your papers for you at the last minute." Cal didn't know whether to be happy that his mother was going to stop trying to control him or sad that she would no longer rescue him.

The consequences of cutting classes or not doing homework are minor compared to those for drunk driving or stealing. It's hard for parents to avoid rescuing their kids when they've been put in juvenile hall. But it will be easier if we remember that choosing not to rescue does not mean abandoning our kids. It means being very loving and supportive while saying to a child who has been hauled off to juvenile hall, "I'll bet this has been a terrible experience for you. I'm so sorry you have to go through this. If you want my help in trying to figure out how you can prevent this from happening again, I'll be glad to talk with you about it. But if you want to figure things out for yourself, I'll respect that, too."

An arm around the shoulders is a good way to show empathy and support without controlling or rescuing.

Allow for Differences

It is highly unlikely that our kids will have the same thoughts and feelings about drugs that we have. First, adolescence is the age of rebellion. Second, their world is quite different from the one in which we were raised.

Third, they form their own conclusions about everything anyway. It is not what happens to us that determines our personality, but the decisions we make about what happens to us.

Even in the same family there will be as many different decisions about drugs as there are kids in the family. Some kids will accept the family values and some will rebel against them. Some kids will be different just to avoid being like one of their siblings. Others will copy a sibling they admire or want to be closer to. There are many factors that promote the differences that make each person unique. We can't expect our kids to be just like us or take it personally when they are not. And it certainly isn't our fault if our kids decide to make decisions that aren't healthy for them.

Show Love and Unconditional Acceptance

A teen reported: "My mother used to give me a hard time about taking my friends for rides and buying gas for the car. She would tell me the only reason my friends liked me was because I had a car. She used to say, 'You wouldn't have any friends if you didn't have a car. They don't really like you. They are just calling to take advantage of you so you will drive them to the game.' The more Mom did that, the more it would put me in a bind, because the most important thing in my life was my friends. But what if Mom was right? I had to either give up my friends to please Mom and keep them from taking advantage of me, or I had to be a sneak so I wouldn't get in trouble with Mom."

We can see that Mom, concerned that people might be taking advantage of her daughter, probably only wanted to be helpful. But because she didn't get into her daughter's world to see the effect of her remarks, she didn't realize she was being more hurtful than helpful. It would have been more encouraging for this teen if Mom had kept her ideas to herself and had been able to accept her daughter, even though she felt differently in this matter. She might even let her teen know that one of the things that makes her special is her joy at helping out her friends. Then, if the teen felt taken advantage of, she would be free to notice and deal with it herself. And if she didn't, she would probably just enjoy helping out her friends.

Many of our kids have decided that our love for them is conditional and that we only love them when they are doing what we want. Some compare themselves to their siblings and decide that we love the siblings more. These thoughts lower their feelings of self-worth.

The important message of love is, "Be just the way you are; feel just the way you feel; do just what you think you want. I love you because you're you. I may not always like or agree with some of your decisions, and I'll probably let you know my thoughts and feelings, but it won't change my love for you."

Many of our kids haven't the faintest idea of what makes them special. As parents, we have countless opportunities to give them feedback on their uniqueness. Often, our kids will say, "Of course, you say that because you're my parent," as if that somehow makes it less so. But they still hear the things we say, and they can return to those positive pictures when they lose faith in themselves.

There are many ways to let our kids know what makes them special. We can tell a friend while our kids are within earshot. We can write our kids notes. We can tell them stories about when they were younger or go through the photo albums and video tapes together.

We can ask for their help in areas of their expertise or their interest. A teenager into heavy-metal music gave his mother a complete course on distinguishing different guitar styles and guitarists, because she was genuinely interested in understanding the music he loved, so that she could know him better. Another teen taught her parents the latest dance steps before they went on a cruise. Many teens have brought their parents kicking and screaming in to the age of electronics, introducing them to computers, VCRs, digital watches, and so on.

In some families, the teen's activities have become a way for the family to spend time together or to participate together. A teen who took up track pulled the rest of the family into jogging with him; they soon started doing weekend ten-kilometer races together. In another family, a daughter into health and nutrition helped the family change from their high-fat and cholesterol diet to one that was better for them.

Another way to help teens know they are special is to tuck them into bed at night. They are not too old for this special treatment, even though they may act embarrassed at first. It's a ritual we can all look forward to. We can also let our teens know it's always okay and important to us, for them to wake us up when they come home late—not because we are checking up on them, but because we sleep better when we know they are safe.

Know When to Get Help

We need to know that getting help does not mean we are failures. It means we are wise enough to make use of all the support that is available to us through friends, therapists, support groups such as Alanon, parenting books, drug-information books, and treatment programs that have intervention specialists. (We explain intervention in detail in Chapter Seventeen.)

We often explain to our clients who seek therapy that they are now in the league of champions who are wise enough to know they need a coach. Olympic champions or championship ball teams would not even consider trying to function without a good coach. The champions still have to do all the work, but the coach can stand back far enough to see with perspective and objectivity. The coach teaches the necessary skills, but the champion still has to practice to apply the skills.

The information in this chapter and the next chapter can help you know when help might be needed. Do not hesitate to choose the championship route, get help, and see mistakes as opportunities to learn.

Have Faith

Alcoholics Anonymous has some of the best suggestions for applying faith. How often have we seen the bumper sticker that says, "Let go and let God," or heard the serenity prayer that states: "God grant me the serenity to accept the things I cannot change, the courage to change the things I can, and the wisdom to know the difference."

The more we are afraid, the harder it is to have faith; yet the more we have faith, the less we are afraid. Think about it. Most teenagers grow up. The teenage years are not forever. We were all teens at one time. We made it, and so will they. It's not up to us to make sure they grow up, but we can do a lot to see that the growing experience is empowering and loving instead of an ordeal. The key ingredient for that is faith.

In this chapter, we've discussed ways to increase our chances of preventing drug abuse. We want to emphasize that we *mean* "increase our chances." Ultimately, we cannot control our teens' perceptions and decisions—but we *can* hope to influence them.

When dealing with the "hard stuff" with teens (alcohol, drugs, sex, etc.), saying "no" isn't the answer. Use all the slices of the pie below to *use* your influence instead of *lose* your influence.

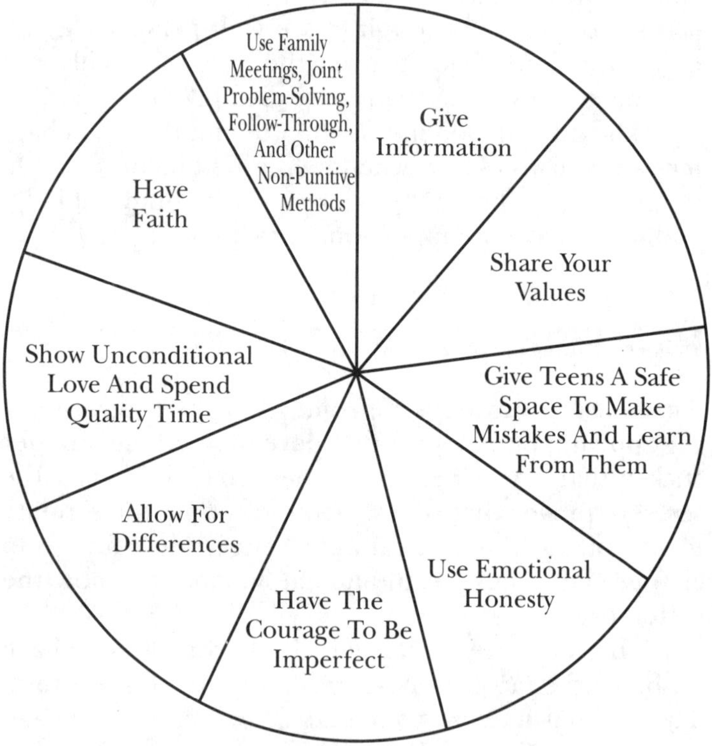

In our next chapter, we'll look more closely at how to tell the difference between normal teenage behavior and dysfunctional behavior and what to do if your kids cross the line into problem drug use or chemical dependency.

▼

Chapter

17

Dysfunctional Teen Behavior

Many of us are sure that when our kids are listening to certain kinds of music, wearing certain kinds of clothes, lying, sneaking off to parties, or participating in other forms of mild rebellion, they are exhibiting signs of dysfunctional behavior. That is probably not the case.

In this chapter, we will discuss the line between normal and dysfunctional behavior in teens; however, what we present here are just guidelines. If you feel that your teen's behavior is not within the realm of normal individuation, we recommend getting into therapy or a support group of some kind. A support group can let you know if other parents are having the same problems. A therapist can offer another set of ears and eyes to observe what is going on in your family. The least that can happen is that you'll spend a little bit of time or money to find out that everything is just fine and relieve your worry.

As soon as some parents spot a few signs of potential problems, they want to send their teens off to therapy to be "fixed" and returned as good as new. However, when teens have problems, the sources often lie within the family relationships. Therefore, it's more helpful to involve the entire family in the therapy process.

Also, what some parents interpret as "potential problems" may be perfectly normal teen behavior that just *looks* dysfunctional to the parents. We've provided a list of various signs to help guide you. We're concerned that our list may be taken too seriously or not seriously enough. Look at the total picture rather than an isolated incident, and follow your inner wisdom as to when you may need help.

The Warning Signs of Possible Dysfunction

The following list is not inclusive but should serve as a guide to determine if behavior is more abnormal than normal. Any of these behaviors may warrant professional help when they represent a pattern rather than isolated incidents.

1. When, for extended periods of time, kids tell us in words that they are unhappy, depressed, feel like killing themselves, hate us, have no friends, and so on. Most teens will express these feelings in isolated incidents that will last only a few hours or a few days.
2. When kids exhibit some of the signs of depression, like loss of appetite, sleeping more than usual, not taking care of their person, spending a lot of time alone or in their rooms, abuse of chemicals, and general despair.

3. When kids start "acting out" extreme behaviors, such as stealing, setting fires, becoming physically violent, completely giving up in school, throwing up, abusing chemicals, or leaving drug paraphernalia around the house.
4. When kids exhibit signs of suicide attempts, cut or mutilate their bodies, get pregnant, or stay "loaded" all the time.
5. When kids start getting their life in order and giving away their possessions to prepare for suicide.

As therapists, we see dysfunction on a continuum. Professional help should be sought immediately for drug abuse, sexual abuse, physical abuse, suicide attempts, pregnancy, and eating disorders. These problems are too difficult to deal with alone and require professional help for the teen and for the family.

Living in a Dysfunctional Family

Being in a dysfunctional family feels a little like getting a popcorn kernel stuck in our teeth. We start working it around with our tongue to try to get it out until we realize we can't. Still, we play with it every now and then, and our tongue gets irritated. After awhile, we give up on it, but it's still there. It doesn't go away by itself. It's a constant irritation—but without dental floss or a toothbrush, it will stay put and we'll just have to get used to it. In a family where there is dysfunction, we've accommodated ourselves to a bad situation for so long that we no longer realize it's not normal.

When we're living with dysfunction, we find it hard to believe that we can get out of it. When we're in crisis, it's hard to picture our lives otherwise. One of the reasons we need outside help is to help us create new pictures of how our lives could be. We can't change anything we can't imagine.

When we're in a dysfunctional situation, we often doubt our own judgment.

When Mrs. Rowe's son was using marijuana everyday, she would smell the dope, notice his dilated pupils and red eyes, and notice the change in his behavior as soon as he came back after being outside a short while. She would ask, "Did you just smoke a joint?"

He would say no and then yell at her about being snoopy, accusatory, and critical.

She would think, "He's right. I am all those things. How can I be that way? How can I do this right? But I think he did smoke it. I'm sure I smell it. But maybe I don't." She would feel like a failure and feel stressed. The next time he went out to smoke a joint, she would do exactly the same thing.

▾ *Stop doing what doesn't work.*

When a teen's behavior becomes dysfunctional, everyone who lives in the family becomes part of the dysfunctional system. Although it seems amazing to an objective observer, when people are caught up in such a system, they keep doing what they've been doing even though it doesn't work. It's human nature to keep doing what doesn't work. Instead of looking at our own behavior, we focus on the person who we believe is causing the problem. While we're waiting for them to change, we give our own power away—and things get worse. We then feel totally out of control.

When we're feeling discouraged and out of control, we often try to find fault. But while we're looking for blame instead of solutions, it's hard for anything to get better. We're caught in a system that often feels like a nightmare with no way out.

▼ *Change yourself first.*

In any dysfunctional system, if we change ourselves just a little bit, the system changes an enormous amount. Having faith in that can help us change. And changing ourselves is something we *can* do, whereas we can't *make* anyone else change. However, when we change our behavior just a small amount, we can affect other people dramatically.

Changing yourself is the basis of Alanon meetings. If you have a teenager who is abusing drugs, find an Alanon support group as soon as possible. Alanon is listed in the white pages of your telephone book or may be a part of Alcoholics Anonymous, which will also be listed in the white pages.

Changing yourself does not mean you don't need to work on changing the family system and helping your teen. Changing yourself means finding out what doesn't work and getting help with what might work.

When Your Teen Is Chemically Dependent

A teen who is chemically dependent may show some of the following signs: change in friends or schoolwork, hangovers, extreme defensiveness or abusive behavior, drug paraphernalia or alcoholic containers lying around, spaciness, red eyes, and withdrawal.

The Guilt-and-Blame Game

Parents often feel confused and unsure—they don't know if they're imagining things or if their teen really is different. They may feel guilty for all the things they think they might have done wrong. They think that either their child is a failure or they are. They beat themselves up for all the times they allowed their child to manipulate them into being wishy-washy rather than maintaining firmness with dignity and respect; or for all the times they gave in, gave up, and yelled and screamed. They believe their actions must be the reason their child is now into drugs. They ruminate for hours, "If only I hadn't done this, if only I hadn't done that, if only I had done this, if only I had done that."

Some parents resort to increased control, based on anger, guilt, and fear, since it seems obvious to them that dignity and respect didn't work. They then tend to lecture, blame, and moralize to the child for his or her lack of moral values and social interest in a last-ditch effort to browbeat him or her into correct behavior.

Other members of the family go through their own sets of thoughts and feelings. Some are sad and try to help. Some watch and copy. Some try to avoid the entire family or simply go away altogether, and some act out even worse than the child with the initial problem. It doesn't feel good for anyone; and everyone is affected and involved in many different ways.

Denial. Most of all, dysfunctional families don't want to face the real problem—that a member of the family is chemically dependent.

When we are able to get out of denial and admit our teen has a drug problem, we can go to Alanon or a treatment program for help. We usually need help getting a teenager into a treatment center through what is called an intervention.

Intervention. Teens who are chemically dependent will do anything to protect their chemical use and can usually out-manipulate their parents. Because the person abusing chemicals wants to keep using them and because the family has a hard time accepting that the teen is chemically dependent, sometimes a trained person is needed to assist the family in getting help with the drug problem. This person sets up an intervention, which interrupts the problem behavior and has the potential for improving the situation.

Most treatment programs have intervention specialists who can help chemically dependent teens face their problem. Many of our high schools have programs to identify kids who are problem drug users and get them help. While the child needs treatment, the family needs help with their co-dependency and enabling issues (as discussed in Chapter Sixteen, these are any behaviors that stop the individual from experiencing the consequences of their own actions).

When we look at chemical dependency in a teenager, we often focus on only one individual, which is like watching a play and forgetting all the other players. We have to remember that teenagers are found within the context of a family, a classroom, or a peer group. We need to see the whole picture and look at how other members of the group act as co-dependents and enablers.

Mr. and Mrs. Graham couldn't admit their daughter, Norma, had a drug problem. She was terrorizing the family, lying on the couch strung out and yelling at everyone who approached her. This had been going on for months and was getting worse. The Grahams met with their therapist to discuss what to do.

Therapist: Your daughter has a drug habit that she has not kicked. Part of your problem is that you yourselves haven't had a drug problem or been around people who have had one. So you keep looking for other explanations for her behavior. You keep dealing with her as if she weren't chemically dependent. She needs help but instead you're enabling her by letting her stay at home and terrorize the family.

Mrs. Graham: But she's our child. How can we tell her she's an addict and can't live here anymore? Where will she go? How will she take care of herself?

Mr. Graham: We know what we should do, but when we say we're going to do it and try to follow through, Norma threatens to kill herself. She says it will be our fault. How can we deal with this?

Therapist: Stop making pronouncements until you're ready to follow through all the way. You need to find a treatment program in your area and find out how to help your daughter get into treatment. This is beyond you. You need help confronting her.

The Grahams decided to follow their therapist's advice on following through. The next week, when their daughter did not come home for three days, they packed her bags and put them on the porch with the following note: "We love you very much. We'll do anything we can to help you if you ever decide to go into treatment for your chemical abuse. We won't do anything to support you in the life-style you are choosing now, so you can't live here any longer until you get help."

They did not hear from their daughter for a week, until she called and asked her mother to have lunch with her. Mom vowed to be loving but not enabling. She was surprised when her daughter told her that she would be willing to talk to the counselors at a treatment program. They went that very day, and the intervention counselor convinced Norma to stay.

The Grahams had done what is called "presenting the bottom line." Once their daughter knew they meant it when they said she could no longer depend on them to support her drug abuse by allowing her to live at home, she made a different choice.

The decision to stop using chemicals must be made by the person who is addicted, but the family can find ways to stop their encouraging (enabling) behavior and help the addict seek treatment.

Interventions can be formal or informal. One person we know, who had been smoking marijuana for a long time, decided to quit when someone asked him how long he was planning to continue to mask his feelings and stop himself from feeling anything. For some reason, that message caught his attention. Another teen talked to a recovering alcoholic. This person said to her, "Using chemicals is like being on an elevator going down. You do not have to hit bottom before you stop using. You can get off at any floor. You can just notice, 'Isn't this interesting? I have just gone down another floor.' And, somehow in yourself, if the decision to stop using is made (it has to be a personal decision; no one can make you do it), you'll do what needs to be done for yourself. That decision can be made at any time." About a month later, without any warning, this teen stopped using chemicals. These were informal interventions.

Other times, a formal meeting is planned, with the help of an expert, to confront the chemical user and encourage him or her to get into treatment. People who use chemicals can make their own intervention, and many do. They get sick and tired of being "sick and tired" and decide to quit using or go for help. The important point is that intervention, however it can be accomplished, is needed to break the cycle of abuse. Without intervention the abuse will continue.

Sexual Abuse and Incest

Sexual abuse is one of the most painful dysfunctional systems for anyone to deal with. The following poem says it all:

Pain

Pain is so sad to see
It hurts so much inside you
But no one cares to see

The pain that is inside you
Hurts like no other
It hurts so much more
That you wish you could die

You know the pain won't last
Not forever at least
As you cry yourself to sleep

No matter how hard you try
To make it cease
But the pain keeps growing
Growing forever deep

This kind of pain leaves deep scars
You feel you can't go on
You know you must so you try

Every day you live like this
Hurts you even more
Your pains are so true and deep
You feel no one understands

You see my friend
I understand because I too
Hurt the same as you

Someday soon you too
Will no longer be feeling blue
Everything will get better
Maybe not so soon

Don't forget though
That happiness is waiting for you
To come and take its hand.

"Pain" was written by a thirteen-year-old survivor of incest. Her experience wasn't uncovered until her mother went to a therapist to deal with some other issues. Mom was feeling a lot of pressure in the family but couldn't put her finger on any one thing. She simply knew it just didn't feel right around her house anymore, so she decided to go in for counseling. As a result, she became more open and emotionally honest. Her improved communication skills started rubbing off on her thirteen-year-old daughter. One day, her daughter told her that one of her relatives was molesting her. It ultimately came out that there had been sexual abuse in this relative's home for years, and nobody had known. This is not unusual in a dysfunctional system. Since denial is such a big part of dysfunction, many of us don't even realize we have a problem until it slips out.

Shelly's upbringing had been very strict, and she was overprotected by her parents. Her family taught her to do as she was told and to listen to grown-ups. Since her siblings had been rebellious, Shelly took the "good, compliant child" role in the family. She focused on doing what others wanted. In some ways, the molestations of Shelly were an extension of her thinking—she couldn't see an alternative to doing what people older than her wanted her to do. When the perpetrators asked her to cooperate, she worried that she wouldn't be loved if she said no. Luckily for Shelly, when she told about the abuse, her mother never questioned the truth of her statements.

We cannot emphasize how important it is to take our kids seriously when they tell us something of this nature. They have already experienced a great deal of shame, guilt, and degradation. They have felt isolated and thought of themselves as "bad." The last thing they need is for their parents to question or blame them.

Once again, this is an area where outside help is essential through therapy or group support. Many communities have Parents United programs and other similar services to help families deal with sexual abuse and incest.

Most often, the perpetrator of incest or sexual abuse will deny that it happened and accuse the victim of lying. Their denial is similar to the addict who is protecting his use. In this case, the perpetrator may also be saving face. Nevertheless, they, too, need help. The healing for the perpetrator begins when they find out they are still a worthwhile human being with certain behavior that must stop immediately. They need to hear that help is available to deal with the feelings, thoughts, and behaviors that brought them to this situation in the first place.

The healing process for someone who has been molested is a long one, but it is much easier if a child can be helped before they repress the information. Otherwise, it can take years and years of pain for the information to surface again so that it can be dealt with. Repression never makes the pain go away. Only talking about the problem and dealing with the feelings can do that.

Just as in chemical dependency, the healing process involves the entire family, as they all have a reaction and a part in the problem. Those family members who are unwilling to participate in therapy and self-help groups continue to suffer until they do get help.

Teen Suicide

Suicide is a choice. When our teens lose self-confidence, suicide becomes one of their choices. A loss of self-confidence coupled with the belief that control is out of their hands may lead to teen suicide. Many teen suicides are also drug-related. If our kids haven't been learning how to cope with life's difficulties themselves, or how to solve their problems and stand on their own feet, suicide may look like the only choice left to them. Many of our kids haven't learned that making a mistake is just an opportunity to try again, and not the end of the world. Unfortunately, because teens can be so intense and dramatic, they may chose a final solution to a temporary problem without a lot of forethought.

Losing a child has got to be one of the most difficult things we as parents could ever face, and losing a child to suicide may be doubly hard. We wish we could give a formula to make sure no one ever had to go through this kind of pain but that isn't possible. However, a review of the warning signs of dysfunctional behavior will help a parent know whether their child is suicidal. It's vital to heed the warning signs and get help immediately.

We must take our teens seriously if they exhibit signs of suicide. We need to encourage them to talk to us or to help them find someone they can talk to. We need to show concern and really listen. They need a ray of hope to let them know that, however bad it may seem now, there is a tomorrow when "this too shall pass." One mother who suspected her daughter might be thinking of suicide told her, "Honey, I remember a couple of times when I felt like committing suicide. I felt so bad I couldn't imagine things getting any better. But they did. I hate to think of how much I would have missed if I had killed myself. For one thing, I would have missed you."

When talking to a child about suicide, it's important to use words like *suicide* and *death* and not shy away from them for fear of introducing an idea which we think our teen doesn't already have. We need to ask if they have a plan or if they've tried already. Finding out their plan shows us how far along they are in their thinking—a teen with a plan is like a loose cannon.

We can ask our child how their life would be different if they killed themselves, and, in doing so, we'll probably find out what is really troubling them. The following conversation shows the *wrong* way to react. We include it here because, unfortunately, it is more typical of parental responses than doing what needs to be done. It shows a lack of compassion, a judgmental attitude, and no listening.

Cliff: No one cares if I live or die.

Dad: You always feel so sorry for yourself.

Cliff: Well, you and Mom split up and you expect me to live with that disgusting person who calls himself my stepfather.

Dad: How dare you use such language like that around me! Your stepfather is doing the best he can.

Cliff: Oh, yeah? Then why does he beat me and pound on me?

Dad: Cliff, I know your stepfather and I know that just isn't true. Why do you tell such lies?

Cliff: Nobody believes me. I hate you all and I wish I were dead! A lot you guys would care!

Dad: Cliff, there you go exaggerating again. You know you don't mean what you say. Now settle down and think about how you can get along better with your stepfather.

In this family, Cliff didn't kill himself, but he did run away at the age of fourteen and no one knows where or how he is.

If Cliff's father had taken Cliff seriously, he would have used the listening skills described in Chapter fourteen. He also would have reassured Cliff that he was concerned and that he would like to go with Cliff to see a counselor so they both could get some help with this problem. When we operate in these ways with our kids —when we see our mistakes—we need to bury the hatchet, admit our mistakes, and try again.

When our kids miss out on compassion, nonjudgment, and attentiveness, they usually can find it elsewhere. Many teens look to initiate relationships with the opposite sex as a way of feeling unconditionally loved. That is one of the reasons a book on teenagers would not be complete without a reference to teen sexual behavior and the dangers of teen pregnancy and of AIDS.

Teen Pregnancy/Teen AIDS

As parents, we love to think our teens are asexual, just waiting until they are older so we can give them the "big talk." Guess again. Not only are many of our teens sexually active but they are at risk for pregnancy and disease because many of us are unwilling or afraid to be realistic about teenage sexual behavior.

The greatest contributor to teen pregnancy is a lack of sex education and a failure on the part of the significant adults in their lives to acknowledge and cope with teen sexual activity. We really can't avoid sex education because it is always happening. Refusing to talk about sex is a form of sex education that invites damaging conclusions, such as "sex is secret, bad, and not to be discussed with your parents." In most cases, these conclusions don't prevent sexual experimentation. They just invite guilt, shame, and silence after it has already taken place.

Even when we are open and willing to discuss sex with our kids, they may feel too embarrassed to talk to us. Teens have a need for privacy, and this is one area where that need is strongly felt. To save their lives and to prevent children from having children, we need to have birth control information and information about safe sex readily available. Prevention of AIDS is best accomplished by using condoms, and yet most teens are not likely to have the nerve, the money, or the desire to go to a store to buy them. Teens are certain they are invincible, and may even think they are immune to AIDS.

Some parents have decided to keep a supply of condoms next to the extra soap, toothpaste, and toilet paper in the linen closet, even though they themselves feel uncomfortable talking with their kids about sex, or their kids feel uncomfortable talking with them. Yet these parents notice the supply has to be replenished from time to time, and they feel it is the least they can do if their teens or some of their friends have decided to be sexually active.

Parents who buy condoms for their teens may or may not approve of their kids having sex, but they don't want to see their children die from AIDS or bring children into the world before their teen is ready to parent and love them.

Eating Disorders

When sex is concerned, parents usually try to ignore

the topic, hoping it will just take care of itself. But when diet is concerned, parents tend to take the opposite approach and become overly involved in an area that is none of their business.

Parental concern for healthy children can get out of proportion around the subject of food, especially since many of us have our own hang-ups about weight, looks, and diet. We try to be good parents by making sure our kids eat properly. Quite often, instead of providing healthy choices and trusting our kids to eat when they are hungry and stop when they are not, we interfere in this natural process and, without knowing it, plant the seeds for eating disorders.

Most eating disorders start in childhood. For many different reasons, some children stop regulating their eating internally, stop listening to their bodies' clues, and no longer trust themselves to eat what is right for them. Since everything can be intense and extreme when kids are teens, problem eating in the younger years can take on serious and even life-threatening proportions in the teen years.

Teens with eating disorders have become dependent on external processes to control their weight. In the most extreme cases, they have completely stopped listening to their bodies' cues to the point of near-death.

Just like chemically dependent people, teens experiencing eating disorders come to a point where they can't stop their damaging behavior without help. Their eating patterns are no longer voluntary.

Some of the most common eating disorders we see in teens are extreme obesity; anorexia or near-starvation by a restricted amount of food intake; and bulimia, a condition in which teens binge on food and then induce vomiting as a means to stay thin. The last two patterns are found mostly in females.

All eating disorders have to do with control issues.

At some point, these teens lost their own sense of power over their bodies and either eat out of control (obesity) or use starvation or vomiting (anorexia and bulimia) to overcompensate for their lack of power.

To say that a teen with an eating disorder is discouraged is an understatement. Why they would chose to act out their discouragement through food, though, is usually a function of the atmosphere created by the parent or society or by the parental style of nurturing.

One of the best ways to prevent or to stop a potentially damaging pattern from getting out of hand is to stop interfering with our kids' food intake. That includes putting kids on diets, nagging, criticizing, taking them to clinics and doctors without being asked, controlling what foods or how much they are allowed to eat, or taking away allowances so they can't buy food. We can also look at our own attitudes about weight and the modeling we're doing of our own eating patterns.

Since any discouraging behavior tends to be a mistaken way of dealing with thoughts and feelings, it is also important to listen to your kids and to not discount or ignore their feelings. Through the communication skills taught in Chapter Fourteen, we can also help our kids learn to express their feelings in words rather than through discouraged behaviors. If we find ourselves focusing on achievement rather than on building competence, we need to back off, since such pressure gives the message that we only love our kids if they are "perfect."

Many teens who have been physically, sexually, or verbally abused, or who have grown up in families where a parent is chemically dependent, have made the mistaken decision that there is something wrong with them, that they are different, and that they are worthless. Not only can they find comfort in eating, but being overweight is an unconscious way of proving their lack of self-worth.

If our kids' eating disorders have moved into the extreme, we must get professional help, which includes both medical and psychological help. In an extreme case, our teen may first need to be stabilized medically before he or she can learn to change the symptoms and deal with the deeper issues in therapy. Once again, the greater the involvement of the family in the therapy process, the faster the healing for the teen.

As frightening as some of these eating disorders can be, most of them can be prevented if we just turn eating over to the child. One mother learned that whenever her teen says she's going on a diet, it's better to say, "That's nice," and see what happens than to lecture, panic, or even help. Usually, her already-trim daughter diets for a few days and then goes back to her normally balanced and healthy eating patterns (which include a certain amount of junk food).

Another way to help our kids is to exercise regularly and set up opportunities for them to do the same, as normal weight is a function to both internal regulation and exercise. Joining a health club, skiing, buying a set of weights and a bench are simply a few suggestions out of many possibilities. Making these available without control may be much appreciated by teenagers.

Young Adults Who Won't or Can't Leave Home

Today we have a new phenomena—kids who won't leave home. These are people in their twenties who have still not become responsible adults with good judgment.

In view of the problems we've been exploring, it

may be surprising to think of kids who won't leave home as exhibiting dysfunctional behavior; but we think children who lack the courage or the drive to start their own lives away from their families have serious problems.

There was a time when mothers dreaded the day of the empty nest when their children all left home and left them feeling no longer needed. Today, many parents *long* for an empty nest, wondering if their grown children will ever leave home and be on their own.

Why are thousands of adult children still living at home with their parents? And why aren't parents delighted to have them?

And how have we created this dilemma?

Many kids want to live at home because they don't know where else they can live in the style to which their parents helped them become accustomed with so little effort of their own. Other kids stay home because their overprotective parents have completely convinced them that they'll never make it on their own and there's no point in trying. They've lost faith in themselves. Some stay home because they have an alcoholic or severly discouraged parent who they are convinced will die without them.

In the first scenario, parents aren't delighted to have their children because they demand the right to live at home but want the freedom to come and go as they please. They want the privilege of home-cooked meals, laundry, and a clean house but don't want to contribute financially. They also refuse to contribute to the upkeep of the home.

This dilemma has been created by parents who have lavished their children with material goods without requiring any effort from the kids—sometimes in the name of love, sometimes by default, and sometimes just because parents want their children to have more than they had. Sometimes it is done to make up for the guilt felt in not spending more time with their children. And sometimes it is done because, even though they know better, it seems easier to give in than to deal with coaxing and hassling.

Overprotective parents may be afraid to let their children go and may actually encourage them to stay home long after the kids are ready to be on their own. These parents may not realize how selfish and debilitating their own behavior is—in their minds, it's for the child's own good.

For severely discouraged and dependent parents, having the child leave could mean the end of their ability to stay dependent. They may be so involved in their own dependency and their own needs that they are unaware of the child's need to leave.

If our adult kids are living at home, the kindest thing that we can do is move them out. We can give them a deadline and offer to help them find a job, make a budget, or find a place to live. But for kids who like the security of their parents' place, sometimes a cold-hearted boot is the first step to show them that they *can* make it.

Choosing a Therapist

If you need professional help, the most important criterion to consider in choosing a therapist is finding one your teen can relate to. Even though it is important for you to feel comfortable, you need to keep shopping until your teen is comfortable. Stay away from therapists who recommend a punitive, restrictive approach for parenting teens. It will just make things worse.

If possible, ask people you know to refer a therapist they have felt satisfied with. If no one you know has been to a therapist, ask Alanon groups or church groups for referrals. When you find a therapist, don't hesitate to ask for a few minutes for a get-acquainted interview where you can learn about his or her basic philosophy.

Remember, when teenagers are chemically dependent, they will not want to see a therapist because they will want to protect their drug use. Find an Alanon group for yourself and work towards intervention.

If your child has dysfunctional behavior, he or she may never change. That is his or her choice. Keeping that in mind, *you* can still learn and grow and do all you can to support yourself and your teenager in ways that might make a difference.

It's Not Your Fault

As parents, we need to remember that what happens to our kids isn't our fault but that we may be inviting discouragement by our actions. Family therapy and parent education can help us get in touch with those behaviors and beliefs that we need to change in order to bring greater health to our families.

We all do the best we can based on our present awareness. It's important to keep in mind that our children are unique individuals who have the power to perceive and choose no matter what we do.

Finding fault is pointless. We can't be looking for fault and looking for solutions at the same time.

Many of the problems we have been discussing are products of dependency patterns that may be a direct result of control, permissiveness, or neglect. The more we learn the language and skills of competence, personal responsibility, and empowerment, the quicker we can change some of these patterns. If we grew up only speaking a certain language (for instance, co-dependence), it's probably all we know. There is no shame in doing the best we can given our current level of skills, but it is a mistake if we don't take advantage of the many opportunities in our culture to learn and to grow.

Conclusion

Growing and Changing

If we aren't changing, we aren't growing. If we aren't growing, we are stagnating. Changing and growing can be exciting and challenging. Our teens provide opportunities for us to change and grow by challenging us to deal with our own unresolved issues. Our teens also challenge us to care enough to learn how to give them the kind of support and skills they need to grow into healthy, independent adults.

Society Changes and Grows

It wasn't too long ago that the word *teenager* could not be found in the dictionary. In those days, adolescents served an apprenticeship to learn a skill, got married, and as adults often did not live past the age of thirty-six.

Political, economic, and health standards have changed dramatically in our society, but we haven't yet caught up with the changes socially or emotionally. In one workshop, we invited participants to look at the different characteristics of teens in the 1920s, the 1960s, and the 1980s. They were amazed to see tremendous difference, and then amazed to see how little parenting had changed. Parenting skills had obviously not kept up with the times. The only major change the workshop participants could see was the importance we now place on helping children develop healthy self-esteem. However, they concluded, this is largely an intellectual understanding since we still use the old methods of overcontrol or overprotection, which make it difficult for children to feel good about themselves.

Our challenge as parents is to grow and change as fast as the times and our teenagers do. The first step is to stop treating our kids like babies, especially our teens. We need to treat them like people who are worthy of respect and who are capable of learning, contributing, and growing.

It's Never Too Late

Many parents wonder if it's too late to repair a severely damaged relationship with their teenage sons or daughters. It's never too late.

Mrs. Green tells of repairing an extremely dysfunctional relationship with her son after learning some of the principles we teach in this book:

"My oldest son left home at the age of fourteen to hitchhike across the country. As I look back on the situation now, I can see how wise and capable he was to leave a situation where I vacillated between overcontrol and overpermissiveness and then always berated him for not cooperating.

"I had just learned about the principles for empowering teens and was able to empower him at a time when it was very scary for me to do so. He was getting involved with drugs. We wondered about his sudden interest in weeding the garden and discovered he was growing pot in our backyard. When I told him this wasn't acceptable, he threatened to leave home. He had run away from home before when we had arguments. I could see that something had to be done to stop the destructive patterns of argument and manipulation we were following.

"I sat down with him one day and decided to be totally honest. I started by telling him I loved him unconditionally. I then told him I didn't agree that using drugs was right, but admitted, 'Who am I to talk? I do stuff that isn't making me happy. I'm a pleaser and a workaholic and I have many insecurities about my worth as a person. All the stuff I do is accepted by society, but it isn't healthy. How do I know drugs are not a better way to go. I don't think so, and I don't understand drug use . . . but I don't know. I know I'm not willing to let you grow pot in my backyard because it's against the law, and I'm not willing to risk the consequences of breaking the law. If you choose to do that you can't live here. If you choose to leave, I hope you'll remember that I love you unconditionally. I hope you'll keep in touch and even feel free to tell me your feelings and experiences with drugs. I hope some day you'll stop using drugs because I know they aren't the answer, anymore than what I do is the answer.'

"He chose to leave saying, 'I guess you would rather have me grow pot out in the open where I can get caught than in the safety of my backyard.' I didn't let that guilt trip hook me. I said, "I wish you wouldn't leave, but I know you'll do what you want to do and that I can't stop you.'

"When he'd run away before, the police would stop him a lot and hassle him. He asked if I would give him a note saying he had permission to hitchhike. I knew a lot of people would think I was crazy, but I knew he was going to go. I knew I couldn't control him. I decided to follow my gut-level desire to let go and support him in what he was going to do anyway.

Sure enough, I got calls from sheriffs in several states who thought I was an extremely neglectful parent. I was sure most people would agree and often was afraid they might be right. To back off and give nothing but unconditional love was scary, but the long-range results speak for themselves.

"At fourteen, my son found jobs so he could survive. He found friends and set up apartments. He became a carpenter's helper, eventually became a very skilled carpenter, and built his own house. It took him eight years to decide drugs did not fit into his life. I may be deluding myself, but I think one reason he was able to come to that conclusion eventually was because I removed one reason for him to continue—rebellion against me.

"He is now an adult, married and has two children. We've developed a wonderful relationship. A highlight of my life was when he called one day and said, 'Mom, you're one of my best friends. No, you *are* my best friend.' And that's the way I feel about him. He's one of my favorite people to be around. We share things with each other now that only best friends would feel free to share. He knows I'll never judge him for anything, and I know he'll never judge me for anything."

▾ *Teenagers are capable.*

It can be very difficult to let go and trust in the basic capability of our teenagers to learn without being controlled by us or overprotected. One reason for this difficulty is not understanding the difference between gutless parenting and courageous parenting.

Gutless Parenting

Gutless parenting is not letting go because it is too scary. It is taking the easy way out rather than facing our fears, seeing our own issues, and growing past them. Gutless parenting is worrying more about what others might think or say than doing what is best for our teenagers, including allowing to let them learn from their mistakes. Gutless parenting means being more interested in perfection than in the growth of our teenagers. Parents who value perfection will overprotect or overcontrol.

Gutless parents don't mean to hurt their kids, but there are many things we do unknowingly that stunts their growth and development. Overprotection, control, rigid rules, and a lack of communication are but a few of the methods that contribute to stealing strength and capability from our teens. We need to stop doing that to them.

Courageous Parenting

Courageous parenting means facing the fear (yes, it *is* scary to let go and allow our children to make mistakes) and doing what needs to be done anyway because of the greater good. Courageous parenting means taking the time to teach skills even though it's easier to just criticize or rescue. Courageous parenting is having faith in the basic capabilities of our teenagers and knowing they can learn when given the room and support they need.

When we think of our teens as competent and capable people who have the ability to learn through experience what is good for them, it's easier to be courageous.

Ruth gives us one example of the capabilities of a

teenager. At fifteen, she was able to plan the menus, shop for groceries, cook, do her laundry, get herself to school, figure out her homework, get to the library to research projects, get good grades in school, bake and wrap cookies for all her friends at school, buy presents for all her friends with money she had earned, saved, and managed.

Ruth figured out how to pay for part of a car and the insurance on that car. By sixteen, she had a car and at seventeen took her first solo long-distance trip to Los Angeles, where she lived on her own for a month while attending dance classes. These capabilities and accomplishments weren't accidental.

In Ruth's family, kids participated in family meetings, did chores, had allowances to manage themselves, handled their own homework without parental interference, and were allowed to pursue whatever they felt ready to do with support and help from their parents.

No one forced Ruth to be independent, but she was given encouragement and taught the life skills necessary to succeed.

Accidental Empowerment

Sometimes teens are allowed to work things out for themselves simply because their parents don't know what their teens are doing so they don't interfere. Mr. Arnold shared an example of accidental empowerment:

"I'm so glad I didn't know Scott was using dope for a year because I know I would have done something stupid and mucked it up. When Scott finally told me about his use of pot, I said, 'How could I have missed all this?' He said, 'Well, aren't you glad you did? This isn't anything you would want to write about in my baby book. I worked it through. I learned what I needed to learn. My only regret is that I used so much. Pot can be fun to use, but I messed it up for myself. I did it so much that I lost the ability to get high from just a little bit of pot. I can't do it anymore at all because I can't enjoy it. That's my only regret.' "

Perspective Helps

During individuation, our teenagers may seem to get all topsy-turvy. We often let our fears run rampant based on the horror stories we hear of the few teenagers who end up badly. But if we keep our perspective, we know that most teens usually end up on their feet.

The Bottom Line—Empowerment

Part of helping our teens come back to themselves is giving them the room to travel experimental roads and try out different roles. Adolescence is a time for tremendous growth and change. Teens need all the support they can get from us. We can be their co-pilots until they are ready to fly solo.

As parents we have a choice—to control or empower, to protect or empower, to feel pity or empower. The choice is ours, and when we choose to stop stealing their confidence and initiative away from them, our teens strengthen their wings so they can fly on their own.

Introduction

This study guide can be very helpful if you are willing to take the time to fill out the exercises in a separate journal, complete the activities, and practice the suggested skills. The activities are arranged to coordinate with the chapters in *Positive Discipline for Teenagers*.

Value and Time Commitment

We suggest you make a commitment to yourself that your relationship with your teenager is valuable enough to spend a specified amount of time each week to complete the study guide assignments and practice the skills.

Less Than Ten Minutes a Week

Each exercise or activity will probably take less than five or ten minutes. We suggest you complete only one or two a week, and spend the rest of the week practicing the suggested skills or new behaviors based on your increased awareness. You will also be encouraged by discovering how much innate wisdom you have given a little guidance in the right direction.

Journal

Take time to write down your successes and failures. Reading about your successes can serve as an encouraging reminder during your "down" days. You will gain insights and learn from your mistakes by writing about them. (We see mistakes as positive learning experiences —which will teach you skills to increase your effectiveness.) You will also find that keeping a journal provides a perspective you often don't see until you start writing. Writing in a journal is an excellent way to tap into your innate wisdom.

Support and Study Groups

It can be encouraging to form a support group of two or more people who go through the study guide together and share insights, experiences, and positive feedback.

It can be fun to go back three to six months later or with the next teen and see where progress has been made and where you might still be stuck.

▼

Chapter 1 Activity

Things Would Be Perfect If . . .

This study guide will be most beneficial if you have a clear picture of what you would like to gain from completing the study of Positive Discipline for Teenagers.

1. Make a list of concerns, problems, or goals you would like to solve or achieve in your relationship with your teenager. Be specific.

2. Go back and prioritize your concerns. Put a number "1" by your most important concern, a number "2" by the second, etc.

3. Give an example of the last time you experienced your number 1 concern. Describe exactly what happened, what you did, the results for you and for your teenager in response to what you did.

4. What insights did you gain, if any, just by completing this exercise?

Skill Pat yourself on the back for being a normal parent who has concerns you would like to solve and goals you would like to achieve—and for caring enough to make the time commitment to do something about it.

Creative Skill What new behavior would you like to practice based on any insights you gained from completing this exercise?

▼

Chapter I Activity

Age Regression

It is easy for parents to forget what it is like to be a teenager and to lose the understanding that can be such an important bridge to close relationships.

1. Think back to your teen years. What were your issues? What did you think about all day?

2. Make a list of things that were important to you.

3. Compare your list with the list of teen concerns on pages 8, 9 and 17 through 19.

4. What similarities do you notice?

Skill Share stories with your teenager of times when you were a teenager and felt the same or had the same concerns and struggles he/she might be having (Do not include stories about how much better you were—like walking five miles in the snow.)

Creative Skill Think of your own special ways to show empathy, understanding, and support. Write them down.

▼

Chapter 1 Activity

Whose Side Are You On Anyway?

It's not what happens to us but how we view what happens to us that influences our decisions about ourselves, which in turn influences our actions. Our behavior affects our perception of our teens. When our teens think we are on their side, their need to act out in extreme ways is greatly reduced.

1. Remember a situation where you treated your teen disrespectfully and write it down.

2. Pretend you are a teenager and imagine what it would be like to have a parent who is acting like you in the above situation.

3. How would you be feeling?

4. What would you be deciding?

5. Would you think your parent was on your side?

6. What are you learning from this activity?

7. Can you think of anything you could do differently as the parent in that situation? Imagine what it would look like and write it down.

Skill Ask your teen if she thinks you're on her side.

Creative Skill Think of places where you could change your behavior so your teen would know you were on her side. What stops you from doing that, if anything?

Chapter 2 Activity

Teen Secrets

We often catastrophize the outcome of normal teenage behavior and believe that how they are now is how they will be forever. Remembering your own teen years—and that you didn't stay that way forever—can relieve your worries and restore your faith in your teenager.

1. List at least three things you did as a teenager that you didn't want your parents to know about.

2. Are there any things on that list that you have still never told anyone?

3. What relationship, if any, do you see between your own teen secrets and your fears or judgments about your teen?

Skill Have faith in your teenager to pass through a normal growth cycle.

Creative Skill Find specific ways to be supportive and show your faith.

▼

Chapter 2 Activity

Nurturing A Plant

When parents appreciate the individual nature of each child and provide the nurturing that helps that child become the best of who he/she is, everyone's self-esteem is raised. We can learn acceptance from nature where it is clear that a cactus needs different nurturing than an orchid; and a rose cannot be a petunia, no matter what you might do to change it.

1. If someone gave you a cactus to take care of for the rest of your life, how would you feel about the plant you received?

2. Would it be your favorite plant?

3. If you received a cactus but wanted a rose, is there anything you could do to turn your cactus into a rose?

4. List all the things it would take to nurture the plant you received.

5. What have you learned from this exercise that could help you with your teenager?

6. In what ways do you violate the concept of gaining knowledge about what your teenager needs (i.e., do you take time to get into the world of your teenager to find out what he/she needs)?

Skill Choose one thing you would do with a plant that you would like to do with your teenager.

Creative Skill Think of what it takes to nurture your teen that goes beyond what a plant needs for nurturing.

Chapter 3 Activity

Draw A Teen

When we hear the word "teenager" we often think in stereotypes. It is important that we create opportunities for a reality check on what is normal and what is not. When we realize that the stereotypes are exaggerations and we get in touch with the individual uniqueness of each teen, we can feel relieved and even grateful for some of the characteristics we have been worried or annoyed about.

1. Describe your picture of a normal teen.

2. Describe your picture of a dream teen.

3. Do you personally know a dream teen or a normal teen?

4. How do you feel about him/her?

5. As a result of this activity, how are you feeling about your teen?

6. How are you feeling about yourself?

Skill What would be the characteristics that you would describe if you were drawing a normal parent and a dream parent instead?

Creative Skill What picture of your teenager have you been holding that you would like to change? How would you change it?

Chapter 3 Activity

Taking Their Behavior Personally

We need to realize that the things our kids do and say are statements about them and not about us, so we can stop blaming ourselves for their behavior or taking it personally. Our kids are separate people from us, and the mistakes and successes they make are theirs to learn from and to own.

Look at the following list and pick a behavior that really bugs you. You can add one of your own if it's not on the list.

- Cutting classes
- Spending time in room
- Refusing to go on family vacation
- Trading outfits you bought for Christmas
- Grumpy mood
- Forgetting to do chores
- Not wanting to sit with you in a movie
- Not wanting to go to college

Read the following two attitudes:

1. Taking it personally means I tell myself their behavior has something to do with my failures or successes (i.e., I'm a terrible parent, I'm a good parent, what will others think, how could they do this after all I have done for them, they must hate me or they wouldn't behave this way).

2. Not taking it personally means I tell myself their behavior has to do with them, not me (i.e., this is important to them, they need to find out for themselves, they are exploring what life and values mean

to them, this is not important to them, I have faith they can learn whatever they need to learn from their mistakes and challenges, I wonder what this means to them).

Go back to the behavior that bugs you and write out how you would act with attitude #1.

Skill Talk with your teen about what you have learned doing this activity.

Creative Skill Think of areas where you are taking things personally and make some changes to attitude #2.

▼

Chapter 4 Activity

Mistakes Baggage

Many of us carry heavy, useless baggage from our childhood about mistakes. Even though this baggage has not effectively served us—and has hurt us a great deal—we pass it on to our children as though it were precious family heirlooms.

1. What are the messages you heard from your parents about mistakes—either stated or implied? List as many as you can think of.

2. What did you decide is the meaning of mistakes for you? What do mistakes say about you?

3. Based on that decision, what kind of behaviors do you do to either avoid making mistakes or keep others from knowing if you do?

4. What messages are you giving your teenager about mistakes?

5. What do you think he or she is deciding?

6. Based on that decision, what kind of behaviors do you think your teenager will do to either avoid making mistakes or keep others from knowing if he or she does?

7. What new decision would you like to make about mistakes for yourself?

8. What kind of decisions about mistakes would you like to foster in your teenager?

Skill Tell your child often that "mistakes are wonderful opportunities to learn."

Creative Skill Think of something you would like to do to foster the kind of legacy you would like to leave your child about mistakes.

▼

Chapter 4 Activity

Mistakes As Wonderful Opportunities To Learn

Parents usually mean well when they try to motivate their children to do better by making them feel bad about their mistakes; however, we fail to check out the results of our good intentions. Only when we see the fallacy of our misguided intentions can we see how empowering it is to see mistakes as wonderful opportunities to learn. We can then replace negative beliefs about mistakes with beliefs about the value of mistakes.

Complete the following:

MISTAKES INTERVIEW FORM

1. What do mistakes mean to you?

2. What do you think mistakes might mean for your teenager?

3. Think of a time when your teenager made a mistake and you were supportive and encouraging.

   A. What did you do?

B. What was the result of what you did?

C. What do you think your teenager learned from that experience?

D. What perceptions?

E. What skills?

F. What did you learn?

4. Think of a time when your teenager made a mistake and you were not supportive and encouraging.

   A. What did you do?

B. What was the result of what you did?

C. What do you think your teenager learned from that experience?

D. What perceptions?

E. What skills?

F. What did you learn?

Is there any way you could use the information from the time you were supportive and encouraging to improve on the time when you were not? Look at the list of affirmations for ideas of how you might adjust your attitude.

Skill Practice supporting your teenager when they make mistakes.

Creative Skill What new affirmations are you willing to make about mistakes?

Affirmations

I will listen and have faith.

She's a normal, healthy teenager.

I trust my instincts.

I give up fear and control.

I stick to the issues.

I respect your opinion.

My kids *are* okay and have what they need.

Your grades are your responsibility.

I'm okay and I have what I need.

I'm doing the best I can.

I won't take it so seriously.

The more I let go now, the less there is to let go of later.

I love ____________ unconditionally and *totally* accept his need to be how he is.

Right action is taking place.

They'll get over it. (Trust their resources.)

It's okay that it's hard for me to have faith.

I balance efficiency with time for people.

I *can* trust my kids.

When I stop "butting in," my kids grow.

I'm a good enough parent.

This is about me—not about you.

▼

Four R's of Recovery (Recognition, Responsibility, Reconciliation, Resolution)

One of the best ways to teach our children that mistakes are wonderful opportunities to learn is to realize this fact for ourselves. Using the Four R's of Recovery allows us to learn from experience that our relationship with our kids can be better after the mistake has been made than without the mistake.

Think of a time when you were disrespectful to your teenager. Write down what happened and how you were disrespectful:

Before you go to your teenager to try out the Four R's of Recovery, go through the steps and write down what you could say in the space provided after each step.

1. RECOGNITION: Realize you made a mistake and that what you did was ineffective. ("It is important to get comfortable with telling you my feelings.") (Responsibility means describing what you did without a feeling of blame or guilt.) How would you take responsibility?

2. RESPONSIBILITY: Take responsibility for your part of the conflict that was created by your mistake. Be specific in telling your teenager the nature

of your mistake: "I yelled at you instead of telling you my feelings." Responsibility means describing what you did without feeling blame or guilt. Write a script about how you could take responsibility.

3. RECONCILIATION: Apologize. "I'm sorry for treating you disrespectfully and for any hurt I may have created." What could you say?

4. RESOLUTION: If necessary work on an agreement of what both of you could do that would be respectful and effective if the problem occurs again. What could either of you do to fix any damage that might have been done? What possible solutions could you offer?

Skill Practice what you have learned with your teenager.

Creative Skill Remember that the feeling behind what you do is more important than what you do. Follow the wisdom from your heart rather than *techniques*.

COMMENT: The affirmations are suggestions other parents came up with to change their negative beliefs about mistakes to beliefs about the value of mistakes.

▼

Chapter 5 Activity

Giving Up Guilt

Guilt is called the stopper emotion. It is a feeling we create when we have decided to do "bad" and look good at the same time—"I'm not going to change, but at least I feel guilty about it." If we feel guilty, we tend to continue our old behaviors. In the following activity, we will zero in on an area of our own guilt, see what decisions we have made that stop us from acting in a new way, decide on a small step we can take if we want to change this, and give ourselves permission to see what we do with the information.

1. Think of a situation with one of your kids where you are feeling guilty. Describe the situation:

2. What are some of the things you do when you feel guilty?

3. What is the price you pay or problems you invite with your behavior when you feel guilty?

4. What is your fear of the worst thing that could happen if you did something differently?

5. What is your picture of a small step you could take to act differently? Write down what that would be.

6. Notice what you do with this information this week. If you decide to take the small step and act differently, record the results.

Skill When you look at the worst thing that could happen, it is probably an assumption that may be very disrespectful to your children. The only way to get to the truth is to have the courage to check it out with them. When we don't, our fears create a barrier between us and our children.

Creative Skill Take the small step you created above. Give yourself permission to be imperfect and tell the truth about it.

▼

Chapter 5 Activity

The Mischief Shuffle

Part of individuation is rebelling against family values such as religion, work ethics, treating adults respectfully, etc. You may feel challenged, afraid, worried about what others think. We need to be aware of the short-range benefits of our "mischief shuffle" reactions and to gain insight about the value of dropping the beliefs that create these reactions.

1. Read the Mischief Shuffle handout.

2. Imagine your teenager having any of the following attitudes:

    a. "I don't want to go to church anymore."

    b. "I don't want to get a job. I just want to have fun."

    c. "I hate going to Grandma's and Grandpa's. Who wants to hang out with a bunch of old people?"

    d. "If I want to drink, that's my business."

3. Now look at some typical (mischief) parenting styles:

    a. You are afraid this might get out of hand, and you try to fix it.

    b. You are afraid of what others might think. You put pressure on your child to live up to other people's expectations—and are sometimes very disrespectful to your child while trying to make her be respectful to others.

c. You want to make sure your child doesn't make a mistake. You can't stand to see him suffer. So you tell him how to do it "right."

d. You are afraid of anger, so you do anything to avoid the wrath of your teenager.

e. You believe it is selfish if you aren't self-sacrificing so you lecture your teenager on what she needs to do to live up to this value.

4. Choose your favorite "mischief" parenting style and describe how it would look in response to one of the above teen attitudes:

Skill Be aware of what your teenager might be feeling, learning and deciding in response to your mischief shuffle; write it down.

Creative Skill Imagine how you would like to be treated if you were a teenager with any of the above teen attitudes. Treat your teenager that way.

▼

Chapter 5 Activity

Alternatives to the Mischief Shuffle

When parents stop dancing the mischief shuffle and instead focus on their long-term parenting goals, they find that they actually have a lot of power to influence their teens. We find that taking care of ourselves and being on our own side is one of the best ways to be on our teen's side at the same time. With this realization, we can decide what we want to say no to, how to express and honor our own limits, how to listen without having to fix or judge, how to ask for help, how to be our "own person" and how to give up guilt and manipulation. This activity will show you the long-range benefits of dropping the "mischief shuffle" beliefs and replacing them with alternatives that show dignity and respect for you and your teenager.

Being on our own side means understanding our own individuality just as we understand the individuality of our teenagers—and supporting our own growth with dignity and respect just as we support our teen's growth with dignity and respect.

1. Refer back to the teen attitudes in the Mischief Shuffle activity.

2. Now look at the following alternatives to the Mischief Shuffle parenting styles:

   a. Decide what you are willing to do rather than what you will make your teenager do. Make sure there is not any revenge or punishment in your decision but just taking care of yourself. Example: "If you don't want to go to Grandma's and Grandpa's, I'm unwilling to explain why. That will be between you and them."

b. Set limits that you are willing to follow through on. Eliminate idle threats and punitive intentions and instead focus on the value of your time and effort to teach life skills. Example: "If you don't get a job and run out of money, I'm unwilling to give you extra."

c. Be aware of your fear of what others might think. Then decide what makes more sense to you—other than living up to their expectations—that will benefit you, your teenager, and your relationship with your teenager. Practice stating your decision with confidence in yourself. Example: "If you don't want to go to church, I'll miss you—and I have faith in you to decide what is important to you."

d. Share from your heart and gut what you feel and what you want, without expecting your teenager to feel the same or to give you what you want. Example: "I'm scared that you are getting into a pattern of drinking that could really hurt you."

e. Be aware of your own unresolved issue around the situation that has been presented by the teenager. Verbalize this issue by stating how you were treated regarding the same situation, how you felt about it, and some decisions you made that may not have been healthy for your own growth. Example: "I hated it when my mother lectured me instead of listening to my feelings about what was important to me—and I realize I just did the same thing to you."

f. See if you can negotiate a "give and take" resolution. Example: "I understand you don't want to go to Grandma's and it's important to me. Would you be willing to go sometimes if I don't ask you to go all the time?"

3. Choose your favorite alternative to the Mischief Shuffle and describe how it would look in response to one of the teen attitudes from the previous activity:

Skill Practice using your favorite alternative the next time you encounter a typical individuation attitude in your teenager.

Creative Skill Make up some of your own alternatives based on how you would like to be treated when you feel rebellious.

▼

Chapter 5 Activity

Give and Take

In many families either the parents "rule the roost" or the children "run the show." Learning the skills of give and take fosters consideration, equality, dignity and respect for self and others.

1. Think of areas where you think you have to do everything your way, or your kids' way:

   TV shows
   Movies
   Music
   Vacation
   Restaurants
   Meals
   Phone use
   Choice of clothing
   Borrowing or lending clothes
   Other ____________________

2. Describe a typical scene around the most common "your way or my way" situation in your home. Include:

   a. What you usually say or do.

   b. What your teen usually says or does.

c. The results of this interaction.

Skill Present one of the listed areas at a family meeting and allow the family to come up with a give and take solution.

Creative Skill Think of a plan for give and take in any one of the listed areas and present it to your teenager.

Chapter 6 Activity

Family Pie

Every child in a family chooses to see himself in certain ways depending on how he decides he can best fit into the family in comparison with his siblings. It is not your job to try to talk your kids out of how they see themselves or their siblings. This exercise is simply to increase your awareness.

1. List each member of your present family.

2. List three or four adjectives to describe each one of them.

3. Ask your kids to do the same without showing them your list first.

4. Compare lists. Are there any differences or similarities? Are there any surprises?

Skill Practice getting into your children's world by understanding their decisions about how they see themselves.

Creative Skill Look for places you might be comparing your children and find ways to appreciate them for their own unique qualities.

Chapter 7 Activity

Mom and Dad Said

As children, we are very impressionable. Our parents often say things that may be intended to motivate us to do better, but instead are very discouraging. We often make decisions—based on these comments—that are detrimental to our self-esteem. To break the harmful patterns, we need to take a new look and make some new decisions.

1. Answer the following:

   a. My mother always said ______________________.

   b. So I decided ______________________.

2. How does that decision affect the way I parent my teenager?

3. Answer the following:

   a. My father always said ______________________.

   b. So I decided ______________________.

4. How does that decision affect the way I parent my teenager?

5. Do your decisions from the past help you or hurt you? In what way?

6. Do your decisions from the past help or hurt your teenager? In what way?

Skill If you wanted to make new decisions, what would they be?

Creative Skill If you wanted to relate differently with your teenager, what would you do based on your new decisions?

▼

Chapter 7 Activity

Healing the Teen Within

Even though we can't change the past, we often can change the feelings that are left from the past by using our imagination to redo the scene the way we wish it would have been.

1. Think of an early memory of something that happened when you were a teenager that you still feel bad about.

2. Write down the incident and be very specific—including how old you were, what was happening in the situation, how you felt at the time, and what decisions you made.

3. Pretend you have a magic wand. Wave it over your early memory and make it just the way you wish it would have been. Write the changes down.

4. Based on the changes you made, how would your feelings change and what new decisions could you make?

Skill Every time you notice yourself feeling the same as you felt in your early memory, use the new decisions you created when you changed your memory with a magic wand to improve your present situation.

Creative Skill Use your magic wand to change other memories that have left you with feelings and decisions you would like to change.

▼

Chapter 8 Activity

The Negative Effects of Punishment

Where did we ever get the crazy idea that in order to make children do better, we first have to make them feel worse? Most people feel misunderstood, humiliated, angry, or like they are bad when they are punished. They usually decide to do one of three things: (1) withdraw, (2) get even, or (3) rebel. Even those who decide to do better do so at great cost to their self-esteem.

1. Think of some ways you are punishing your teenager. Are you using any of the following typical punishments?

   Grounding
   Taking away privileges
   Withdrawing love
   Taking away or withholding money
   Making rules without agreement
   Giving orders

2. Think of a time when you were punished as a teenager. Write about a specific example.

   A. What kind of punishment was used?

B. How did you feel?

C. What did you decide about the person who punished you and about yourself?

D. What did you do?

E. How does the decision you made then still affect your actions today?

Skill Stop punishing. Often we can improve a situation simply by stopping what doesn't work.

Creative Skill Learn and practice alternatives to punishment.

▼

Chapter 8 Activity

Alternatives to Punishment

There are many respectful discipline skills we can learn that are more effective than punishment. Even though humiliating punishment may stop misbehavior, the cost is usually lowered self-esteem, which takes the form of rebellion, revenge, or feelings of inadequacy.

1. Think of a time when you punished your teen. Grounding, taking away privileges, withholding money, etc., are all forms of punishments. Write down the incident.

2. Did you notice your teen express resentment, revenge, rebellion, or retreat (sneakiness and lowered self-esteem)?

3. Picture yourself choosing one of the alternatives on the following list:

- Decide what *you* will do, not what your teen will do.
- Use follow-through (see Chapter 10 or the "Follow Through" activity).
- Say how you feel.

- Expect your teen to be who she is and act accordingly.
- Support your own growth.
- Say "I can't make you and I would like your help."
- Work on an agreement with your teen using the "Joint Problem Solving Steps" and "Follow Through."

4. How would you handle the problem situation using one of these skills?

5. How do you feel when you think about letting go of punishment?

Skill Notice the places you are currently using punishment.

Creative Skill Try out one or more of the alternatives to punishment or add to the list yourself.

▼

Chapter 9 Activity

Legacy

It is easy to get caught up in day-to-day living and concerns and to forget about the big picture and long-range parenting.

1. Pretend your teenager is ready to leave home to begin the adventure of life on his own.

2. Make a list of at least four things you would like your teen to have as a legacy of your parenting:

   a.

   b.

   c.

   d.

3. After each thing you have listed, write down at least one thing you are doing to build this legacy for your teen.

Skill Repeat this activity once a month.

Creative Skill What things could you stop doing that are detracting from the legacy you would like to leave?

Chapter 9 Activity

Long-Range Parenting

We need to be aware of the difference between long-range and short-range parenting and aware that most of us operate within the short-range parenting style. One of the main differences is that long-range parenting is pro-active and leaves teenagers with life skills. Short-range parenting is reactive and robs teenagers of the opportunity to learn life skills.

1. Read "The Growing Process" on page 385.

2. Now imagine your teenager has come home three hours after curfew. Refer back to the short-range parenting list and write down some of those reactions that feel familiar to you.

3. How do you feel after reacting this way?

4. Write down how you imagine your teenager feels:

5. What is she learning about herself?

6. What is he learning about life skills?

7. Now refer back to the responses from the long-range parenting list. Write down the ones you would like to use in response to your teenager coming home late.

8. How do you think you might feel after responding this way?

9. Write down how you imagine your teenager might feel.

10. What is she learning about herself?

11. What is he learning about life skills?

Skill Think of a recent encounter with your teenager. Which reactions or responses did you use? Visualize yourself using the ones you would like to use the next time you have a similar encounter.

Creative Skill Choose one skill from the long-range parenting list that would be easiest for you to use and practice for one week.

The Growing Process

Long-Range Parenting Promotes the Growing Process

Teach life skills, such as handling money and the art of negotiation

Solve problems

Learn from mistakes

Focus on relationships

Increase self-awareness

Short-Range Parenting Stunts the Growing Process

Look for immediate solutions

Control

Punish

Neglect or give up

Overprotect or rescue

Chapter 9 Activity

Separate Realities

If you would like to know how your teenager sees things, sometimes all you have to do is ask. The hard part is to just listen instead of arguing, trying to change them, wanting to fix things, etc. We can really get into the world of our teen by learning to listen and respect separate realities.

1. Choose one of the following:

   a. Cutting school

   b. Not doing homework

   c. Not doing chores

   d. Not keeping room clean

   e. Staying out after curfew

   f. Too much TV

   g. Too much phone use

   h. An issue of your choice

2. Ask your teen any of the following questions using the issue you chose:

   a. What is your picture of (doing chores)?

   b. What's your plan for (homework)?

   c. How do you see that (not keeping your room clean) working?

d. What is your story about (staying out after curfew)?

3. Sit quietly while he answers. The only exception for breaking your silence is to show interest by asking such questions as, "Anything else?" "Could you tell me what you mean by that?" "Will you tell me more?" "Could you give me an example of when that happened?"

4. How does it feel just to listen?

5. Do you think your teen trusts you to tell you her thoughts and feelings?

6. Is there anything you could do to improve the relationship?

Skill Practice listening without talking unless being curious.

Creative Skill Listen to yourself communicating with your teen and pick out places you try to fix, argue, or use other means to cut off communication. Can you find a way to change any of that?

Chapter 9 Activity

Empowering vs. Enabling

Enabling behavior is anything parents do that is getting between young people and life's experiences to minimize the consequences of their choices. Empowering behavior is anything parents do to turn control over to young people as soon as possible so they have power over their own lives. The purpose of this activity is to learn the concept and skills of empowering young people—and long-range benefits.

Read the "Helpful Hints for Empowering vs. Enabling" on page 140.

1. Pretend you are a teenager who has not been doing your homework.

2. Now read through the enabling statements and imagine your parents are responding to you with each of the enabling statements.

3. In your imagination (as a teenager) how were you feeling? What decisions were you making about the adults in your life? What decisions were you making about yourself? What were you deciding to do?

4. Now read through the empowering statements and imagine your parents are responding to you with each of these statements.

5. In your imagination (as a teenager) how were you feeling? What decisions were you making about the adults in your life? What decisions were you making about yourself? What were you deciding to do?

Skill Practice using at least one empowering statement with your teen this week.

Creative Skill Realize that adults do not necessarily feel comfortable with empowering statements and actions.

Chapter 10 Activity

Follow-through

Parents of teenagers usually use consequences to control or to punish. That could be one reason why teenagers often see logical consequences as punishment. Follow-through is one effective alternative that avoids this dilemma. Teens are usually willing to make an agreement during a friendly discussion. However, it is very normal for them not to keep the agreement and thus the need for follow-through. Follow-through is about what the parent does and not what the teen does. It is not an attempt to control the teen's behavior, but rather an action on the parent's part that involves helping your teen control his own behavior.

1. Write down a situation where a teenager doesn't keep agreements, such as mowing the lawn, cleaning up messes, doing laundry, etc.

2. Describe how you would normally handle this situation. Most parents use nagging, criticizing, judging, punishing, and other similar methods.

3. Your priorities are probably different from those of your teen. What are yours? What are his?

4. Read the "Four Steps to Follow-through," "Four Traps that Defeat Follow-through," and "Four Hints for Effective Follow-through" on p. 160, 166.

5. Visualize yourself using follow-through on the situation you described above. Describe how it might look.

Skill Notice if you follow-through or if you lecture, nag, or punish instead.

Creative Skill Pick a trouble spot with your teen and work on the "Four Steps to Follow-through" together.

▼

Chapter 11 Activity

Using Anger Constructively

Anger is a feeling. It's okay to feel any feeling because feelings aren't good or bad, right or wrong. When we become aware of our feelings and know what they are about, we have more choices of how we wish to act. Learning to identify anger and the object of the anger (what we are angry at) helps us take control of our lives and improve all our relationships. In this activity, the idea is to learn to say, "I'm angry," and then to figure out what the object of the anger is.

1. Think about a time when you felt angry. Sometimes we use other words instead of "anger" to describe those situations, so if nothing comes to your mind, try to remember a time when you felt frustrated, irritated, upset, a little peeved, etc. Write it down.

2. Refer back to the incident you just wrote down and fill in the blank: "I'm angry at ____________." Is this "object of your anger" another person, someone else's anger at you, life, yourself, a situation, or an absent other (someone who has died, moved away, or appears to be here but is either drunk, under the influence, or just "emotionally distant")?

3. Use The Five Objects of Anger chart to see if you mismanaged your anger at the time of the incident

or used your anger constructively in a mutually respectful way. Write down what you did and the results of what you did.

4. What does this activity teach you about yourself?

Skill Decide what you will do differently next time you experience a similar situation. Write it down and then visualize yourself practicing this new behavior.

Creative Skill Think of areas where you could speak up about what you feel (without expecting anyone else to feel the same), and say what you want without expecting anyone else to give you what it is you want. Write it down and visualize yourself practicing this new skill.

The Five Objects of Anger
(Adapted from the work of Mitch Messer)

Object	Mismanage	Constructive, Mutually Respectful Use of Anger
1. My anger at another person	Fight, stop, run away, hold it all inside, eat, blow off steam, yell, hurt someone	Tell the truth. Say, "I'm angry." Decide what I will do and do it instead of trying to change the other person.
2. Another person's anger at me	Say, "I seem to make you angry." Question his/her right to be angry. Disappear, defend, give away my power, take his/her mischief seriously or literally, argue with him/her, try to fix the other person—make him/her sane.	Remember I am worthwhile and it's his/her anger. Validate, validate, validate by saying any of the following: "I'm sorry you're angry. Did something make you angry? What angered you the most when that happened? You sound angry. I'd be angry, too." Change myself if it is what I would like to do.

3. My anger at life.	Same as #1.	Write an anger letter, but don't send it. Talk to a friend who will validate my anger. Know this anger is between "me" and "me."
4. My anger at the absent	Shut down, drink, take it out on someone else, keep it all in.	Same as #3. Join ALANON or ACA group.
5. My anger at myself	Think I'm stupid because I can't solve problems. Feel inferior, so increase overcompensation, self-contempt; invite others to stop treating me nicely because I don't deserve it.	Get out of childhood role. Do homework in the real world by trying a new action. Be an adult. Stop saying, "I'm stupid." Write a letter. Try again—succeed. Stop looking for faults. Forgive myself.

Chapter 11 Activity

The Value of Money

Teens learn the value of money from their personal experiences. Money is one of several mediums which give teens the opportunity to learn life skills.

1. What were your experiences about money from your childhood?

2. What did you learn from them?

3. How do you deal with money today?

4. How do you help your teenager deal with money today?

5. Read the article on money.

6. What ideas did you get from the article that will help you deal more effectively with your teen and money?

Skill Sit down with your teens and have them make a list of their expenses. Be curious and don't lecture.

Creative Skill Work with your teens to provide ways for them to acquire money. Consider an allowance or clothing allowance.

What Does Your Child Know About Money?

The Johnson family was about to complete their weekly grocery shopping when five-year-old Jimmy started coaxing for a toy car. Mom asked politely, "Have you saved enough money from your allowance to buy it?"

Jimmy looked sad and said, "No."

Mom suggested, "Maybe you would like to save your money so you can buy that car."

Of course Jimmy never saved enough money to buy the car. He wanted it bad enough to spend Mom's money, but not enough to save his own money.

Five-year-old Sally wanted a new bicycle. Dad worked out a plan with Sally that as soon as she could save $5 toward a bicycle, he would pay the rest. They got a glass jar, pasted a picture of a bicycle on it and Sally put her whole allowance (four quarters) in the jar the first week. Since Sally's allowance was only $1 a week, and it was difficult for her to resist the ice cream truck, it took her three months to save $5. This seemed like an eternity to Sally, but every time she brought up the subject of a new bike, her Dad would ask, "How much have you saved?" They would go to the jar and count the quarters. They would figure out how many more quarters she needed to reach her goal of $5, and Dad would encourage her that she could do it.

In the sixth grade, Amy was given a school clothing allowance. Mom and Amy went through her closet together to figure out what she needed, and then sat down to work on a budget to see how much she could spend for each item she wanted to purchase. Amy had to make decisions such as: would she buy two pair of expensive jeans or four pair of less expensive jeans? During their shopping expedition, many times Mom heard Amy say, "I like this a little bit, but I don't like it a lot. I'm not going to buy anything I don't really like a lot."

In the seventh grade, Sam started saving diligently for a car because his parents had taken the time to discuss with him that they would not be willing to buy him a car when he was 16 unless he put in as much effort as they did. They agreed to match what he saved by the time he was ready for a car, if he had a job so he could buy the gas and insurance. Together they investigated the cost of insurance, and Sam learned that it was much less expensive if he had a "B" average on his report cards. Sam decided he would work hard to maintain a "B" average.

Jimmy, Sally, Amy and Sam are all learning the value of money. They are learning delayed gratification, goal setting and the need to work and plan for what they want. They are also learning many side benefits such as cooperation, responsibility and appreciating what they get. They all made poor decisions along the way. Amy learned to buy only what she "really liked" after buying some things she didn't like so much and then not having money left for things she really liked. Sally finally learned that she wanted a bicycle more than she wanted ice cream. Sam did not save enough money for the car of his dreams, but learned to fix the clunker he purchased because he was too impatient to wait and save a little longer.

Providing allowances is a tool parents can use to teach children many valuable lessons. Too many parents give "handouts" instead of allowances. Handouts are often based on the whims of parents and/or the ability of kids to coax, whine and manipulate. Kids believe that checks and credit cards provide an unlimited supply of money. It is a very disrespectful system that leaves everyone feeling bad—parents who feel manipulated by coaxing, crying or other forms of demand for money, which is never appreciated by their children; and children who do not learn the confidence and self-respect that comes from dealing with money responsibly.

The allowance system is respectful to all concerned. It is negotiated in advance based on what the family can afford and the needs of the kids. If the children's needs are greater than the family budget, they can be encouraged to supplement their income by baby-sitting, washing cars or mowing lawns.

Many problems can be avoided when allowances are not tied to chores. A four-year-old may enthusiastically make her bed for 10 cents, but will ask for 50 cents by the time she is eight. By the time she is 14 she won't want to do it even for a dollar. Connecting chores to allowances offers too many opportunities for punishment, reward, bribery and other forms of disrespectful manipulation. Each child gets an allowance just because he/she is a member of the family, and each child does chores just because he/she is a member of the family. It can be helpful to offer special jobs for pay that are beyond regular chore routines, such as weeding for $2 an hour or cracking nuts for $1 a bag. This offers opportunities for kids who want to earn extra money, but does not cause problems if they choose not to take the opportunity.

Allowances can be started when children first become aware of the need for money—when they start wanting toys at the supermarket or treats from the ice cream truck. Some families start with a quarter, a dime, a nickel, five pennies and a piggy bank. A small child loves the variety and enjoys putting the money in the piggy bank. As children get older, allowances can be based on need. Children learn budgeting when parents take time to go over their needs with them. A child of six may need 25 cents for gum and 25 cents for savings. A child of 15 may need $5 a week for a movie, $5 for school lunches and $4 for savings and or snacks.

If kids run out of money before the end of the week it is important to empathize but not rescue. They need the freedom to spend their allowance as they wish. If they spend it all at once they have the opportunity to learn from that experience—so long as parents don't interfere or make judgments. This does not mean that allowances cannot be renegotiated. Renegotiation is an important part of the learning process as kids get older and their needs change. Birthdays or the start of a new school year is a good time to sit down together and look at needs and go over budget planning.

A clothing allowance is a good addition to a regular allowance as soon as kids are old enough to be aware of fashion and want more clothing than is really necessary. A clothing allowance provides limits and encourages responsible decision making. When children are younger there may be two shopping trips each year—one in the spring and one in the fall, each with a certain dollar amount allotted. As children get older they may get a certain amount each month for them to budget.

Allowance and clothing budgets help children learn what their values are, to make decisions and live with the results, and to use money responsibly. By the time they leave home, they are ready to manage their finances entirely.

This article is by Jane Nelsen and Riki Intner. It can be found in the *Teaching Parenting* manual by Lynn Lott and Jane Nelsen, available through Sunrise Books, Tapes & Videos, 1-800-456-7770.

Chapter 12 Activity
Letting Go

Letting go is not easy for parents. Our fears often get in the way of allowing our children to grow through normal developmental stages. Trying to stop pre-adolescents from going to the mall or a teenager from talking on the phone too much, driving a car, or going to a party is similar to trying to stop a toddler from walking because she might hurt herself. If our goal is to empower our kids and help them grow, then the five steps of letting go can help us accomplish this task. We need to deal with our own fears that get in the way of empowering kids so we can turn power over to them by letting go.

1. Think of an area where you are having a hard time letting go with one of your kids (an area where you know in your heart you are holding on too tight). Write it down.

2. What are the issues?

   A. Yours (usually your fears)?

   B. His or hers (usually what he/she wants)?

3. Are you willing to practice letting go? There's no point in going on to the next two steps if you know you are not willing to let go.

4. What is a small step you could take to let go? Be specific.

5. When would you be willing to start your small step of letting go and how long are you willing to do it even though it may be a little uncomfortable for you?

Skill Using the insights you gained from this activity, put into practice what you decided as your small step for letting go.

Creative Skill Think of other areas where you could practice the skill of letting go.

Chapter 12 Activity

Teen Within, Teen Without

When we remember our own teen years, it helps us gain perspective on how our teens might be thinking and feeling. When we operate from a position of fear, we tend to forget how it really is for teens, and we do things that make the situation worse.

PART I

1. Think of an early memory from your teen years and write it down. Be specific.

2. In the memory, what were you telling yourself?

3. How were you feeling?

4. What were you doing?

5. What were others around you doing?

6. What did you decide?

PART II

1. Think of a situation with your own teenager where you are angry, confused, scared, or where you believe he or she is making a mistake. Write it down.

2. In the situation, what are you telling yourself?

3. How are you feeling?

4. What are you doing?

5. What is your teen doing?

6. What are you deciding?

7. What do you think your teen might be deciding?

PART III

1. Go back to your memory of yourself as a teenager and pretend you have a magic wand. How would you change that memory with your magic wand so it would be the way you wish it would have been? Describe how the information from doing that might help you deal more effectively with the current situation with your teen.

(Example: I changed my early memory so that my parent listened and understood instead of putting me down. I can see now how I need to listen more and understand rather than trying to motivate with "put downs.")

PART IV

1. Can you create an affirmation for yourself based on the work you just did that can help you improve your relationship with your teen? An affirmation is a positive statement that you can believe and tell yourself over and over.

(Example: I will listen and understand.)

Skill The next time you're discouraged with your teen, remember back to your own teen years for perspective.

Creative Skill Use the affirmation you created to change your thinking during a conflict with your teen.

Chapter 13 Activity

Joint Problem Solving

When we operate on the principle of mutual respect, we learn that parents and kids have different issues and different feelings about the same subject. If we try to force our way on them or give in to their demands, any solution is short-lived. It's only when we all feel understood that resolution is possible. Follow the steps of joint problem solving to learn a process for finding solutions with your teenager that you both can live with.

1. Think of a disagreement you have with your teen, such as getting chores done, cleaning rooms, use of the family car, telephone use, curfew, etc. Write down your issue.

2. What do you think your teen's thoughts and feelings might be about this issue? You could even ask him and write down the answer. Make sure you don't argue, blame, or attack if he tells you his ideas. If he tells you his ideas, make sure he knows you understood by saying, "You feel __________ because __________ and you wish __________." You can ask him if there is more. Write down your teen's issues.

3. If your teen will listen to you, could you tell her

your thoughts and feelings? Fill in the blanks:

I feel __________ because __________ and I wish __________.

Practice saying this to yourself and then see if your teen will listen as you tell her your thoughts and feelings. Ask your teen if she will tell you what she just heard you say. This doesn't mean she sees it the same way.

4. If you and your teen have different ideas about the problem, ask if you can brainstorm some ideas so you can find a solution that you both could live with for one week. Brainstorm. It helps the brainstorming process if the parent comes up with wild and crazy ideas. If you are not ready to try this out with your teen, you could brainstorm yourself. Write down all suggestions.

5. Choose a suggestion you're both willing to try for one week. Write it down.

6. Appreciate each other for listening. Agree on a review date.

7. If you did this without your teen, think about what is stopping you from talking to your teen and doing the activity with her.

Skill Practice until you feel comfortable trying out joint problem solving with your teen.

Creative Skill Make a date to go through this activity with your teen.

Chapter 14 Activity

Effective Communication Tools

Parents complain that kids won't talk to them and that they don't have good communication. Another problem parents complain about is that teenagers like to have the last word. Unfortunately, so do parents. This activity is guaranteed to open up communication with teenagers.

PART I

1. Describe the last time your teenager started talking to you about something you have a lot of opinions about, such as not wanting to do homework, not wanting to go to church, wanting to go to parties, and thinking school is irrelevant.

2. Visualize yourself saying anything you want in your mind, just don't let your lips separate; try saying "uhm" in different intonations. When your teen runs out of things to say, you say, "It was really nice talking to you." Describe your visualization.

3. How difficult was this for you to do even in your imagination?

PART II

1. Visualize yourself in an argument with your teenager about something like doing his chores when you want him to, what he is wearing, how he spends money, or telephone use.

2. In the middle of the argument, visualize yourself stopping and letting your teen have the last word.

3. How difficult was it for you to stop? Do you still have smoke coming out of your ears because you let your teen have the last word?

Skill Find opportunities to practice keeping your lips together and letting your teen have the last word.

Creative Skill Realize that even though you don't get your own way, you will invite your teenager to communicate with you—and that the purpose of these activities is not to solve the problem but to improve the relationship.

▼

Chapter 14 Activity

The "I Feel" Process—Emotional Honesty from the Head, Heart or Gut

Most of us have learned to talk from our heads instead of our hearts or our guts—our judgments instead of our feelings. The purpose of this activity is to give you practice sharing feelings rather than judgments.

1. Become familiar with the "Feeling Words" chart.

2. Describe an area where you don't think you're getting anywhere and are feeling frustrated with your teenager. You are feeling that no matter how many times you try to communicate, your teen is just not getting the message.

3. Write down how you have been handling the situation that concerns you—such as lecturing, nagging, guilt tripping, punishing.

4. Now go back to the same situation and—with the following simple process—share your feelings instead of your judgments:

   I feel __________ because __________ and I wish __________.

Check the "Feeling Words" chart if you are having trouble using feeling words and are using "like," "that," or "you" instead (these are not feeling words).

5. Imagine how your teen might feel when you handle the situation in your usual way, and how he might feel when you share your feelings using the "I feel" process. How do you feel in each situation?

Skill Practice the "I feel" process with your teenager in the area that has been frustrating you.

Creative Skill When you forget to use the "I feel" process, use the "Four Rs of Recovery" and then the "I feel" process.

"FEELINGS LIST" BY WILLHITE & ASSOCIATES
AGGRESSIVE
AGONIZED
ANXIOUS
APOLOGETIC
ARROGANT
BASHFUL
BLISSFUL
BORED
CAUTIOUS
COLD
CONCENTRATING
CONFIDENT
CURIOUS
DEMURE
DETERMINED
DISAPPOINTED
DISAPPROVING
DISBELIEVING
DISGUSTED
DISTASTEFUL
EAVESDROPPIN
ECSTATIC
ENRAGED
ENVIOUS
EXASPERATED
EXHAUSTED
FRIGHTENED
FRUSTRATED
GRIEVING
GUILTY
HAPPY
HORRIFIED
HOT
HUNGOVER
HURT
HYSTERICAL
INDIFFERENT
IDIOTIC
INNOCENT
INTERESTED
JEALOUS
JOYFUL
LOADED
LONELY
LOVESTRUCK
MEDITATIVE
MISCHIEVIOUS
MISERABLE
NEGATIVE
OBSTINATE
OPTIMISTIC
PAINED
PARANOID
PERPLEXED
PRUDISH
PUZZLED
REGRETFUL
RELIEVED
SAD
SATISFIED
SHOCKED
SHEEPISH
SMUG
SURLY
SURPRISED
SUSPICIOUS
SYMPATHETIC
THOUGHTFUL
UNDECIDED
WITHDRAWN

Chapter 14 Activity

I Love You, and the Answer is "No"

Most parents can't just say "no." They add anger, criticism, blame, character defamations, want to teach lessons or make kids suffer—and then give in later. We need to learn to say a simple "no" with love.

1. Imagine your teenager asking you the following questions and using every coaxing and manipulative skill she can think of to get you to say yes:

   "Can I use the car?"

   "Can I borrow $5 for lunch money?"

   "Can I wear your new sweater?"

2. Write down what you usually do.

3. What do you think your teenager learns from your typical response?

4. How do you feel when you have let yourself be manipulated into saying yes when you want to say no?

5. What behaviors or manipulations were hardest for you to resist? Which ones do your kids use most with you? What worked for you as a kid? Are there any similarities?

6. Now visualize yourself saying "no"—and nothing more—with dignity and respect to each request and argument from your teenager.

7. In your visualization, what happened? How did you feel? What did you visualize your teenager feeling and learning?

Skill Say "no"—and nothing more—with dignity and respect once in the following month.

Creative Skill Be aware of how often you say no when it's not appropriate and how often you say yes when you don't want to. Get in touch with what you feel and what you want before you respond to your teen.

Chapter 15 Activity

Fun Things to Do

If we did nothing more than remember to have fun with our teenagers on a regular basis, we would be surprised how much our relationships would improve—and how much more we would enjoy life in general. Unfortunately, we get caught up in busy schedules and dealing with problems. The purpose of this activity is to serve as a reminder of the importance of having fun and to provide inspiration and motivation to do it.

1. Make copies of the "Fun Things To Do" form for each member of your family. Fill out your own form privately first and ask each member of the family to do the same.

2. Schedule a "Fun Things To Do" meeting, and ask everyone to bring their completed forms. Take turns sharing your lists of fun things to do. Circle the items that more than one person has in common.

3. Have a brainstorming session to see how many more things the family can think of that they would like to add to their lists.

4. Get a calendar. Have each member of the family present one thing they would like to do for fun as a family. Schedule it on the calender on a date that suits everyone. (There should be a date planned for each member of the family's favorite thing to do for which the rest of the family agrees to participate.) Have fun together on days that are planned.

Skill Repeat this activity at least once a month.

Creative Skill Schedule at least one fun thing you like to do alone once a week for a month.

FUN THINGS TO DO

TOGETHER		ALONE	
Things That Cost $$	Free Things	Things That Cost $$	Free Things

Chapter 16 Activity

Learning About Drugs

Most parents of teenagers think one thing when they hear the word "drugs": not my kids! Learning more about the complexities of this topic help us deal more realistically with our kids.

See how many items you can list for each of the following categories of drugs to start realizing how many different things the word "drugs" covers:

Drug Categories

OKAY	HOUSEHOLD	PRESCRIBED
i.e., caffeine, sugar	i.e., aspirin, cough medicine	i.e., valium

APPROVED OR NOT	ILLEGAL STREET	UNRESTRICTED
i.e., alcohol	i.e., cocaine, crank, marijuana	i.e., over-the-counter varieties of painkillers

Skill Ask your teen to do this with you.

Creative Skill What are your attitudes about some of the categories of drugs other than "illegal street?" Look for conflicting messages you may be giving your kids about drugs, i.e., valium or alcohol is okay; other drugs are not okay.

Bibliography

Adler, Alfred. *What Life Should Mean to You.* New York: Capricorn Books, 1958.

Adler, Alfred. *Superiority and Social Interest.* Illinois: Northwestern University Press, 1964.

Adler, Alfred. *Social Interest.* New York: Capricorn Books, 1964.

Adler, Alfred. *Cooperation Between the Sexes.* New York: Anchor Books, 1978.

Albert, Linda. *Coping with Kids.* New York: E. P. Dutton, 1982.

Allred, G. Hugh. *How to Strengthen Your Marriage and Family.* Provo, UT: Brigham Young University Press, 1976.

Ansbacher, Heinz and Rowena. *The Individual Psychology of Alfred Adler.* New York: Harper Touchbooks, 1964.

Bayard, Robert and Jean. *How to Deal with Your Acting Up Teenager.* San Jose, CA: The Accord Press, 1981.

Beecher. *Beyond Success and Failure.* New York: Pocket Books, 1966.

Christianson, Oscar. *Adlerian Family Counseling.* Minneapolis, MN: Educational Media Corp., 1983.

Corsini, Raymond, and Genevieve Painter. *The Practical Parent.* New York: Harper and Rowe, 1975.

Corsini, Raymond, and Clinton Phillips. *Give In or Give Up.* Chicago: Nelson Hall, 1982.

Deline, John. *Who's Raising the Family?* Madison, WI: Wisconsin Clearing House, 1981.

Dinkmeyer, Pew, Dinkmeyer. *Adlerian Counseling and Psychotherapy.* Monterey, CA: Brooks/Cole Publishing, 1979.

Dinkmeyer, Don, and Rudolf Dreikurs. *Encouraging Children to Learn: The Encouragement Process.* Englewood Cliffs, NJ: Prentice-Hall, 1963.

Dinkmeyer, Don, and Gary McKay. *Parents Handbook: Systematic Training for Effective Parenting.* Circle Pines, MN: American Guidance Service, Inc., 1989 (3rd edition).

Dinkmeyer, Don, and Gary McKay. *Raising a Responsible Child.* New York: Simon & Schuster, 1973.

Dreikurs, Rudolf, Bronia Grunwald, and Floyd Pepper. *Maintaining Sanity in the Classroom.* New York: Harper & Row, 1971.

Dreikurs, Rudolf, and V. Soltz. *Children: The Challenge.* New York: Hawthorn Boos, 1964.

Dreikurs, Rudolf. *Psychology in the Classroom.* New York: Harper & Row, 1966.

Dreikurs, Rudolf. *Social Equality: The Challenge of Today.* Chicago: Contemporary Books, Inc., 1971.

Dreikurs, Rudolf, R. Corsini and S. Gould. *Family Council.* Chicago: Henry Regnery, 1974.

Dyer, Wayne. *Your Erogenous Zones.* New York: Avon Books, 1976.

Glenn, H. Stephen and Jane Nelsen. *Raising Self-Reliant Children in a Self-Indulgent World.* Rocklin, CA: Prima Publishing, 1988. (1-800-456-7770)

Glenn, H. Stephen. *Developing Capable People* (audio cassette tape set). Fair Oaks, CA: Sunrise Press. (1-800-456-7770)

Glenn, H. Stephen. *Bridging Troubled Waters* (audio cassette tape set). Fair Oaks, CA: Sunrise Press, 1989. (1-800-456-7770)

Glenn, H. Stephen. *Involving and Motivating People* (audio cassette tape). Fair Oaks, CA: Sunrise Press. (1-800-456-7770)

Glenn, H. Stephen. *Introduction to Developing Capable People* (video tape). Fair Oaks, CA: Sunrise Productions, 1989. (1-800-456-7770)

Glenn, H. Stephen. *Empowering Others: Ten Keys to Affirming and Validating People* (video tape). Fair Oaks, CA: Sunrise Productions, 1989. (1-800-456-7770)

Glenn, H. Stephen. *The Greatest Human Need* (video tape). Fair Oaks, CA: Sunrise Productions, 1989. (1-800-456-7770)

Glenn, H. Stephen. *Six Steps to Developing Responsibility* (video tape). Fair Oaks, CA: Sunrise Productions, 1989. (1-800-456-7770)

Glenn, H. Stephen. *Developing Healthy Self-Esteem* (video tape). Fair Oaks, CA: Sunrise Productions, 1989. (1-800-456-7770)

Glenn, H. Stephen. *Teachers Who Make a Difference* (video tape). Fair Oaks, CA: Sunrise Productions, 1989. (1-800-456-7770)

Goldberg, Herb. *Hazards of Being Male.* New American Library, 1976.

Janoe, Ed and Barbara. *Dealing with Feelings.* Vancouver, WA: Arco Press, 1973.

Janoe, Ed and Barbara. *About Anger.* Vancouver, WA: Arco Press, 1973.

Kvols-Reidler, Bill and Kathy. *Redirecting Children's Misbehavior.* Boulder, CO: R.D.I.C. Publications, 1979.

Losoney, Lewis. *You Can Do It.* New Jersey: Prentice-Hall, Inc., 1980.

Lott, Lynn, Marilyn Kentz and Dru West. *To Know Me Is To Love Me.* Santa Rosa, CA: The Practical Press, 1983. (1-800-456-7770)

Lott, Lynn. *Changing Your Relationship With Your Teen.* Santa Rosa, CA: The Practical Press. (1-800-456-7770)

Lott, Lynn, and Dru West. *Together and Liking It* (formerly Married and Liking It). Santa Rosa, CA: The Practical Press, 1987. (1-800-456-7770)

Lott, Lynn, Riki Intner and Dru West. *Family Work: Whose Job Is It?* Santa Rosa, CA: The Practical Press, 1983. (1-800-456-7770)

Lott, Lynn and Jane Nelsen. *Teaching Parenting Manual.* Fair Oaks, CA: Sunrise Press, 1990.

Manaster, Guy J., and Raymond Corsini. *Individual Psychology.* Itasca, IL: F. E. Peacock Publishers, Inc., 1982.

Nelsen, Jane. *Positive Discipline.* New York: Ballantine Books, 1987. (Originally published in 1981 by Sunrise Press, Fair Oaks, CA. 1-800-456-7770)

Nelsen, Jane. *Understanding: Eliminating Stress and Finding Serenity in Life and Relationships.* Rocklin, CA: Prima Publishing, 1988. (Originally published in 1986 by Sunrise Press, Fair Oaks, CA. 1-800-456-7770)

Nelsen, Jane. *Positive Discipline* (audio cassette tape). Fair Oaks, CA: Sunrise Press. (1-800-456-7770)

Nelsen, Jane. *Positive Discipline Video.* Fair Oaks, CA: Sunrise Press, 1988. (1-800-456-7770)

Nelsen, Jane. *Positive Discipline Study Guide.* Fair Oaks, CA: Sunrise Press, 1988. (1-800-456-7770)

Nelsen, Jane, and H. Stephen Glenn. *Time Out: Abuses and Effective Uses.* Fair Oaks, CA: Sunrise Press, 1991. (1-800-456-7770)

Nelsen, Jane, Riki Intner and Lynn Lott. *Clean and Sober Parenting.* Rocklin, CA: Prima Publishing, 1992. (1-800-456-7770)

Nelsen, Jane, Lynn Lott and H. Stephen Glenn. *Positive Discipline in the Classroom.* Rocklin, CA: Prima Publishing, 1993. (1-800-456-7770)

Nelsen, Jane, Lynn Lott and H. Stephen Glenn. *Positive Discipline: A-Z.* Rocklin, CA: Prima Publishing, 1993. (1-800-456-7770)

Nelsen, Jane, Cheryl Erwin and Carol Delzer. *Positive Discipline for Single Parents.* Rocklin, CA: Prima Publishing, 1993. (1-800-456-7770)

Pew, W. L., and J. Terner. *Courage to be Imperfect.* New York: Hawthorne Books, 1978.

Smith, Manuel J. *When I Say No I Feel Guilty.* NewYork: The Dial Press, 1975.

Walton, F. X. *Winning Teenagers Over.* Columbia, SC: Adlerian Child Care Books.

Information on Special Problems

Alcoholics Anonymous World Services. *Alcoholics Anonymous "The Big Book."* 3rd edition. New York: Alcoholics Anonymous World Services, 1976.

Al-Anon Family Group. *Al-Anon: Is It for You?* New York: Al-Anon Family Group Headquarters, 1983.

Beattie, Melody. *Co-Dependent No More: How to Stop Controlling Others and Start Caring for Yourself.* San Francisco: Harper/Hazelden, 1987.

Black, Claudia. *It's Never Too Late to Have a Happy Childhood.* New York: Ballantine Books, 1989.

Black, Claudia. *My Dad Loves Me, My Dad Has a Disease.* Hazelden Educational Materials, 1989.

Gaetano, Ronald J., R.Ph., with James J. Masterson. *Teenage Drug Abuse: 100 Most Commonly Asked Questions about Adolescent Substance Abuse.* Union, NJ: Union Hospital Foundation, 1989.

Hafen, Brent Q., with Kathryn J. Frandsen. *The Crisis Intervention Handbook.* Englewood Cliffs, NJ: Prentice-Hall, 1982.

Hollis, Judi. *Fat is a Family Affair.* San Francisco: Harper/Hazelsen, 1986.

Kimball, Bonnie-Jean. *The Alcoholic Woman's Mad, Mad World of Denial and Mind Games.* Center City, MN: Hazelden Educational Materials, 1978.

McCabe, Thomas R. *Victims No More.* Center City, MN: Hazelden, Educational Materials, 1978.

Pickens, Roy W., and Dace S. Svikis. *Alcoholic Family Disorders: More Than Statistics.* Center City, MN: Hazelden Educational Materials, 1985.

Powell, John S. *Why Am I Afraid to Tell You Who I Am?* Allen TX: Argus Communications, 1969.

Wholey, Dennis. *The Courage to Change.* Boston: Houghton Mifflin Company, 1984.

Woititz, Janet Geringer. *Adult Children of Alcoholics.* Hollywood, FL: Health Communications, 1983.

Woititz, Janet Geringer. *"Co-Dependency: The Insidious Invader of Intimacy," in Co-Dependency, An Emerging Issue.* (Hollywood, FL: Health Communications, 1984), 59.

Index

About the Authors

Jane Nelsen, Ed.D. is a popular lecturer and the author of *Positive Discipline* and *Understanding: Eliminating Stress and Finding Serenity in Life and Relationships*. She has coauthored many books, including *Positive Discipline in the Classroom, Raising Self-Reliant Children in a Self-Indulgent World,* and *I'm on Your Side: Resolving Conflict with Your Teenage Son or Daughter*. She has appeared on "Oprah," Sally Jessy Raphael," "Twin Cities Live," and was the featured parent expert on the "National Parent Quiz," hosted by Ben Vereen. Jane is the mother of seven children and the grandmother of eleven.

Lynn Lott, M.A., M.F.C.C., is also an in-demand speaker and therapist. She has authored and coauthored many books including *Family Work: Whose Job Is It?, Together and Liking It, I'm on Your Side, To Know Me Is to Love Me, Clean and Sober Parenting,* and *Positive Discipline in the Classroom*. She has appeared on "The Joan Rivers Show," "The Home Show," "The Today Show," and "Phil Donahue." She lives with husband Hal and is the mother of two children and two stepsons.

For a free newsletter and information on lectures and workshops by Jane Nelsen or Lynn Lott call 1-800-879-0812.

PRODUCTS BY THE AUTHORS

To: Empowering People, P.O. Box 1926, Orem, UT 84059
Phone: (800) 456-7770 (credit card orders only) Fax: (801) 762-0022

	Price	Quantity	Amount
BOOKS			
Positive Discipline for Teenagers by Nelsen & Lott	$14.95	_______	_______
Positive Discipline A-Z by Nelsen, Lott & Glenn	$14.95	_______	_______
Positive Discipline in the Classroom by Nelsen, Lott & Glenn	$15.00	_______	_______
Positive Discipline: A Teacher's A-Z Guide by Nelsen, Duffy, Escobar, Ortolano & Owen-Sohocki	$14.95	_______	_______
Raising Self-Reliant Children in a Self-Indulgent World by Glenn & Nelsen	$12.95	_______	_______
Positive Discipline by Nelsen	$11.00	_______	_______
Positive Discipline for Preschoolers by Nelsen, Erwin & Duffy	$14.00	_______	_______
Positive Discipline for Single Parents by Nelsen, Erwin & Delzer	$12.95	_______	_______
Time Out: Abuses & Effective Uses by Nelsen & Glenn	$6.95	_______	_______
Understanding: Eliminating Stress... by Nelsen	$12.00	_______	_______
Positive Discipline for Parenting in Recovery by Nelsen, Intner & Lott	$12.95	_______	_______
The Family That Works Together... by Lott & Intner	$9.95	_______	_______
To Know Me Is To Love Me by Lott, Kentz & West	$10.00	_______	_______
Together and Liking It by Lott and West	$7.95	_______	_______
TAPES & VIDEOS			
Positive Discipline cassette tape	$10.00	_______	_______
Positive Discipline video	$49.95	_______	_______
Building Healthy Self-Esteem through Positive Discipline by Nelsen	$10.00	_______	_______
Positive Discipline in the Classroom cassette tapes	$49.95	_______	_______
Positive Discipline in the Classroom video	$9.95	_______	_______
MANUALS			
Teaching Parenting the Positive Discipline Way	$39.95	_______	_______
Positive Discipline for Parenting in Recovery	$19.95	_______	_______
Positive Discipline for Single Parents	$19.95	_______	_______
Positive Discipline for Preschoolers	$19.95	_______	_______
Positive Discipline in the Classroom	$39.95	_______	_______
Student Assistance through Positive Discipline	$19.95	_______	_______

SUBTOTAL _______

Sales tax: UT add 6.25% ; CA add 7.25% _______

Shipping & Handling: $2.50 plus 50¢ for each item _______

TOTAL _______

(Prices subject to change without notice.)

METHOD OF PAYMENT (check one):

_______ Check made payable to Empowering People Books, Tapes & Videos

_______ Mastercard, Visa, Discover Card, American Express

Card #_______________________________ Expiration _______/_______

Ship to_______________________________________

Address_______________________________________

City/State/Zip_________________________________

Daytime Phone_________________________________

Workshops and Seminars

The authors offer workshops and seminars on Teaching Parenting the Positive Discipline Way for parents and parent educators; Positive Discipline in the Classroom for teachers, administrators, and school personnel; and Developing Capable People for parents, educators, and others who are in a position to influence youth development.

Workshops, seminars, and facilitator trainings are scheduled throughout the United States and Canada each year.

For information on Jane Nelsen, contact:
Positive Discipline Associates
P.O. Box 788
Fair Oaks, CA 95628-0788
(800) 879-0812

For information on Lynn Lott, contact:
Summerfield Workshops
930 Mendocino Avenue
Santa Rosa, CA 95401
(707) 573-8888

The authors are also available for lectures, teacher inservice training, and conference keynote and workshop presentations.